GENDER AND THE DIGITAL ECONOMY

GENDER AND THE DIGITAL ECONOMY

Perspectives from the Developing World

Editors

CECILIA NG
SWASTI MITTER

SAGE Publications
New Delhi ❖ Thousand Oaks ❖ London

First published in 2005 by

Sage Publications India Pvt Ltd
B-42, Panchsheel Enclave
New Delhi 110 017
www.indiasage.com

Sage Publications Inc
2455 Teller Road
Thousand Oaks, California 91320

Sage Publications Ltd
1 Oliver's Yard, 55 City Road
London ECIY ISP

Published by Tejeshwar Singh for Sage Publications India Pvt Ltd, phototypeset in 10/12 pt Sanskrit-Palatino by Star Compugraphics Private Limited, Delhi and printed at Chaman Enterprises, New Delhi.

Library of Congress Cataloging-in-Publication Data

Gender and the digital economy: perspectives from the developing world/editors, Cecilia Ng, Swasti Mitter.
    p. cm.
    Includes bibliographical references and index.
    1. Women in economic development—Developing countries.
2. Information society—Developing countries. 3. Information technology—Economic aspects—Developing countries. 4. Women—Effect of technological innovations on—Developing countries.
5. Women—Developing countries—Economic conditions—21st century.
    1. Ng, Cecilia, 1950– II. Mitter, Swasti, 1939–

HQ1240.5.D44G463   305.42'09172'4—dc22   2005   2005021889

ISBN: 0–7619–3410–3 (HB)   81–7829–573–3 (India–HB)

Sage Production Team: Ridhima Mehra, Ashok R. Chandran and Santosh Rawat

CONTENTS

Part III
The Politics and Policies of Gender and ICTs

ACKNOWLEDGEMENTS

This volume comprises selected articles from various issues (Volume 6, No. 3; Volume 8, No. 1; and Volume 9, No. 2) of the journal *Gender, Technology and Development (GTD)*, an international refereed journal based at the Gender and Development Field of Study, the Asian Institute of Technology (AIT), Thailand and published by Sage Publications, India. We would like to thank the former President, Jean-Louis Armand, Provost Mario Tabucanon, and Dean Chongrak Polprasert of the Asian Institute of Technology, and Sage Publications for allowing us to reproduce these articles, all of which have been revised and updated by the respective authors. For this, we appreciate the efforts of the authors in re-working their essays based on the comments of the reviewers whom we thank as well.

Our foremost thanks must go to Veena N. and Emilyn Madayag who provided the impetus to begin and end this project. Without their commitment, editorial skills, and organizational ability to bring the different talents together, this book would not have gone off the ground. To Jonathan Shaw, Mari Osawa, and Bernadette Resurreccion, whom we harassed at different phases of this long process, we owe our deepest gratitude. We thank Kyoko Kusakabe and Thanh-Dam Truong for their support and encouragement. We also thank Govind Kelkar and Pierre Walter for editing the articles published in the special issue on 'Women and Digital Divide' (6: 1). Ritu Vajpeyi-Mohan and Tejeshwar Singh of Sage Publications have been most kind in accommodating our innumerable foreseen and unforeseen delays in this project. We also thank Ridhima Mehra at Sage who edited our book for final publication. We enjoyed working with all of you. We are indebted to Elsa Ramos and Siham Friso of the International Confederation of Free Trade Unions, Brussels, for locating the origin of the photograph in Swasti Mitter's paper.

But most importantly, we thank the women and men who made this book possible by interacting and sharing with us, and the authors. The thoughts, feelings, and experiences which they shared so generously have enriched our work and our lives. We hope we have done you justice in bringing forth your voices in this Information Age.

Gender and Empowerment in the Information Economy: An Introduction

Swasti Mitter and Cecilia Ng

In the last three decades, we have seen the acceleration and spread of new technologies, particularly information and communication technologies (ICTs),[1] throughout the world. This is generating a modern day industrial revolution leading to a paradigm variously called the 'new' economy, the information economy or the digital economy. The rise of an Information or Knowledge Society, of which the digital economy is a key component, is significantly changing the way we live and work together. However, in the current context of ICTs-driven globalization, there is no guarantee that the inequalities and asymmetrical power relationships between the rich and poor countries and among different groups will be reduced. Indeed, there are serious concerns that the digital divide within and across nations will simply exacerbate existing material disparities with consequent social tension. To be sure, only a very small percentage of the world population is connected in the Network Society and the majority of women and men in the developing world are affected by exclusion rather than inclusion. Moreover, women in both the developed and developing countries, embedded within patriarchal contexts, are most probably heavily disadvantaged compared to men, in both the access to and control over ICTs.

It is against this existing and growing digital and gender divide that we have heard this question repeatedly: Can ICT be a driving force for the empowerment of women and make a difference in development? (Mitter, Fernandez, and Varghese, 2004) Some have

argued that ICTs divert the focus—in terms of attention and funding—from more basic issues and needs such as food, water, clothing, shelter, health, security, and literacy. While these concerns are
critical, especially in the poor countries, we also argue that addres-
sing the digital divide is an urgent task—for several reasons. Firstly,
the digital divide could exacerbate already existing inequalities in
society between high-, middle-, and low-income countries, communities and peoples, and within them as well. Secondly, due to
asymmetrical power relations in society, it is naive to assume that
all countries and individuals automatically gain equally from
globalization and ICTs. Thirdly, if we do not engage with the information society in its formative years, women's voices will not be
heard in the future as well. Fourthly, women's active involvement
is essential to ensure that a plurality and diversity of views are accepted in the information society. This engagement is another step
towards promoting gender equity in the information society.

We now ask ourselves: *How* can ICTs empower women and
make a difference to development? The focus of this volume, therefore, is economic empowerment.[2] We acknowledge that economic
empowerment, while insufficient, is a necessary condition for
the empowerment of women and other disadvantaged peoples.
The essays in this book take a critical view of the relationship
between ICTs and development and the ways in which this could
empower women within their families, workplaces, communities,
and cultures.

This book is not oblivious to the negative consequences of
ICT-led development. However, it wants to alert the readers to
the positive aspects of the introduction of ICTs. Several scholars
and activists have raised concerns about the problems associated
with the information society, especially the masculine nature of
ICTs, the patriarchal structure within which ICTs are introduced,
feminization of low-skill ICT jobs, the unequal gendered access to
technological education, and the degradation and devaluation of
women employed in certain sectors (Ghosh, 2004; Gothoskar, 2000;
Lie, 1991; Stanworth, 1998; Wajcman, 1991). There are others who
have pointed out some of the benefits that ICTs have brought to
women in developing countries and how women themselves have
negotiated gender relations at the household and community levels
(Kelkar and Nathan, 2002; Jamie Lee, 2004).

There is no doubt that ICTs have, for the first time, opened up windows of opportunities to a vast number of young women who would have remained unemployed or underemployed despite their relatively high levels of education. In the late 1970s, the development of micro-electronics and computers led to the emergence of the global assembly line creating employment opportunities for women in the developing world. Initially, the outsourcing of work from high-waged countries to low-waged ones was confined mainly to manufacturing. With today's networking technologies, outsourcing is spreading at a much faster rate to services work giving rise to a 'newer' international division of labor and global trade in digitized information. Women are playing important roles in this transnational restructuring as employers, employees, entrepreneurs, as well as civil society activists on the Internet, among others.

Despite these opportunities, there are reasons to assess further, if women remain as vulnerable to patriarchal controls in the new economy as in the old. We felt it would be worth exploring whether early marriages, lack of decision-making power in the family, low esteem in society, and sexual harassment at work are just some of the problems they face. For them, even relatively low value added operations such as back office activities, which do not need access to elite and expensive technical institutions, bring relatively high incomes, some degree of mobility, personal freedom, and negotiating power within the family. Once empowered, women themselves can, perhaps, decide whether, or when and how to opt for the use of ICTs in coping with their basic livelihood needs.

The message of this anthology is historically specific; it captures and conveys the aspirations and anxieties of women in the developing countries in the emerging information economy and society. The authors are mainly from the developing world; some of them, not so uncommon in our globalized world, live in developed countries but retain umbilical relationships, personally and professionally, with the countries of their origin. Again, there are those who come from the developed world, yet, identify themselves with the destinies of women in the developing countries where the power of ICTs is transforming their lives. The anthology, thus, offers a dimension that is understandably distinct from those of professional consultants and experts from the outside. The various chapters offer the insiders' points of view. They are not necessarily more valid or more functional, but different from the outsiders' evaluation of the relevance of ICTs for improving employment and livelihood opportunities. All too often, in the discourse on ICTs, the media has focused on the relocation of jobs from the First World. The increasing unemployment in the North, the great technological leaps of this era, and of course, the consequences of these technological advances on daily lives and lifestyles in the North are also mentioned. There is little, however, from the perspectives of poorer countries, and far less, from the women in them.

This volume in essence aims to raise certain key questions about the implications of the digital economy for women's lives in the South.

The Issues and Challenges

Globalization as Context

As noted earlier, the arguments in this volume are placed within the context of globalization, which itself is driven by ICTs. Globalization does not necessarily obliterate the unequal power relationships between rich and poor countries. The power of ICTs might even exacerbate these inequalities without the right policy interventions at the national and international levels,. In this context, the issues raised by Swasti Mitter and Martha Roldan in their essays in this volume are crucial.

The discourse of ICTs is rooted in the conviction that access to networking technologies is an empowering tool for women of poorer countries. But Swasti Mitter asks: Is this necessarily so? Mitter contends that it has been difficult to find evidence to assess its liberating potential on the lives of women from underprivileged backgrounds. In her essay, 'Globalization, ICTs, and Economic Empowerment: A Feminist Critique', she evaluates the problematic of ICT-led globalization from the perspectives of women of poorer countries. She does so by documenting the opportunities and challenges that women in the developing world encounter in the global digital economy. Women, because of their responsibilities as care givers and homemakers, encounter certain common predicaments in the world of paid work. Yet, she argues, it would be wrong to treat women as an undifferentiated group.

The discourse of economic empowerment through the use of ICTs by traditionally disadvantaged groups, such as women, refers to the growing anxieties, as expressed in anti-globalization movements and in the writings of a number of eminent non-European scholars on the subject. The roots of such anxieties, particularly in the South, lie in the hegemony of the North, both in technologies and in trade. In this context, the essay reflects the visions and concerns of women of the developing world regarding ICTs and digital trade in communities that often lack basics such as electricity and clean water. Hence, Mitter makes a case for including women's groups in policy dialogues for assessing the significance of ICT-led globalization in the developing world. However, she stresses the need to be critical of the concept of universalism in the priorities and aspirations of women. Mitter passionately concludes that it is crucial to ask the women themselves, especially those from the poorer countries, what they want from ICTs, as the silencing of their voices poses a threat to peace, stability and sustainability in development.

Is it possible to talk about the prospects for women without placing them in the background of their own countries? Does the digital divide along gender lines pose more of a challenge than the divide along local, national, or regional lines? Interweaving feminist agenda and regional priorities, Martha Roldan contributes in an interesting and incisive piece to the ongoing debate over the nature and dynamics of information- and knowledge- based development which she terms as Informational Capitalism. Placing the question of women in the context of the wider issue of development, her essay examines the underlying possible transitions from Information to Knowledge Societies, and reflects on its gendered implications on the basis of the Argentine experience. To this effect, she argues that it is necessary to distinguish between the neo-Liberal and Liberal (institutional) theoretical paradigms in order to elucidate, from a Critical Political Economy perspective, the dynamics of the 'Virtuous Circle' linking information, knowledge, work organization and development, and the regulatory framework deemed necessary to translate that virtuosity into practice in different regions of the world. This debate, Roldan feels, is still a missing component of the feminist agenda in southern Latin America.

Using the principles enshrined in the International Covenant on Economic, Social and Cultural Rights (1966), Roldan makes a case for the designing and enactment of humane forms of work organization in the search for information-cum-knowledge development paths. The agency of workers in the production and control of knowledge and information is hence a key perspective in the essay. Based on this position, she examines the viability and some of the gendered consequences of the application of the neo-Liberal project on Information Societies in Argentina, in the context of contemporary regional 'Globalization' expressed in the construction of MERCOSUR (the Common Market of the South).

On the basis of her analysis, Roldan posits that the introduction of Information Technology within the context of regional globalization exacerbates the vulnerabilities of non-core workers, of whom women form a large part. Women are doubly vulnerable in countries such as Argentina which are viewed by multinational companies as peripheral sites for tapping cheap labor. It seems that within such a context, ICTs have neither empowered women nor have they brought the desired development benefits to women in poor countries. She concludes by drawing lessons from this exercise as a contribution to the theoretical and political construction of a renewed national and regional 'gender-aware' information-cum-knowledge development agenda, and to the defense of the economic, social, and cultural rights, as indivisible dimensions of human rights of women (and men).

ICTs, Work, and Empowerment

The debate about whether technology oppresses or liberates society is a long standing one. Feminist scholars in the 1980s noted that the unequal gender division of labor, both in production and at the family level, proved remarkably resilient despite technological advancement (Cockburn, 1985). Later, research in the electronics industry pointed out that technological upgradation led to increased sectoral and occupational segmentation by gender, increasing the divide between women and men workers, and decreasing the number of women workers hired (McKay, 2002). Would ICTs be any different when they are introduced into the workplace and to new environments, particularly in the services sector? Indeed, Czarina Saloma argues that the barriers to entry in the development of business applications based on global standard ICTs are not as high as those in the development of semi-conductors and standard proprietary hardware and software. Subsequently, it has been shown that women's opportunities lie more in this ICT-driven global economy. The visionary work of Castells on the network society argues that technological changes, in particular network technologies, have transformed patriarchy into a 'contested domain, rather than a sphere of cultural repro-duction, leading to fundamental redefinitions of gender relations, family and sexuality'(Castells, 2000: 2–3).

Of course ICTs in and of themselves will not necessarily trans-form gender relations, nor automatically empower women, as much also depends on the socio-cultural and political context in which they are being introduced. To further this debate, Saloma argues that the presence of high-skill technological fields in the so-called developing countries, and the presence of women in these fields make previous theorizing on dependent technological work inadequate. She addresses this issue by suggesting a framework based on Schutz and Luckmann's (1973) concept of social distri-bution of knowledge and Lachenmann's (1997) notion of female spaces. On the basis of an examination of the Philippine ICT indus-try, she discusses the development of female spaces in the industry and its implications for the feminization of labor, and other related issues. Underlying the emergence of this group of women Infor-mation Technology (IT) workers are 'user-friendly' technologies, horizontal learning structures, and the hybridity of some arenas of IT.

Saloma argues that the nature and structure of ICTs and ICT work have resulted in the presence of fields in the Philippine ICT industry that require a non-technical/interdisciplinary back-ground, discourage gender tracking in the compensation structure, and promote recognition of women's epistemic privilege and standpoint. All this, she notes, prevents the feminization of labor in these fields. The findings support the argument that creating a context conducive to the entry of more women into hitherto male spaces is currently a more important concern than the question of the feminization of labor in the ICT industry. In a nutshell, she claims that the Philippines ICT industry has not resulted in a devaluation of women's labor, at least at the more highly skilled levels.

The special nature of the IT industry is also taken up by Kelkar, Shrestha, and Veena who examine women's agency in the IT industry in India based on field research in two cities: Bangalore and Delhi. They point out that the nature of work in the IT industry is different as networking capacities, tools, as well as the individualization of these capacities have increased women's capacities to take decisions, thereby constructing greater spaces to enhance their agency. ICTs have led to a broadening and diversification of technological activities and actors. Kelkar, et al. looked at both the software industry and IT-Enabled Services (ITES), particularly through the perceptions of women and men workers, and managers within the industry.

What is interesting is their discussion of how working in the IT sector has affected the gender division of labor at home. Single women are more mobile and less hindered by family concerns, when compared to married women, who are bound by the contradictory demands of their families, jobs, and children. At the same time, the prestige attached to the IT industry allows young women to work night shifts, live alone in cities, and control their incomes. They conclude that while a large number of women continue to work in gendered homes and paid work sites, balancing work and domestic responsibilities, they also carry an ongoing struggle to challenge the embedded patriarchal relations within the family and in the industry. In contrast to the gender egalitarian tradition of the Philippines, the socially-sanctioned gender inequalities in the market in India seem more rigid. Despite this, Indian women prefer to work outside the home in order to improve their social position. This also allows them greater scope to enhance their agency, and resist family-based dependency and coercion.

This autonomy for women is especially relevant when we discuss outsourcing, as women are getting some kind of equality at the workplace. A very special case is that this is the first time we are documenting new opportunities for women in the formal sector in response to globalization and the growing trade in the service sector. The essay by Cecilia Ng and Swasti Mitter examines the experiences of women workers in the emerging Information Technology Enabled Services sector (ITES), in particular call centers, representing customer services at both national and globally outsourced sites. Although the Malaysian and Indian cases are not entirely comparable, the case studies give a certain insight into the changes in the lives and career patterns of women in the developing world. The interesting aspect of these new types of jobs is that women's opportunities do not depend on an effective search of the labor market, rather it is the expanding market that draws women into employment in the formal sector. Although the women call center workers do not come from the poorer classes, without new opportunities, Indian women have very few alternatives: be housewives or take up lower-paid jobs.

The essay on call centers contributes to the debates about whether these institutions replicate the run-away manufacturing firms in the export-oriented sector of the developing world of the 1980s. By producing new empirical data and privileging the voices of women workers themselves, Ng and Mitter ask: is there a devaluing of women's work and skills or have women workers empowered themselves through these new employment opportunities? It is indeed a double-edged sword as even though the women workers feel stressed and their work is closely monitored, the industry does seem to recognize their (soft) skills and rewards them accordingly, thus questioning the feminization of labor position—a point also argued by Saloma.

In this discussion on call centers, issues of cultural hegemony and identity brought up by some Indian writers, including Mitter in this volume, have not been taken up for deeper investigation and analysis. This issue needs further exploration in future research, particularly so, in the light of the recent controversy around it. For example, as stated by Roy and Barsamian (2004: 90), 'So Indians must take on false identities, pretend to be Americans, learn a "correct" accent. It leads to a psychosis.' This notion of cultural imperialism has been countered by Basi (2005), whose research pointed out, that the women themselves do not feel that they have lost their Indian identity despite having to practice 'accent neutralization' or learn about the culture of another country.

Trading and Networking through the Net: Different Facets of Empowerment

Having dealt with economic empowerment of employed women in urban areas, we now turn to two case studies of women using the Internet—for trading and networking. While one does not want to dismiss the possibilities of ICTs and self employment, at this moment in history, it is very difficult to assess the power of ICTs to strengthen entrepreneurship and self-employment. It is important to collect and document case studies which can assist us to highlight the potentials of this approach. However it is equally important to remember that there are so few examples of such case studies that they may not have any scientific validity for replication and policy making. One has to remember that the success and failure of an ICT pilot project may be rooted in the history, tradition, and culture of the locality, and hence, be cautiously optimistic.

Susan Schaefer Davis provides a valuable and concrete case study of the challenges rural women from the poorer parts of the world face in utilizing the Internet for selling their products in the global market. Through her experience as a development practitioner from the North, she discusses in some detail how one can be instrumental in initiating a process that enables home-based women weavers in Morocco to overcome the hurdles of trading through the Internet. In a pilot project, illiterate women in two sites in rural Morocco use the Internet to sell the rugs and other textiles they weave. This could provide a solution to the perennial problem of marketing the products of isolated rural women, in addition to demonstrating how ICTs could be used to improve the lives of women who are disadvantaged by class, location, and culture. It allows women to keep a larger share of the final profit, which often instead went to middlewomen/men. The essay describes the process of getting rural women to sell their textiles online, including both benefits and constraints.

The two sites provide interesting contrasts in terms of gender differentiation, communication challenges, and the transmission of payment internationally. It also cautions us not to impose canons of Western feminism in assessing the benefits of e-trade in societies where social norms are different. In this unusually interesting case study of successful trading both for the women and the community, Davis reveals how through this networking mode, women obtain a greater share of the profits generated by their work, and also some degree of empowerment and freedom, even though the profits are used mainly to support the family and to pay for children's education. At one site, rug sales are assisted by the Village Development Association, which receives a percentage of the profits. This is then used for projects like latrines for the school.

In addition to economic empowerment, this anthology also acknowledges the importance of networking to bring together people from the North and South to exchange and learn from each others' experiences. Such virtual networking could empower women from both locations, as discussed in the essay on the Virtual International Women's University (vifu) by Isabel Zorn. This essay describes an experiment initiated by women from the North, in connecting and supporting women from the South, particularly in sharing and accessing information on gender issues. At the same time, they are also critically conscious that this virtual project is supporting only those women who have access to computers— that is, women in the South who are more privileged. Highlighting how the design of technology can include or exclude women, Zorn informs us that the incentive for setting up this Project was the belief that while ICTs are being used to support development, women do not profit from them as much as men do. Therefore, she describes how the founders looked into how Internet Technology could be designed and applied to improve women's lives and women's access to information, education, and autonomy.

This essay suggests an 'avenue' to empower women in the North and South by building virtual international communities as one of the tools for women to participate in and benefit from international exchange. It discusses the social and technical aspects of building an enabling environment for women through vifu. What was important in enabling the sustainability of this communication, was the conscious implementation of a development procedure characterized and guided by feminist principles of inclusion, participation, user-developer-interaction, and transparency with the aim of enabling sociability and the transfer of technological know-how. Zorn argues that when ICTs are going to be promoted and used for developmental issues, their specific technical and social design, particularly the human-computer interaction, and the interdependence of social and technical issues will play an important role in the success or failure of any initiative.

Implementing the Change

The final section of the volume looks at the possibility of implementing changes at the macro-level as well as within institutions at the micro-level. Dora Inés Munévar and Juan Aburto Arrieta start with a proposition that gender discrimination determines women's exclusion in all societies and social estates, so that they constitute the poorest people. As such they argue that gender inequality comprises an almost insurmountable impediment to the enjoyment of all kinds of resources, including technological resource, and communication technologies, in particular. To surmount this discrimination, and to enhance women's empowerment, they propose the configuration of Gender-Net as a decisive tool to promote the quality of life of women through the use of community-based human communicative processes. Underlying the establishment of this networking strategy are critical sociocultural and political goals including democracy, citizenship, and empowerment. Munévar and Arrieta force us to think about the power relations unfolded by the Internet as a technological product and, simultaneously, as the technological input to reach empowerment goals.

Through the medium of telecenters at the community level, Gender-Net hopes to provide a basis for the opening up of questions and discussions about technology and life and, more closely, the issue of technology and gender discrimination. The authors remind us that the successful usage of Gender-Net as a telecenter is determined by how flexible it is to the changing communication needs of a community, and by how it can offer equitable opportunities for personal and professional growth. Additionally, the provision of ICTs to various segments of society requires expertise in the potential of that kind of tool to serve different kinds of needs. These include strategic expertise in planning large-scale innovation projects, technical expertise related to hardware, and educational expertise in using new technologies for the advancement of empowerment, knowledge, learning, and gender. By consciously factoring in these principles into the creation of Gender-Net, the essay concludes by suggesting three phases in this initiative, based on the premise that ICTs will contribute towards development and gender equality.

The last essay by Marcelle points to the urgent need to fill the gap between the concept and practice of gender equality in the ICTs arena and to develop effective strategies for concerted action. While the essay by Munévar and Arrieta focuses at the community level, Gillian Marcelle proposes strategies to gender sensitize, through a process of continuous interaction, the ICTs arena comprising scholars, activists, policy makers and technologists. Based on a reading of existing literature by feminist scholars and policy oriented work, as well as her experiences as a gender expert with the United Nations and women's NGOs, she interrogates this conceptual silence and ambiguity regarding gender equality, ICTs, and human development. What is also useful is her definition of the ICTs arena which includes in an all encompassing sense, ICTs production units, ICTs services and applications, ICTs equipment, ICTs policy and regulatory bodies, as well as technical bodies involved in establishing ICTs infrastructure and services standards.

She subsequently outlines a conceptual framework, which can be used to open spaces for gender equality and women's perspectives to contribute to reshaping the ICTs revolution. It sets out a three-phased approach: Buy-in, Implementation, and Growth and reinforcement (BIG). These actions are needed to ensure that women secure access to the potential benefits of ICTs and minimize potential problems associated with the ICTs revolution. Marcelle rightly points out that ICTs cannot fulfill their potential for use as a tool for gender equality, women's empowerment, and human development unless decision-making and participation in the ICTs sector undergo a fundamental change. She then uses this action oriented conceptual framework to analyze four critical areas of intervention—ICTs policy making, ICTs applications for promotion of women's economic empowerment, ICT-enabled health and education services, and ICT-mediated public life participation. In including all the strategic actors in the ICTs arena, Marcelle's recommendations in the BIG framework would be a useful starting point for the international players concerned about developing ICTs for development. Gillian Marcelle complements Martha Roldan by espousing the critical role of negotiation at the policy level. Hers is a strategic approach to ensure that the feminist agenda gets included in the ICTs policy arena. Whereas Roldan makes a case for a more fundamental shift in power relations between the North and the South, Marcelle highlights the way forward within existing institutional and regional power structures. She envisages a people- rather than profit-centered ICTs revolution, where democracy, transparency, and participation become the bases for governance, rather than just empty rhetoric.

Global Actors in the Information Society

This volume hopes to contribute to the above discussions and engage with national and international forums, including the forthcoming World Summit on the Information Society (WSIS)—a gathering of ministerial bodies and policy makers intending to develop a better understanding of the information revolution and its implications for the international community. One of the key issues, as the first Summit in 2003 revealed, will be to continue the discourse on the role of ICTs in stimulating growth, creating greater social and gender equality, and improving living and working conditions.

The 2005 WSIS Summit in Tunisia coincides with the first five-year review of the world's progress towards attaining the Millennium Development Goals (MDGs). The essays in this volume are also framed within the context of the current exploration by policy makers and donor agencies implementing the MDGs which include poverty reduction and gender equality. It is important to stress the fact that some of the benefits of ICTs exclude some of the poorest people, but this does not make ICTs irrelevant to the MDGs, as women are always at a disadvantage. In addition, the 2000 Beijing Plus Five meeting in New York stated clearly that the priority of policy makers should be to use ICTs for economic empowerment, and not just to combat the negative portrayal or abuse of women in the media.

In our anthology, we try to raise issues which should be useful not only for international bodies, but also for other actors such as NGOs, the corporate sector, and trade unions. For example, at the third meeting of the International Telecommunication Union Working Group on Gender Issues in 2004, it was recognized that the international community is just beginning to understand the way in which the digital divide is intensified by women's and men's access, or lack thereof, to resources which enable them to actively participate in the development of their communities and countries.

Missing Bytes

The materials in this anthology hope to provide answers to some of the questions raised in the international arena in the context of

ICTs and development. But perhaps the most important contribution of the authors has been to raise important questions, debunk myths about ICTs and women in developing countries, and to highlight and pinpoint the direction that future research could take in order to make the world a better place and to uplift women's position in it. This book attempts to remedy the relative lack of scientific material to back up the demands and claims of NGOs and activists and strengthen the communication links between policy makers and civil society.

The authors are from different parts of the world and from diverse backgrounds. Yet they all make a case for further research in the field where so little is known and yet so much is talked about. None of the essays in this volume explores the impact or potential of ICTs in strengthening women's position in agricultural occupations and perhaps future research should be directed towards this. Stewart (2004) offers some analysis of how the use of ICTs by women in the North does not necessarily liberate them in their lives and work. Based on her work in cotton farms in Queensland, Australia, Stewart argues that the use of mobiles and computers has not transformed the unequal gender division of labor and power relations among farm families. Rather, it has exacerbated the existing imbalance in gender roles and ideologies. It would be useful to extend this to the rural sector in the developing countries and to see how e-business, as in the Moroccan situation, can be replicated in an agricultural context.

There are anxieties about the paucity of data and of evidence, but there are even greater concerns about the absence of conceptual frameworks for critiquing the emergent Informational Capitalism. The essays in this volume indicate a way forward to redress the lacunae and stress that the perspectives of women must be included in the negotiation process at the global, national, and local levels. In this context, it would be useful to research and document the technical and social processes whereby women, through networking technologies, are involved in enhancing their own agency either individually, or through solidarity campaigns. More research is needed, for example, into the innovative ways in which women, especially disadvantaged women, in the developing world have used the Internet. At the end of the day, it is women's experiences and voices that count in how they apply ICTs: to transform their lives; to redesign the world they live in; and also to shape the future of technology itself.

Notes

1. We try to be as precise as possible about the definition of ICTs. It refers to networking technologies arising out of the convergence of information and communications technologies and the Internet, extranet, intranet, and associated technologies.
2. Economic empowerment is defined as economic change as well as increased bargaining power and/or structural change which enables women to secure economic gains on a sustained basis (Carr, Chen, and Jhabvala, 1996).

References

Basi, Tina. (2005) 'Faces and Places: Women Working in Delhi's Call Center Industry', *Conference Proceedings on Gender, Development and Public Policy in an Era of Globalization*, Asian Institute of Technology, Bangkok, Thailand.

Carr, Marilyn, Chen, Martha and Jhabvala, Renana (eds). (1996) *Speaking Out: Women's Economic Empowerment in South Asia*, IT Publications on behalf of Aga Khan Foundation Canada and United Nations Development Fund for Women (UNIFEM), London.

Castells, Manuel. (2000) *The Rise of the Network Society*, Blackwell Publishers, Oxford, UK and Maden, USA.

Cockburn, Cynthia. (1985) *Machinery of Dominance: Women, Men and Technical Knowhow*, Pluto Press, London.

Ghosh, Jayati. (2004) 'Globalisation and Economic Empowerment of Women: Emerging Issues in Asia', Paper presented at the High-Level Intergovernmental Meeting on the Beijing Platform for Action, UN-ESCAP, 7–10 September.

Gothoskar, Sujata. (2000) 'Teleworking and Gender: Emerging Issues', *Economic and Political Weekly*, 35(26): 2293–98.

Kelkar, Govind and Nathan, Dev. (2002) 'Gender Relations and Technological Change in Asia', in *Current Sociology*, 50(3): 427–41.

Lee, Jamie Cistoldi. (2004) 'Access, Self-Image, and Empowerment: Computer Training for Women Entrepreneurs in Costa Rica', *Gender, Technology and Development*, 8(2): 209–29.

Lie, Merete. (1991) 'Technology and Gender: Identity and Symbolism' in Lehto, Anna-Maija and Eriksson, Inger (eds), *Proceedings of the Conference on Women, Work and Computerization*, 30 June–2 July, Helsinki.

McKay, Steve. (2002) 'Hard Drives and Glass Ceilings: Gender Stratification in High-Tech Production', Paper presented at SSSP Annual Meeting, 15 August.

Mitter, Swasti, Fernandez, Grace, and Varghese, Shaiby. (2004) 'On the Threshold of Informalization Women Call Centre Workers in India' in Carr, Marilyn (ed.),

Chains of Fortune: Linking Women Producers and Workers with Global Markets, Commonwealth Secretariat, London, pp. 165–83.

Mitter, Swasti. (2002) 'Offshore Outsourcing of Information Processing Work and Economic Empowerment of Women', Paper presented at World Bank, Washington DC, 2 June (Available at http://www.dgroups.org/groups/worldbank/Gender-ICT/docs/SwastiMitterJune02.pdf).

Roy, Arundhati and Barsamian, David. (2004) *The Cheque Book and the Cruise Missile,* South End Press, Cambridge, MA.

Stanworth, Celia. (1998) 'Teleworking and the Information Age', *New Technology, Work and Employment,* 13(1): 51–62.

Stewart, Julianne. (2004) 'Gender as a Factor in the Uptake and Use of ICTs on Family Farms in Southern Queensland, Australia', *Gender, Technology and Development,* 1(8): 97–117.

Wajcman, Judy. (1991) *Feminism Confronts Technology,* Polity Press, Cambridge.

PART I

Theorizing Gender, Development, and ICTs: A Reality Check

2 GLOBALIZATION, ICTs, AND ECONOMIC EMPOWERMENT: A FEMINIST CRITIQUE

SWASTI MITTER

This essay has a history. It is an extended and updated version of a paper that I wrote in September 2001 at the request of the Economic and Social Committee of the United Nations General Assembly.[1] The Assembly that year, in New York, was gearing up to discuss the role of globalization and its implications for developing countries. One of the preparatory panels, in that context, was to explore the possibilities of ICTs giving poorer countries, and disadvantaged people such as women, access to the global economy. The invitation to participate in the panel as an Expert came to me in August and I wrote my contribution for the session scheduled for mid–September on the eve of the planned Assembly meeting. Then came the events of 9/11, leading to the postponement and subsequent shifting of the site of the General Assembly meeting to Geneva. The panel where I was to participate, however, took place in New York, not exactly on the planned date but only a few days later, on 20 September to be precise. I arrived at the shell-shocked UN headquarters with a revised text and a moral obligation to contribute, however modestly, to bridge the gap between the haves and have-nots in our polarized world. This is part of what I presented at the panel:

> The catastrophic events of September 11 ... have made me acutely and painfully aware of the advantages and disadvantages of our networked, interlinked world ... the convergence of computer and communication, culminating in Internet Technologies, has given rise to a network society, where alliances could be forged, on a supranational level, in many spheres. The global nature of terrorism is a sinister consequence of such networking possibilities.... Yet, as I see it,

the same networking technologies could be used as harbingers of new opportunities for the poor in developing countries. At this point in time the international development community has a moral obligation to highlight the potential of ICTs in reducing inequities on national and international levels that pose threats to peace and stability.

I am writing this essay as a continuation of the one I presented in New York precisely out of a moral obligation that I feel as a researcher serving the development community. Historically, this is an opportune moment, as I wish to urge the World Summit on the Information Society[2] to address concerns that many women and men in the South have about globalization and network technologies. Their concerns are rooted in the anxiety that arises from the hegemony of the North over trade and technology. Redressing the balance will require fundamental changes in policies towards trade agendas and intellectual property rights. It takes a long time to initiate or implement such changes; in the short run it may be prudent to be strategic and explore the possibilities of ICTs in improving the quality of life within the prevailing North-South relationship. I shall, hence, draw attention of diverse constituencies to areas where information is scant and research is necessary for assessing the origin, extent, and significance of the digital divide. The knowledge, I hope, will be useful if the development community wishes to counter the material disparity arising out of asymmetrical access to ICTs. At the end of the essay, I shall make a case for respecting the voices of the people on the ground, some of whom question the importance of connectivity as a bread and butter issue. The focus of my essay is women as they form the majority of the poor in developing countries. While economic empowerment is the major focus of my analytical and synthesizing exercise, I am aware that it is not a sufficient condition of social empowerment in tradition bound societies.

Concerns

The vision of globalization is by no means an uncontested terrain. Based on the Washington Consensus of the World Bank, the IMF, and the Treasury of the United States, the principle of globalization advocates liberalization of trade as one of the conditions of structural adjustment and reform. The breaking down of artificial barriers to the flow of goods, services, capital, knowledge, and to (a far lesser extent) people has benefited some countries; but the majority of the developing countries remain unconvinced. The philosophy of globalization, often described as free market fundamentalism, is seen to contribute to the swelling numbers of people living below the poverty line (Stiglitz, 2002). Africa plunges deep into misery as incomes fall and the standard of living declines. Members of the civil society take to the street to join the anti-globalization movement in order to express their anxiety.

Indeed, it will not be fair to treat ICTs as value-free, neutral technologies; they play a key role in the present phase of globalization and the implementation of the free market philosophy. By reducing the cost of communication and transport to a dramatic extent (Mitter and Efendioglu, 1999), they have not only enhanced the speed of commercial transactions but have also changed the composition of global trade. Globalization is not a new phenomenon; but the distinguishing feature of the present globalization is that countries, developing and developed, have become increasingly connected through trade in digitized information. Combinations of computer and communication technologies, culminating in networking technologies, have enhanced the speed and reduced the cost of communication to such an extent that the question of distance has become less relevant in commercial and business transactions. With the digitization of information, it has become possible, and generally cost effective, to transfer information processing work, both in manufacturing and in services, to offices and work units that are remote from main premises, within and across national boundaries. In OECD (Organization for Economic Cooperation and Development) countries, it has given rise to the outsourcing of a vast range of information processing work both to subcontracting and satellite units within a country as well as to some developing countries that possess a low-waged, computer-literate, and English-literate workforce (Braga, 1996; Mitter and Efendioglu, 1999). In some developing countries, as in India and the Philippines, women have become major recipients of this globally distributed work.

Despite some such visible gains, women and men in developing countries have not seen the specter of ICTs as an unquestionable blessing. Islamic scholars, for example, have raised doubts about the appropriateness of this imported technology on philosophical and ethical grounds. The cyberfuture has been seen by some only as an accentuation of European Civilization that is dynamic, yet, aggressive and unstable in style (Sardar and Ravetz, 1996: p.12). There is some unease that social and cultural disjuncture arising from ICT-enabled occupations does not get mentioned in the Northern discourse of science and technology. This deliberate separation between technology and ethics, or between science and religion, is viewed as purely Eurocentric, a legacy of hostilities between those who claimed to be the custodians of Christianity and those who challenged their intellectual and territorial powers (Sadr, 1984). Such a separation is culturally specific and is contrary, as Vandana Shiva (2000) puts it, to more holistic notions prevailing in non-Christian and non-European societies. The 9/11 event, however, has made a section of the intelligentsia in the West reappraise their *Weltanschauung* with the confidence in the universalities of European Enlightenment values giving way to skepticism and doubt. As John Gray (2003) put it in his book, *Al Qaeda and What it Means to be Modern*, there are many ways of being modern, yet, the belief in the West that there is only one way and that it is always good, has deep and disturbing roots:

> Western societies are ruled by the myth that, as the rest of the world absorbs science and becomes modern, it is bound to become secular, enlightened and peaceful—as, contrary to all evidence, they imagine themselves to be. With its attack on the Twin towers, Al Qaeda destroyed that myth (ibid.: 118).

This concept of universalism is being similarly questioned in the context of empowering women with the help of ICTs. The Aristotelian notion of universality in human rights and values has influenced a large part of the contemporary feminist philosophy in North America (Nussbaum, 2000). However, the emerging discipline has, as I see it, overlooked the multiplicity in the aspirations of women in non-European countries (Mitter, 2001). The discourse has similarly ignored the difference in the priorities of women in rich and poor countries. Women, in no society, form an undifferentiated group. In the information economy as in other economies, a woman's position within her country is crucially determined by her access to productive resources, and by the privileges of her

Figure 2.1

Global B2B and B2C E-commerce Spending by Region, 2000 and 2005

Country/Region	2000						2005					
	B2B		B2C		Total		B2B		B2C		Total	
	Value ($B)	Share (%)	Value ($B)	Share (%)	Value ($B)	Share (%)	Value ($B)	Share (%)	Value ($B)	Share (%)	Value ($B)	Share (%)
United States	117	41	44	60	161	45	1,561	36	256	36	1,817	36
Western Europe	57	20	13	18	70	20	1,465	34	253	36	1,718	34
Japan	69	24	6	8	75	21	504	12	75	11	579	11
Asia/Pacific	13	5	6	8	19	5	516	12	83	12	599	12
Canada	11	4	2	3	13	4	135	3	23	3	158	3
Latin America	5	2	1	1	6	2	71	2	9	1	80	2
Rest of the World	10	4	1	1	11	3	77	2	8	1	85	2
Worldwide	282	100	73	100	355	100	4,329	100	707	100	5,036	100

Note: Percentages may not add up to 100 due to rounding error.
Source: International Data Corporation (2002).

class and ethnic background. In India, women software programmers in the state of Kerala (Arun and Arun, 2002) encounter life chances and challenges that are very different from those faced by women street vendors in the city of Ahmedabad. In the global economy, a woman's space is defined also by her country's place in the international trading league. It will thus definitely be prudent to place the issue of women in the context of the competitive position of the country and the region in which they reside. I illustrate this point with a reference to trade in digitized information, internationally.

Figure 2.1 shows two segments of the trade in digitized information: Business to Business (B2B) and Business to Consumer (B2C). The current share of developing countries in both B2B and B2C as the figures show, is minute. Asia is the leading region among the developing countries in B2B and B2C, followed by Latin America, while the share of Africa and other developing countries is virtually nil. Even within Asia, it is concentrated in a handful of countries such as India, Malaysia, China, and the Philippines. In this scenario, one needs to be cautious in expecting substantial benefits accruing to women and men in developing countries, irrespective of their class backgrounds, from the global trade in digital economy.

GIVE WOMEN A CHANCE

Questioning universalism in women's rights and priorities does not mean a lack of acknowledgment of certain common predicaments shared by the majority of women in all strata of society. The biological and social roles of women as mothers, homemakers, and carers circumscribe their ability and opportunity to function on an equal basis with men in most economic spheres. It happens in traditional occupations and sectors, loosely described as the Old Economy, and is likely to persist even in the so-called Digital or New Economy.

Societal roles or biological attributes do not always work against women. The patience and persistence needed for repetitive work or the ability and inclination to work in a team are the qualities that managements often associate with women. This perception, real or stereotyped, partly explains the feminization of the workforce in the manufacturing industries of export-processing zones in the developing world. Similar considerations now lead to recruiting of young women in large numbers, as I discuss later, in emerging institutions of the digital economy, such as call centers. It has created new opportunities but has led to a flexible and non-unionized workforce. The quality as well as the quantity of work should thus be part of a feminist evaluation of the impact of ICT-led globalization.

Women also often find it more difficult than men to engage in new forms of self-employment. Businesses in telekiosks or cyber cafes often elude women who do not have the same access as men to family property or institutional finance (Gothoskar, 2000; Mitter, 2000). Women also have to face greater barriers than men in receiving education and training that can equip them with computer literacy, English literacy, and business skills. Parents tend to invest more in the education of the boy rather than the girl child as daughters leave the parental home at marriage and in many societies the family has to save for a dowry to marry the daughters off.

The introduction of networking technologies is a new phenomenon. It is thus difficult to find enough evidence to assess its liberating potential on the working lives of women from underprivileged backgrounds. In this essay, all I shall attempt to do is highlight the barriers that women, more than men, face in being linked to the global economy. The link to the global economy comes either through a greater access to the international market or being the recipient of globally distributed work in information processing. I have thus distinguished two different ways of earning livelihood—self-employment and employment in the globalized information economy.

TRADING ON THE NET

In the majority of the developing countries, self-employment is the most important means of survival for women. Again evidence is scant and one should be cautious about the sustainability and replicability of isolated success stories. The limited evidence available so far shows that women have found some scope in obtaining a market niche in the purchase and sale of information. A much discussed example is the Grameen Phone in Bangladesh, where women run a successful business selling communication services via mobile telephones to other women (Hafkin and Taggart, 2001) who have relations and contacts abroad. In India and Malaysia, women use online delivery of services as freelance journalists to newspapers and other publishers (Ng, 2001a) within and across national boundaries (Mitter, 2000). In Peru, a nationwide network of housewives called Tortasperu (see www.tortasperu.com) involved in baking confectioneries sold over the Internet, showcased lucrative work for women taking care of children at home and yet, delivering much needed foreign exchange to the country. Similar cases have been documented in Africa such as Ethiopia's virtual gift shop (see www.ethiogift.com) where traditional Ethiopian costumes, food items, and spices produced by women are sold over the Internet to customers abroad. One should, however, be cautiously optimistic as there are considerable barriers that, as I see, women face in engaging in trade.

The number of women Internet users is miniscule in most countries where there is an insignificant amount of Internet access for the entire population. The International Telecommunication Union (ITU) in 2002 released some statistics on female Internet usage (Figure 2.2) which show that in most poorer countries, women represent a much smaller proportion of even this insignificant number of users.

The International Data Corporation in 2002 reported that 90 percent of Internet usage is located in industrialized countries, where about 60 percent are already dominated by the USA and Canada. However, with an annual growth rate of 38 percent by 2005, the forecast is that the US would fall to third place in terms of Internet usage, trailing behind Asia-Pacific, which would capture 27 percent of the market and Europe, which would garner more than 30 percent.

Aggregate statistics on the rapid deployment of telecommunication infrastructure and facilities within Asia and the Pacific are, however, misleading: the region is vast and diverse in terms of ICTs. For example, apart from the spectacular progress made in China, Singapore, Taiwan, South Korea, and Japan, the rest of the countries in Asia-Pacific are languishing. At the present rate of development, Bhutan, for example, would take until 2050 to achieve the teledensity that Singapore has today. The ITU reports that fewer than two in 10,000 Cambodians and Vietnamese use the Internet, while nearly 3,000 out of every 10,000 Singaporeans do so. Of the more than 300 million people connected to the Web

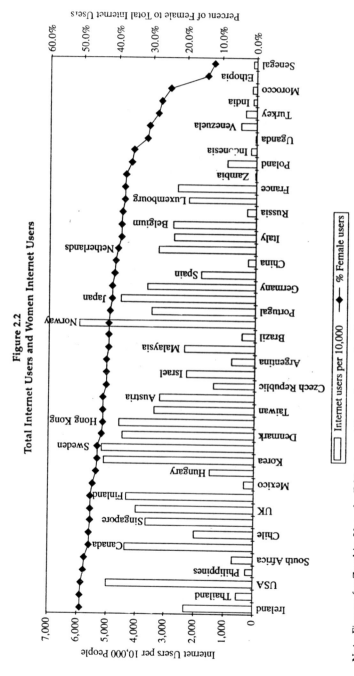

Figure 2.2
Total Internet Users and Women Internet Users

Percent of Female to Total Internet Users

Internet Users per 10,000 People

Internet users per 10,000 ■ % Female users

Note: Figures for Zambia, Uganda, Ethiopia, and Senegal were taken from Hafkin and Taggart (2001) and refer to the year 2000.
Source: World Teleconmunication Development Report 2002, ITU.

in the world today, only 3.2 million or just over 1 percent live in Southeast Asia. Worldwide, UNDP reports that more than three quarters of Internet users live in high-income countries which contain 14 percent of the world's people.

Accessing the Internet is one thing, owning a computer another. Home access to a computer and to the Internet in developing countries is hardly a phenomenon. Even privileged professional women in many parts of Asia and Africa encounter difficulties in accessing the Internet not only because they do not own computers, but simply because they do not even have telephone lines which is a basic Internet infrastructure. The highest total Internet monthly charges in US dollars were found in Ethiopia ($95), Argentina ($92), Kenya ($82), and Tanzania ($74) compared to the much lower average costs of $14 for Europe and $26 for the Americas. If purchasing power parity (PPP) conversion rates were used instead, (that is, the number of local currency units required to buy the same amount of goods and services in the domestic market as a U.S. dollar would buy in the United States), the ISP charges reach as high as $646 in Ethiopia!

There are other barriers that pose even greater challenges for trading. The language of the web pages is predominantly English and hence excludes a large number of women who lack formal education, especially in English. The Association for Progressive Communications (APC) Women's Networking Survey in 1996 (Hafkin and Taggart, 2001) reported that the language of the Internet was the major barrier for women in the use of network technologies. The picture, however, is changing and perhaps for the benefit of women who generally have less chances than men to learn English. Results of the IDC's World 2001 Survey revealed that about 43 percent of all websites are now multilingual. If we count multilingual together with monolingual English sites (17 percent), English still dominates as the language of the Internet with 56 percent. On the positive side, one can discern that the dominance of English is somehow weakening. In 1999, 95 percent of web pages were in English; the figure has declined to 68.4 percent in 2000.

As with most issues on ICTs, the language of the net is a problematic one. Familiarity with the common global language for the Internet, English, gives women entrepreneurs greater chances to enter the international market; training for women in English should thus become important—a rare opportunity for the majority of women in poorer countries.

Lack of technical competency also creates hurdles. Unlike the telephone, the use of Internet requires more complex and demanding skills including those of troubleshooting. Women experience a greater sense of techno-fear as compared to men because of the lack of encouragement in solving technical problems in schools and families. Again, for women, the questions of quality control or of regulatory policies such as the restriction on and the cost of international transactions may appear daunting (Box 2.1).

> **Box 2.1**
> **Small Businesses Face Difficulties in Global E-commerce**
>
> We sell art calendars with photos taken by young women in our cooperatives and sell them abroad. We publicize their availability over the Net to customers abroad. We find customers but it is not easy to sell. It costs us nearly US$3 to cash a cheque or a draft of US$5, the maximum price we can get. In addition, there are bureaucratic wrangles to receive payment from abroad.
>
> Source: Interview by Swasti Mitter with Shahidul Alam, DRIK Picture Gallery, Bangladesh, at a workshop organized by IDRC in Delhi, 3 March 2002.

In Africa, Asia, and Latin America, employment, particularly in the formal sector, is a privilege that only a minority of women enjoy. The digital economy is no exception where women, generally from relatively affluent educational and social backgrounds, receive a certain amount of globally distributed work. The majority of the employment in the digital economy, for women as well as men, has so far come from the export-oriented segment of the market of which software is one major sector. This expansion has broadened the job prospects of women in new areas. The limited statistics that we have so far, indicate that women in some of the Asian countries occupy more than 20 percent of professional jobs (Mitter, 2000; Ng, 2001b). This figure in the field of software services is higher than any other field of engineering.

Assessing the parity between women and men in the digital economy is a complex task, which involves looking at the quality as well as the quantity of work. Women are not always losers.

As the Survey by Cecilia Ng in Malaysia in 1999 shows (Ng, 2001a), in the software sector women in Malaysia are getting numerically almost as visible as men. However, they are generally clustered at the low-skilled end of the hierarchy with little future for career progression. Male workers dominate the technical and managerial occupations.

It is not necessarily the discrimination by employers that accounts for this skewed distribution. Often women themselves settle for less demanding jobs as they have to be responsible for looking after the children (Arun and Arun, 2002). A Survey in Kerala shows that some mothers gave up work in software development because of the stress involved in meeting deadlines; however they continued to use their skills by taking up more flexible jobs such as teaching in computer training.

Although impressive, the prospects for women lie more in the Information Technology Enabled Services (ITES) than in software services. The worldwide demand for ITES is expected to grow at a dramatic rate in the coming decade and is expected to be US$ 671 billion by the year 2005 (Communiqué India, No. 2, Feb. 2002). With revenues of US$ 870 million from ITES (also called Remote Services) in 2000–1 and an annual growth rate of 66 percent, India currently has the potential to address a large part of the market (ibid.). In 1999, NASSCOM projected that for the year 2005, employment figures in ITES in India would be nearly 1.1 million. There are no gender-disaggregated statistics on employment that arise from this outsourced ITES in South and Southeast Asia. According to the Deputy Director of the Confederation of Indian Industries (CII), at least 40 percent of these newly-created jobs are given to, and taken by, women (Field Survey, 2002).[3] The share of women is likely to be similar in countries such as the Philippines. The Remote Services or ITES that refer to relocated back office operations open up opportunities for women. Yet, one has to be cautious about the future (Box 2.2). There are various types of back office services requiring different levels of skills from women and men, and there is a discernible trend in hiring women in operations that require less complex skills.

The recent qualitative case studies in India (Mitter and Sen, 2000) indicate that women are concentrated in those areas that need routine or discretionary skills. Women are less visible in specialized areas of back office operations. The next round of technological changes in the areas of voice recognition and image processing may make some of these routine skills less saleable in the international market.

Box 2.2
Gender Structure in Back Office Services

Routine: requiring only basic skills—Women predominate
- Data capture and processing.
- Customer call centers—for routine queries, order taking, and referrals.
- Hotel or rental car reservations.
- Virtual service centers (e.g., home delivery pizza companies).

Discretionary: requiring technical training and problem solving—Women predominate
- Data verification and repair (e.g., optically scanned documents).
- Claims processing.
- Mailing list management.
- Remote secretarial services.
- Customer call centers—account queries, after-sales support.

Specialized: requiring specific expertise and managerial authority—Men predominate
- Accounting, book-keeping, payroll processing.
- Electronic publishing.
- Customer call centers—problem/website design and management.
- Dispute resolution.
- Technical transcription (e.g., medical, legal).
- Medical records management.
- Technical online support.
- Indexing and abstracting services.
- Research and technical writing

Source: Adapted by Swasti Mitter from *I.T. Information Technology* Vol. 11, No. 2, December 2001, EFY Enterprises Pvt Ltd, New Delhi, p. 29.

It will be wise to assess where the future lies in the short as well as in the long run for both women and men. Volatility in the US economy and in Wall Street currently has affected the volume of e-business in software. Even a NASDAQ-listed company such as

Infosys, India's second largest listed exporter of software services, has come under pressure as US clients sharply cut spending on technology services (*Financial Times*, 11 April 2002, p. 27). This turnaround in business has had a serious impact on the recruitment and salary grades of Indian graduates in ICT-related courses (Box 2.3). Significantly, Infosys is investing US$ 5 million in setting up a business process outsourcing unit for receiving back office tasks such as bill processing. This business is seen as low margin and high volume, requiring repetitive skills, feminized and amenable to automation. It may not survive in the next phase of technological change, but currently provides much needed cushion against impending recession.

Box 2.3
No Jobs for Kharagpur Indian Institute of Technology (IIT)
Finalists

Recession has finally hit the ultimate bastion of job security—Indian Institute of Technology (IIT), Kharagpur. More than 40 percent of this year's BTech finalists—ranked top among all IITs—are still jobless. Many have settled for projects less than Rs 5,000 (US$100) a month. 'Anguished' IIT authorities have sent desperate messages to its 'high-profile' alumni requesting them to hire the students. Last year saw a 'crazy rush' over recruitment, with more than 85 percent of students 'well-placed' by December 2000. Year 2001 came as a rude shock, 'sans salaries, sans job security, or for that matter, sans a job'. And with less than five months to go before 'campus days are finally over', it is 'grab what you get' for the fourth year students.

Source: *The Statesman*, Kolkata, 31 December 2001, p. 1

The relatively brighter prospect of the ITES segment of e-commerce bodes well for women. Yet, there are reasons to be vigilant. There are threats of redundancies from technological changes and the jobs are footloose in nature. There is growing competition among developing countries to attract these jobs. African countries such as Ghana that have made visible entries into the Internet economy are receiving jobs that went previously to India. Wages in African countries are much lower than those prevailing in Asia and the lower cost makes these countries attractive sites for outsourcing companies in the US. The average wage of a data entry operator is US$ 480 per annum in Ghana; wages for comparable skill is US$ 1,250 in India and US$ 25,000 in the USA. These 'footloose jobs', no doubt, open up new opportunities and higher pay for women, yet, there are also reasons to be concerned (Box 2.4).

Box 2.4
Electronic Sweatshops?

If you are caught playing your radio too loudly in Times Square, selling ice cream while parked in a Harlem crosswalk or dumping your kitchen trash in Prospect Park, your ticket does not just go to City Hall to be processed. It goes to Ghana. Just days after the tickets are written out on New York City streets, they are scanned and sent as digital photographs to computers in a small office in downtown Accra, Ghana's hot and crowded capital. From New York's perspective, it hardly matters whether the work is done in Africa or Delaware: the contract is simply a way to process the half-million environmental tickets the city hands out every year. It is good work, by Chanaian standards. The typists earn 500,000 cedis a month (almost $70—three times the Ghanaian minimum wage and more than twice the average per capita income) to type the offender's name, address, fine and offence location into a searchable database that is sent back to New York. It can then be stored electronically and used to generate payment notices. The company's contract requires it to return the transcribed information with an error rate of no more than 1 percent and within 48 hours of pickup. The employees work in revolving eight-hour shifts that run 24 hours a day. They are immaculately dressed and sit silently at computer terminals, typing as fast as they can in a plain office. The workers get one 30-minute and two 10-minute breaks per shift to use the bathroom, eat and call friends. Their computers have no e-mail because it could be a distraction. Soon, workers will be paid by the keystroke, with deductions for errors. Data Management, the name of the office, is the largest Internet center in West Africa. Visitors at the Internet center downstairs jokingly call Data Management an 'electronic sweatshop'. But the jobs are so popular that dozens of people apply for each opening, even when the company does not advertise. And to many people in this city of open sewers and vast unemployment, the data entry operation represents a beacon of hope.

Source: Worth (2002)

Women in Call Centers

One of the most publicized relocations of e-business, from the developed to the developing countries, is in the area of customer care services in call centers. Call centers are characteristic institutions of the Internet economy and represent distant and/or external sites of companies for answering business queries of the customers. The offshore call centers are located in low wage, multilingual countries where the overhead costs are relatively small.

There has been a steady growth of call centers in this region, providing white-collar employment to women who would have found it difficult to obtain employment after a modest education. These new opportunities are welcome in the region where youth unemployment is particularly high. There is no uniform pattern in the dynamics of call centers. The business is not always export-oriented. In Malaysia, call centers are geared primarily towards finance, banking, and airlines companies of Malaysia. In India, in contrast, entrepreneurs in the business of call centers target multinationals, such as British Airways or American Express. Surveys in India and Malaysia by my research colleagues indicated that the proportion of women in the total workforce varies from 40–70 percent. The women tend to be between 20–25 years of age and in most cases this is their first job (Gothoskar, 2000; Ng, 2001b). They are, to quote a 22-year-old programmer in Kolkata, 'too young and career-oriented to think of maternity leave and childcare' (Mitter, 2000).

In view of the projected growth of these call centers worldwide (Figure 2. 3), women in the Asia-Pacific region are likely to benefit, at least in terms of quantity of work, from this segment of e-commerce. This is plausible as Figure 2.4 shows that of all developing countries, the countries of this region are the main recipients of call center revenues and jobs. The questions that need to be addressed in this context are those of sustainability and desirability of these jobs.

To start with, changes in technology may alter the volume and the nature of call center service provisions. Instead of providing a central base for teleworking, call center services may be provided virtually, supported by fast data communication linkages among a network of home-based teleworkers. The deployment of a portfolio of web-based technologies (Internet, Intranet, and Extranet)

Figure 2.3
Value of Call Center Operations Worldwide

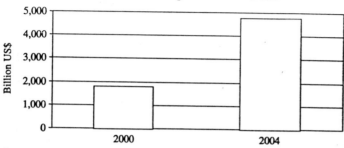

Source: www.idc.com

Figure 2.4
Geographic Distribution of Worldwide Customer Support
and Call Center Revenues, 2000

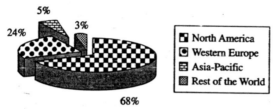

- North America
- Western Europe
- Asia-Pacific
- Rest of the World

Source: www.idc.com

may also reduce the market for call center service provisions. In banking, for example, customers may directly arrange their own transactions. In this new techno environment, instead of focusing upon a single task, call centers will be engaged in multi-dimensional tasks. Women need to have access to generic training and life-long education in order to retain their share of the call center jobs in the future.

The impact of call center jobs on the quality of lives, as has been documented so far, gives rise to concerns. First, in the export-oriented segment of the business, employees generally have to pretend to be European or American, in order to convince the customers that the answers are not coming from offshore countries and that their personal information is not sent outside the country of their residence. The cultural schizophrenia that this pretence entails on the part of the employees (Box 2.5) has its cost.

Box 2.5
Hi, I'm in Bangalore (But I Dare Not Tell)

With frosted glass and funky amber lights playing off the turquoise walls, the offices of Customer Asset look more like a Santa Fe diner than a telephone call center in southern India. The cultural vertigo is complete when employees introduce themselves to a visitor.

'Hi, my name is Susan Sanders, and I'm from Chicago,' said C. R. Suman, 22, who is in fact a native of Bangalore and fields calls from customers of a telecommunications company in the United States. Ms. Suman's fluent English and broad vowels would pass muster in the stands at Wrigley Field. In case her callers ask personal questions, Ms. Suman has conjured up a fictional American life, with parents Bob and Ann, brother Mark and a made-up business degree from the University of Illinois. 'We watch a lot of *Friends* and *Ally McBeal* to learn the right phrases,' Ms. Suman said. 'When people talk about their Bimmer, you have to know they mean a BMW.'

'Or when they say "No way, Jose," there is no Jose,' added Ms. Suman's co-worker, Nishara Anthony. Anthony, goes by the name Naomi Morrison and, if asked, says she comes from Perth Amboy, N.J. The point of this pretence is to convince Americans who dial toll-free numbers that the person on the other end of the line works right nearby— not 8,300 miles away, in a country where static-free calls used to be a novelty. Call centers are a booming business in India, as companies like General Electric and British Airways set up supermarket-size phone banks to handle a daily barrage of customer inquiries. The companies value India for its wide-spread use of English and low-cost labor.

Source: *New York Times*, 21 March 2001

Second, there is a prospect of the 'burn out' syndrome. As Ng reports: 'While most call center workers expressed job satisfaction, there were also complaints about how stressful the job was. One reason given was the highly competitive environment as incentives are given to top performers in call success rates (for example, in debt collection efforts), implying reprimands and threats of dismissals for low success rates. These employees have to deal most civilly with their recipients many of whom tend to be abusive or even hysterical. While the call center industry has the ability to provide young women with the means of entry into the banking sector, the danger lies with its being a dead-end job, with limited career promotion prospects' (Ng, 2001b: 121). While welcoming the new opportunities that the digital trade brings to their lives, young women employees in India too view this type of job simply as a brief interlude in their lives (see Box 2.6).

Box 2.6
The Mixed Reaction to Call Center Jobs (India)

'But to tell you the truth, the work itself is very boring. There is nothing creative or challenging in the work itself. Sometimes, we wonder what are we doing here.'

'As compared to other factory jobs, getting 5,000 rupees as a start seems damn good. That is only till you have family responsibilities.'

'We work 5 days a week. The off-days may vary from one month to another. But that is fine. Besides, we have meetings of the teams every once a month. We can raise any issue we want to in these. Like if we have problems with taking leave or anything. But there are no problems at all for us to raise. So we do not raise anything at all.'

'But the main thing is that all of us want to leave at some point; so there is not much of an interest in improving things. You talked about some organization or collective body of employees. No, we don't have any such thing. That is the reason. There is not that sort of interest.'

Source: Gothoskar (2000)

TELEWORKING: A BLESSING FOR WOMEN?

In the context of globalization and ICTs, there has been experimentation with modes of working including that of telework. Tele means distance and teleworking refers to ICT-mediated distant work. The term usually implies home-based work or telecommuting. Strictly speaking, telemediated remote work covers also institution-based work as in telecenters, neighborhood centers, and satellite offices, in addition to telecommuting.

Home-based teleworking, in theory, could enhance the participation of women in e-commerce as it allows certain flexibility, both, in the timing and location of work (Mitter, 2000). Women, with caring responsibilities at home, welcome this flexibility, but as surveys in India and Malaysia indicate, not without reservations. Whereas some women celebrate the opportunities that teleworking brings, the majority fear that the home-based work will deprive them of the status of working women and dignity at work. In addition, activists like Sujata Gothoskar rightly fear that teleworking may lead to insecure flexible employment which may lead to isolation, loss of career prospects, and difficulty in engaging in any kind of collective action to achieve dignity at work. This can lead to new types of informalization of work (quoted in Mitter, 2000: 2241)

Prevalence surveys by my research colleagues revealed that home-based telework is miniscule even in dynamic cities like Mumbai and Kuala Lumpur (1 and 0.35 percent respectively). The survey of women's attitude towards telework on the other hand, gave some insights for the reasons women showed a preference for institution-based teleworking as in telecenters. As Cecilia Ng reports, in Malaysia,

> interviews with women's groups indicated that the telecenters, commercial and state sponsored, may be the ideal site for externalized work that will: allow women (and men) to combine work with collective childcare facilities; enable women (and men) to have interaction with peer groups and thus allow them to acquire and improve their tacit skills; and provide facilities for state and corporate sector supported vocational training in the field of computer literacy (Ng and Khay Jin, 2000).

Managerial concerns may also explain the low prevalence of teleworking in India and Malaysia. In a survey of management perception of teleworking, most respondents reported that in Malaysian culture, face-to-face interaction was essential (Ng, 2001a). In India too, research revealed a cautious attitude of management towards home-based teleworking. In the financial sector, for example, companies find it prudent to outsource work to call centers rather than to teleworkers.

In institution-based teleworking it is easier to monitor and supervise employees in the traditional way, while widespread implementation of home-based teleworking will require a fundamental shift in the culture of management from direct supervision to a basis of trust. For self-employed and freelance workers, home-based teleworking will involve skills in self-management and time management. These skills are important for women to acquire in order not to get distracted by household chores, nor to overwork while teleworking from home. In spite of the difficulties in attaining these skills, some women opted for teleworking. Age and stage of life are key factors in molding women's preference for telework. In Mumbai, while young women work in call centers or offices of foreign airline companies in the export processing zones, older women, with young children, opt for and receive home-based telework. Companies such as Datamatics—a rapidly growing software house, receive assignments from their international clients. In turn, they pass these to women teleworkers who work from their homes, mostly on-line, and with their own computers. These home-based teleworkers represent a wide range of women: house-wives, doctors, lawyers, chartered accountants. All that they have in common is that they had to give up regular employment for the sake of their families. Teleworking gives them a welcome and much needed opportunity to be in touch with the world of work. Yet, it is difficult to ensure that these women can progress, with adequate access to training and childcare, to high value-added jobs (Mitter, 2000).

The experience of Malaysia is similar. As Ng and Khay Jin report, 'the case studies in software, as well as in printing and publishing, indicate that some women often opt for and find satisfaction in home-based work, either as freelancers or as employees. This happens in a particular phase of their life cycle, especially when there are inadequate childcare facilities' (Ng and Khay Jin, 2000: 2311). The provision of childcare thus remains a key issue in recruiting, retaining, and retraining women in the New Economy as it was in the Old Economy. As the French adage has it, *plus ça change, plus c'est la même chose*. In other words, although things appear to change they remain the same.

VOICES FROM BELOW: GLOBAL OR LOCAL?

While extolling ICT-led globalization, it would be wise to remember that too heavy a reliance on export-oriented activities leads to a new kind of dependency for the poorer countries, which have no control over the factors that influence the demand for skills, services, and goods in the richer ones. Besides, the discussion of globalization and ICTs does not address the needs and aspirations of the majority of the people who live in rural areas and below the poverty line. It tends to have an elitist focus and diverts attention from the needs of those who operate beyond the peripheries of the market but contribute crucially to the survival of the family and the community. Women's work forms a very large part of such unpaid, yet, essential labor.

The discourse of ICTs is rooted in the conviction that access to networking technologies is an empowering tool for women of poorer countries. But is it necessarily so? Until and unless we have adequate and well-formulated research, it will be difficult either to substantiate or to refute this belief. In any case, no one, so far, has asked women themselves whether they think it is of any importance to them to be connected to the global economy. Or, if they have to choose, whether they would rather have support in having access to more basic facilities, such as clean water, and cheap medicine. There may be the anxiety that diverting resources to networking technologies may restrict the power of the local community to address more urgent needs. One needs to know the answers, as it is the local tensions and concerns over limited resources, that often threaten the world's peace and stability. Yet it will be unreasonable to expect a straightforward and uniform answer as the diversity in historical and cultural contexts is likely to elicit a more nuanced response from the target beneficiaries. We can have some notion of such complexities already; from passionate and articulate statements from leading politicians and activists of poorer countries. Lalla Ben Barka, of the Economic Commission for Africa (2002), for example, forcefully argues that the problem (for Africans) has always been an approach that imposes 'knowledge' from the outside: 'Putting computers in rural schools when there is no electricity, a shortage of trained teachers and little or no African content is a wasted investment ... let us proceed in stages.'

Winnie Byaniama, a Member of the Parliament and a leading feminist from Uganda, on the other hand, told me at an UNCSTD meeting in 1998 that African women need to be told about the possibilities of ICTs: 'We, women, in Africa, feel that information and communication technology is passing us by; and, sisters, we are hungry for it.'

The risk of misinterpreting aspirations or requirements of women can, perhaps, be minimized by including poor women, as much as possible in the relevant feasibility studies. The distance from the object of our study, I feel, adds to the confusion that we

Figure 2.5

Source: Originally published in *Free Labour World*, 1997. Present copyright holder unknown.

professionals encounter in assessing the effectiveness of ICTs. It is in this context that I so cherish a picture that I came across several years ago: it tells me the role of subjectivity in distilling messages from a text, visual or written (Figure 2.5). Could she be from Africa? Or perhaps from Bangladesh? Does she appear to be empowered?

Or does she project a disgruntled disdain? What is she telling me? Is it that the computer presents her with an exit route to the global economy? Or is it that she dreads having to cope with a machine that is irrelevant to her everyday needs? When there is no dialogue with the signifier herself, we, researchers, experts, and consultants project our own mindsets and economic philosophy in constructing the meaning, and act on it. The action, however, may not be right or for that matter, disastrously wrong. It is on the grounds, both of ethics and scientific enquiry, therefore, that I urge the development community to network with women's groups in poorer countries. It is a challenging but worthwhile task as the silenced voice contributes to terror and instability. In any case, it will save us from the fallacies of elitism that claim: we must speak for them as they cannot speak for themselves.

Notes

1. A high-level dialogue on responding to globalization facilitating the integration of developing countries into the world economy in the 21st century was organized by the Economic and Social Committee of the United Nations General Assembly from 20–21 September 2001. I was involved in the Panel entitled 'Enhancing the Integration of Developing Countries in the Emerging Global Information Network, Facilitating Access to Information and Communication Technology for Developing Countries'.
2. The World Summit on the Information Society provides a unique opportunity for all key stakeholders to assemble at a high-level gathering and to develop a better understanding of the information revolution and its impact on the international community. It aims to bring together Heads of States, Executive Heads of United Nations agencies, industry leaders, non-governmental organizations, media representatives, and civil society in a single high-level event. The roles of these various partners in ensuring smooth coordination of the practical establishment of the information society around the globe, will also be at the heart of the Summit and its preparations. It was decided that the Summit would be held under the high patronage of the UN Secretary-General, with ITU taking the lead role in preparations.
3. Interview by Swasti Mitter with Sushanto Sen, the Deputy Director of CII, India on 8 March 2002.

References

Arun, Shoba and Arun, Thankom. (2002) 'ICTs, Gender and Development: Women in Software Production in Kerala,' *Journal of International Development*, 14(1): 39–50.

Ben Barka, Lalla. (2002) 'For Africa to Jump, it will need legs' in Special Issue on 'Africa in the Age of Information Technology,' *Africa Recovery*, 13(4) (Available at http://www.un.org/ecosocdev/geninfo/afrec/vol13no4/21lalla.htm).

Braga, Carlos A Primo. (1996) 'The Impact of the Internationalization of Services on Developing Countries,' *Finance & Development*, 33(1), World Bank, http://www.worldbank.org/fandd/english/0396/articles/070396.htm.

Gray, John. (2003) *Al Qaeda and What it Means to be Modern*, Faber and Faber, London.

Gothoskar, Sujatha. (2000) 'Teleworking and Gender: Emerging Issues,' *Economic and Political Weekly*, 35(26): 2293–98.

Hafkin, Nancy and Taggart, Nancy. (2001) *Gender, Information Technology, and Developing Countries*, USAID, Washington, DC.

Mitter, Swasti. (2000) 'Teleworking and Teletrade in India: Diverse Perspectives and Visions', *Economic and Political Weekly*, 35(26): 2241–52.

———. (2001) 'Universalism's Struggle,' *Radical Philosophy*, Issue 108 , July/Aug, pp. 40–42.

Mitter, Swasti and Efendioglu, Umit. (1999) 'Is Asia the Destination for "Runaway" Information Processing Work? Implications for Trade and Employment' in S. Mitter and Bastos, M.I. (eds), *Europe and Developing Countries in the Globalised Information Economy: Employment and Distance Education*. London, New York, Routledge, pp. 9–27.

Mitter, Swasti and Ashish Sen (2000) 'Can Calcutta Become Another Bangalore', *Economic and Political Weekly*, 35(26): 2263–68.

Ng, Cecilia (ed.). (2001a) *Teleworking and Development in Malaysia*. UNDP Malaysia Southbound Penang.

———. (2001b) 'Teleworking: Blessings for Malaysian Women in the Information Age?' in *Teleworking and Development in Malaysia*, UNDP Malaysia Southbound Penang, pp. 111–25.

Ng, Cecilia and Khoo Khay Jin. (2000) 'Teleworking in Malaysia: Issues and Prospects,' *Economic and Political Weekly*, 35(26): 2308–13.

Nussbaum, Martha C. (2000) *Women and Human Development: The Capabilities Approach*, Cambridge University Press, Cambridge, UK.

Sadr, M Husain. (1984) 'Science and Islam: Is There a Conflict?' in Ziauddin Sardar (ed.), *The Touch of Midas: Science, Values and Environment in Islam and the West*, Manchester University Press, Manchester.

Sardar, Ziauddin and Ravetz, Jerome R. (ed). (1996) *Cyberfutures: Culture and Politics on the Information Superhighway*, Pluto Press, London.

Shiva, Vandana. (2000) 'Bioethics: A Third World Issue', http://www.nativeweb.org/pages/legal/shiva.html.

Stiglitz, Joseph E. (2002) *Globalisation and Its Discontents*, W W Norton & Company, New York, London.

Worth, Robert. (2002) 'In New York Tickets, Ghana Sees Orderly City', *New York Times*, 22 July.

3

FROM 'INFORMATION' TO 'KNOWLEDGE' SOCIETIES? ARGENTINA IN THE CONTEXT OF ENGENDERED REGIONAL GLOBALIZATION

MARTHA ROLDÁN

During the decade of the 1990s, a vast spectrum of the Social Sciences focused on the dynamics of 'End of the Century' capitalist development, and highlighted its informational, scientific, and technological features that a number of scholars associated with the construction of *Information or Knowledge Societies*. Information or Knowledge Societies are understood as societies in which *expanding flows of information-communication* and *knowledge*, facilitated by kindred systems of work organization, are signified as crucial dimensions of any project of long-term socio-economic growth. This Virtuous Circle would be linked to the generalized use of Information and Communication Technologies (ICTs) within a 'global', regional, national, and local regulatory framework deemed to be conducive to that development goal. When arguing that the relationship as posited by economic schools among knowledge, information-communication, and work organization is embedded in the theorization and practices of development (or to the absence of development), I am referring to a broad definition of development implying 'success in the display of the human and productive potential' of a given society (Aronskind, 2001: 11). This implies, development signified as the articulated construction of contexts that guarantee the exercise of economic, social, cultural, civil, and political rights of women and men as indivisible dimensions of human rights.[1]

This demand is urgent as despite the International Covenant on Economic, Social and Cultural Rights, (ICESCR, 1966) pledging to guarantee the exercise of these rights without discrimination of any type—race, color, sex, language, religion, and others (Article 2) —the evolution of an increasingly informational world economy during the last decades violates human rights to development in majority of the countries of the world.[2] The long cycle of decline in the rate of growth of the world product that started in the 1970s is associated with the acceleration of the internationalization of capital on a regional basis—a process commonly known as Globalization—and facilitated by the generalized utilization of ICTs. Globalization has brought about new polarizations and exclusions, and a growing but articulated gap between developed (central) and developing (peripheral) economies whose informational dimensions are yet to be assessed (Chesnais, 1996).

Argentina and other countries in Latin America, Africa, and Asia, have not remained outside this general trend. I argue, therefore, that the construction of contexts of development constitutes a goal, and a main theoretical and political challenge of our time. Moreover, any attempt to revert that trend involves multiple theoretical, conceptual, and political challenges raised by one fundamental question: How are we to think genuine development paths in the era of information–knowledge 'Globalization'?

The objective of this chapter is to contribute to the ongoing debate over the nature and dynamics of information and knowledge-based development, underlying possible transitions from information to knowledge societies, and to reflect on its engendered implications on the basis of the Argentine experience (1990s–2000s). To this effect I argue, in the first part, that it is necessary to distinguish between the neo-Liberal and the Liberal (institutional) theoretical paradigms embedded in that debate. The drawing of this distinction is essential in order to elucidate, from a critical perspective, the dynamics of the 'Virtuous Circle' linking information, knowledge, work organization and development, and the congenial regulatory framework deemed necessary to translate that virtuosity into practice in different macro regions of the world. I take the European experience as one illustration of these possibilities. Last, but not the least, I argue that the problematic of this chapter is still a missing component of the feminist agenda in southern Latin America.

The Theoretical and Conceptual Framework

I argue that it is important to distinguish among socio-economic theories in order to clarify the significations given to the Virtuous Circle linking information, knowledge, work organization, and the multi-level regulatory framework defined as a necessary condition for the construction of information or knowledge societies as tools for the attainment of 21st Century capitalist development. This acquires distinct features according to the macro-region being considered, be it central, industrialized North America, the European Union, or the Japanese-led Asian space; or peripheral, often transnationalized industrializing areas, such as southern Latin America. I will briefly summarize the neo-Liberal (neo-classical) and the Liberal (institutional) economic paradigms, and their application to the information and knowledge societies debate that developed in Europe in the 1990s, proceed to the critiques raised from Critical Political Economy, and then to the challenges that feminist scholarship in southern Latin America must face in order to effectively contribute to this ongoing debate in the 2000s.

The Neo-Liberal Vision: The Bangemann Report

By neo-Liberalism, I mean the renewal of neo-classical or conservative economics. Its philosophical support is utilitarianism, a vision that signifies the rationality assumed to characterize human nature and, hence, the 'good society' that will satisfy it—through the market—strictly on individual preferences in the search for pleasure maximization and suffering minimization (Ebert, 1996). This philosophical underpinning was born in the United Kingdom in the 18th Century, blossomed in the last decades of the 19th and 20th Centuries, and still holds its ground at the dawn of the 21st Century by being embedded in contemporary neo-Liberal rational-utilitarian economic discourse on 'Information Societies'.

By giving priority to equilibrium, and ignoring the broader social and historical variables, and the conditioning factors inherent in the concrete and real environment of the process of production, this approach equally ignores the tensions and contradictions that mobilize 'from the basic units of accumulation to the society as a whole' (Tauile, 2001: 35, my translation from the original Portuguese text).

During the 1950s, information[3] became a synonym for valuable news, a fact or event that exerts influence on business or social behavior, stock market prices, and government decisions. Knowledge, in turn, became codified technical information, which is typically generated in the Research and Development (R&D) offices of specific firms; a type of good whose production, diffusion, and uses are endowed with economic values, and lead to beneficial results. It is also an exogenous variable, which is replicated through ICTs, and is available by paying royalties, or licenses in case it is protected by patents or copyrights. (Chudnovsky and López, 1995). The crucial issue of intellectual property rights, a theme of the Second Industrial Revolution, has once again come to the fore.

With regard to work organization, management literature celebrates the transference of the Japanese informational 'lean production' model of work organization (teamwork) to all companies.[4] New workers must be problem-solvers, creative, responsible, and have the skills and attitudes that might be developed by their employers (SCANS, 1991).

Although denied in discourse, public policies do exist in real life situations: nation-states and local governments actively intervene in all economies through de-and re-regulatory strategies, in pursuit of 'market-friendly' growth. This requires nation-states to participate in macro-regional negotiations as the Bangemann Report illustrates (Comisión Europea, 1994). This Report, entitled *Europe and the Global Information Society: Recommendations to the European Council*, is the most widely quoted source of *neo-Liberal* thinking on 'global' information societies in Latin America. Briefly stated, it sponsors the adoption of public policies that would lead to the emergence of a world information society under the auspices of the (European) private sector by guaranteeing: generalized access to ICTs, the reduction of the digital divide, and free competition for European ICTs manufacturers and/or telecom operators, which 'are at the forefront of these technological developments and should reap the benefits' (ibid.).

To this effect, this market-driven revolution mobilizes the private sector and European nation-states to guarantee a needed competitive environment, by breaking national telecom State monopolies (through privatization and market liberalization) and, simultaneously, attempting to control the free flow of information through the struggle in defense of intellectual property rights. As a result, *supra-national*, regional regulation (institutionalization) are now necessary. Given that the information society is global, 'the Group thus recommends that Union action should aim to establish a common and agreed regulatory framework for the protection of intellectual property rights' (ibid.).

The Liberal Vision: The HLEG Report

I understand the Liberal theoretical approach as the equivalent of 'institutional', 'structural' or 'heterodox' economics, one of the theoretical offshoots of classical economics. Its philosophical support gives a signification that oscillates between morality and instrumentality to the rationality that would characterize human nature, and, hence, the 'good' society that may satisfy this rationality. The Liberal approach—that has been historically associated with the growth of capitalism and demands for democracy and political liberties based on the *moral* conviction of the equality of all 'men'—is, nowadays, the main focus of Latin American debate. Can this school, that equates long-term economic growth, based on industry, to the development of endogenous technological competencies, and the consolidation of new institutions, be 'the' unique alternative to the neo-Liberal hegemony of the 1990s, as some authors claim?

A sub-branch of this school associates the possibility of genuine development to the emergence of a Knowledge, and/or Learning Age, that would be articulated to contemporary 'Globalization' trends (Dosi, 1996; Lastres and Ferraz, 1999). The common element of this literature is the attribution a key role in innovation and, therefore, in the degree of competitiveness attained by different economic agents to the accelerated generation and diffusion of knowledge. Information, knowledge, and work organization, optimized by, but not equivalent to, the generalized use of ICTs, constitute the foundations sustaining the successful restructuring in production and services that took place during the last decades of the 20th Century, and which continues into the new century.

However, while information is assimilated to codified, structured data, knowledge is classified as either codified or tacit. Codified knowledge is that type of knowledge that can be transformed into a message and manipulated as information and, therefore, be easily transferable using ICTs. Tacit knowledge is inherent in people, and in the accumulation of their lived experiences in the world of productive (and reproductive) work, and in organizations and specific places that share a common action and language. Hence it is not available in the market, and requires a specific type of social interaction, that is assimilated to learning in order to be transferred (Lundvall, 2000; Cowan and Foray, 1998).

Codified and tacit knowledge complement each other, and are embedded in practices common to each firm, sector, or region (network of firms). Hence, successful knowledge generation and transference cannot be ensured by discourse only. Innovations are based on knowledge originated in a social and collective environment, and the education necessary to understand the use of local codes can only be attained through a network of relationships, and the process of interactive learning. ICTs should then be viewed as essentially complementary to investment in human resources and skills (HLEG, 1997).

This perspective, by promoting the distinction between types of knowledge, and by insisting on the importance of learning for innovation, simultaneously *legitimizes* the new forms of work and productive organization based on the 'Japanese model' ('Ohnist/ Just in time (JIT)'). This is so because this model counts with mechanisms for the production and appropriation of tacit knowledge and aptitudes, which are structured (embedded) in the same process of capitalist production and circulation (Jürgens et. al, 1993).[5]

The trenchant critique of neo-Liberal thinking advanced by the structural school is translated to the emerging European 'Information Economies' by the High Level Final Policy Report to the European Commission (HLEG, 1997). It conveys a mature reflection on information-based European capitalism after the negative implications of neo-Liberal growth policies applied in the 1980s and 1990s, and promoted by the Bangemann Report (1994) had already taken their toll.

Two focal points are pertinent to this essay: First, the critique of technological determinism sponsored by earlier reports that ignore the nature of the new, digitized ICTs-based technological clusters and their 'social embeddedness'. Second, the excessive responsibility left to private sector interests should be corrected through adequate nation-state and European Union regulatory coordination, including complementary investments in human resources and skills that are not yet forthcoming, to ensure that the Wise Society finally emerges.

To overcome these deficiencies, the HLEG suggests a continuum of policy challenges derived from the recognition that 'despite innumerable analyses on the subject, there is still insufficient recognition, in our view, that the new ICTs embody a radically different set of parameters for potential growth and development opportunities'. I stress the need to regulate the information society markets to tackle the *abuse of market power* and; the coordinating regulation required to reduce the threat of market dominance and abuse in particular ICT market segments.

Liberal Literature from the Perspective of Critical Political Economy[6]

Without dispute, the Liberal (institutional) approach to socio-economic growth and its corollaries prove to be very useful theoretical and political instruments for overcoming a number of biases inherent in neo-classical thinking on development. However, Critical Political Economy theorization as well as recent empirical evidence show the limitations implicit in any attempt to promote information-knowledge-based development on one unique foundation: the construction of knowledge and learning societies defined exclusively according to Liberal tenets. Several reservations must, then, be posited to the institutional economic paradigm and to the viability of the public policies derived from this approach, when applied outside the European Union. From current discussions on ALCA (Free Trade Area of the Americas)/MERCOSUR (the Common Market of the South), the following observations are in order.

At the supra-national level, the 'heterodox' approach takes for granted, but does not investigate, the origin, nature, concrete dynamics, and implications of the regional 'globalization' context whose accelerated transformations impose pressures not only on the firm's behavior and competitiveness, but also on any broad conception of development. These 'globalization' processes—while seeking regional markets and resources (such as the Latin American MERCOSUR)—have become key elements in the configuration of the contemporary world economy, thereby recreating and intensifying the Center, 'developed' vs. Periphery, 'developing' economies divide.[7]

The above transformations, in turn, are closely related to the supra-national institutional construction (both *de facto* and *de jure*) led by the United States, the Group of 7, the IMF (International Monetary Fund), the World Bank and its Washington Consensus, which has been formalized in Europe by the Maastricht Treaty and the WTO. These multinational bodies elaborate the context of liberalization demanded from national economies, while also shaping the parameters of regional markets, such as the Latin American MERCOSUR.

At the national/regional level, Policies of Science, Technology, and Innovation directed to the construction of National Systems of Innovation (NSIs) proper to the institutional approach take for granted that these national or regional spaces are often the sites of MNCs headquarters, or of national-capital enterprises accruing innovation-based profits through effective competition in the industrial plane. However, the existence of innovative, national-capital industrial firms that could serve as platforms for the construction of NSIs in the already highly-transnationalized MERCOSUR region is still to be shown. Another related issue concerns the limitations inherent in peripheral NSIs, taking into consideration the restrictions imposed by the enforced opening of these economies, which have been subject to successive structural adjustment plans by the WTO, IMF and other international organizations, and perhaps in the future, also from Agreements originating in the approaching World Summit on the Information Society (WSIS).

In addition, the domination of financial capital endangers the viability of public policies in Science and Technology even in the central economies.[8] It is no surprise, therefore, that investments in R&D are among the most concentrated types of world investments and that information-knowledge privatization via intra-firm trade in manufacturing and services constitutes an inherent feature of *Mondialization* and, as such, forms a crucial part of the negotiations taking place in North American Free Trade Agreement (NAFTA), ALCA and now the WSIS. We must, therefore, conclude that a process of global technological diffusion does not take place. Instead, there is a concentration of production of scientific and technical knowledge, and strategic technologies in very limited places (Chesnais, 1996), and the new competition between MNCs has intensified the centralization of knowledge at their head-quarters, and in the economies of the Triad.

Last but not the least, **at the world, regional, national or local levels,** the institutional theory mostly ignores the conflicting nature of capital-labor relations, as well as its gender dimensions manifested in the concrete reality of capitalist work organization. That is, it does not raise the issue of the limits of what are to be deemed as legitimate management practices concerning work organization, to the extent that the latter is functional and conducive to successful (profitable) innovations. Hence, it cannot examine the negative implications of the 'Japanese model', for the society as a whole, and for women and men workers in particular.

21st Century Informational Capitalism

Another offshoot of the Critical (Radical) theoretical approach can advance to the examination of 'informationalization' processes, a complex dynamics deemed by some authors to constitute *the* main feature of contemporary capitalism (Dantas, 2001, 2002a, 2000b and 2000c; Castells, 2000; Lojkine, 1995). My reading of this approach is based on the work of Marcos Dantas, who re-semantizes Information Theory (IT) in radical, critical terms, to subsequently apply this renewed IT to the analysis of human labor and the valorization and accumulation of capital. His objective is to explore and explain why central, developed capitalism is assuming increasingly informational-communicational features since the first phase of the Second Industrial Revolution (1880s–1920s), a revolution based on the application of Science and Technology to production. The following points are crucial for a debate on the polemical issues raised by institutional economics and for incorporating Dantas' main tenets into this essay.

All human labor, Dantas (2002b) argues, is informational labor, that is, labor devoted to perceiving, processing, registering, and communicating information. Information is perceived by Dantas (2002a: 146) as 'a process that gives orientation to the action (*trabalho*) performed by any living organism in its efforts to recover part of the energy that it dissipates because of the laws of thermodynamics' (my translation from Portuguese, emphasis added). Information is, thus, produced when an object that conveys potentially significative signals starts an interaction with an agent who is capable, competent, interested and willing to extract its significations (Dantas, 2002b). It is therefore, not a unidirectional process, but a bi-directional one, ingrained in codes, as suppliers of orientations to action. Information, therefore, is an activity of living labor, and should not be conflated with some result of the process of capturing and processing it (a book, electric signals, etc). Neither should 'data' or 'knowledge' (which are the products of past labor) be conflated with informational dynamics per se.

In this fashion, Information Theory helps to clarify the nature of interaction that presides over capitalist informational labor; and to delve into the nature of human communication in the world of toil; IT also illuminates the capacities and skills of the labor force, which assumes the existence of codes. Without communicative activities, workers would not know which tasks to perform. Communication is thus a constitutive component of the labor process, and an element for the negotiation of the use value of labor power vis-a-vis capital.

Simultaneously, this critical approach is useful in explaining the growing magnitude of human labor over information itself in the context of a new information-based division of labor in productive activities. This is because, in former times, the information necessary for the performance of this type of activities was captured, processed, and communicated directly by the senses of the body, and that information was free to be captured by the mind and the body of the worker, in her/his own social and natural environments. Increasingly, since the Second Industrial Revolution, immediate production came to be congealed in the forms and movements of machinery systems, while living labor, continued expanding in the growing and more encompassing activities of processing, registering, and the communication of social information. Hence, living labor, Dantas argues, that is labor endowed with knowledge useful for production, will never cease to be the type of labor necessary for capitalist accumulation. However, the value of labor for capital, the type of labor that allows for capital accumulation, increasingly becomes a function of information processing activities taking place along the productive chain, hence implying the presence of new international divisions of labor and suitable coordination mechanisms to sustain that growth.

New Center-Periphery Relationships: This division of labor takes place between firms whose value-generating activities are based on labor connected to scientific-technological research, creation or innovation of products and processes, and firms whose value activities are based on repetitive, elementary, routine labor. Hence, informational capitalism does not count with a homogeneous labor collective (among countries). The extension of the productive chain signifies the concentration of creative labor in the *center* and of redundant, routine labor in the *periphery*. Thanks to the extended world networks of communication, firms linked via ICTs and working as a unit in real time, can locate labor where its costs are as low as its low informational level.

In synthesis, contemporary informational capitalism mobilizes labor to process and communicate information by means of adequate (digital) processing and communication. The reductionism of previous approaches is corrected by showing that ICTs transport signals whose codes must be captured, and shared by 'recipients' for interaction-communication to be completed. But this capitalism devalues the use value of routine labor in the international informational hierarchies, with catastrophic consequences, as shown by statistics on social exclusion globally.

A STILL MISSING FEMINIST AGENDA

To my knowledge, feminist scholarship in Latin America, outside the NAFTA region at least, has largely neglected the information-knowledge development problematic. This is unfortunate for two reasons. On the one hand, southern Latin American informational development perspectives cannot be easily dissociated from the outcome of the world 'trade war' among North American, European, and Asian MNC suppliers of networks and services in the telecom business (among other sectors) that continue to compete for the promising 'emerging' MERCOSUR region of the 1990s. This process persists in the current but still undecided fate of the ALCA vs. MERCOSUR dispute, and is also reflected in the WSIS agenda and WTO negotiations. An early feminist intervention may influence *ex-ante* crucial decisions concerning the future development of the region. On the other hand, women's gender subordination in the spheres of production, (reproduction) and circulation has not disappeared but has probably increased in the last decades in the Latin American periphery with variations according to class, and race/ethnicity.

Southern Latin American feminist scholars, to the extent that they have examined issues related to the information and knowledge societies debate, have carried out this task on an individual discipline basis only (mainly sociology, political and communications sciences, psychology, and anthropology), thus neglecting the underlying development discourse. As a result, the feminist intellectual and political project of liberation in the region has so far not been able to confront the challenges that Liberal and Radical Political Economy raise in the still insufficiently-explored field of information-knowledge-based capitalist development.

An example of 'missed opportunity' is the lack of contribution by gender experts to the WSIS PrepCom meeting, convened by the Economic Commission for Latin America and the Caribbean (ECLAC) and other organizations, and held in the Dominican Republic in 2003. Unfortunately, no congenial feminist text accompanied the male economic development experts' contribution to this meeting. In my view, this example might well reflect the remnants of gender discrimination still pervading supra-national organizations that are officially committed to gender equity, especially in the world periphery. An intra-institutional division of labor that assigns engendered perspectives to a separate unit, always runs the risk of relegating feminist social scientists to 'dated' issues once male economists have already given the theory (code) that defines the meaning of ongoing or future regional socio-economic development.[9]

This is also plausible if we take into consideration the ECLAC sponsored Experts Meeting on Globalization, Technological Change and Gender Equity, 2001 (my translation from the original Spanish title). This was not an opportunity for high level Latin American feminist development experts to constitute an inter-disciplinary group to develop an *autonomous* report on the subject, as illustrated by the European (mainly male) HLEG. At that time their ECLAC male counterparts were already elaborating a very ambitious research agenda that resulted in a number of documents, a book on the transition from the Industrial to the Digital Economy, plus the main official ECLAC Document written for the PrepCom meeting in early 2003! The (Gender) Experts Meeting's proposals

and recommendations included several measures such as conducting research into the components of globalization, macroeconomic policies, and gender, race and ethnic dimensions;
establishment of data banks bearing on education levels, age, social
strata, and gender; promotion of women's strategic uses of accessible technologies, specially ICTs. References are also made to the
digital divide, telecenters, e-government, and public services and
to the most effective exercise of citizenship.

These are, of course, fair recommendations in their own right,
but they are not preceded by an explicit discussion of the underlying theory and model of development it is engendering: the roots
and dynamics of the private sector 'export-led model of economic
growth' to which the same report refers, and to which it attributes
opportunities and restrictions as far as gender equity is concerned.
An emphasis on this main theme would have allowed an examination of the structural consequences of the application of that
economic model for the countries of the region, its linkages with
'globalization', and the particular categories of women who would
be willing and able to participate in the construction of information-
knowledge-based development. Feminist scholars already have a
menu of possible 'transitions' to address themselves to, each model
involving theoretical assumptions and political challenges that can
no longer be neglected.

Yet, if the neo-Liberal model of growth adopted in the region
has already failed in terms of human rights-oriented development
by excluding the majority of the area's population, no proper engendering could correct that outcome. On the contrary, one may
then enquire into the meaning of gender equity in processes leading to underdevelopment. The experience of Argentina, to which
I now turn, illuminates this effect.

CONSTRUCTING A PERIPHERAL 'INFORMATION SOCIETY'

Towards an Argentine Information Society?

The construction of an information society as an instrument for
development has been present in the Argentine official government
discourse since the beginning of the 1990s.[10] Already in the 2000s,
a National Program for an Information Society was already drafted

by decree 252/2000 during de la Rúa's Presidency, in the framework of the Secretariat of Science, Technology, and Production Innovation. This Program continues the Argentine Internet for Everyone Plan. The difference between both the schemes is that the latter Plan, designed during Menem's Presidency in the 1990s, did not have any social repercussions, while the Program explicitly states the need to coordinate a major goal, the social diffusion of Internet together with other objectives, to generalize the use of ICTs in all societal sectors; and to increase competitiveness in the production of goods and services; and to expand the use of telemedicine and teleeducation plans. The Program had almost no application and how it is continued or discontinued under the present administration is yet to be seen.

A retrospective analysis with a focus on the context of origin of those Plans, allows us to perceive the logic of this adverse outcome. I have referred in other texts to the extensive literature bearing on the orthodox application of the neo-Liberal model of economic growth in Argentina during the 1990s and to its New Public Policies (NPPs) involving the privatization of State enterprises, (including ENTEL, the National Telecommunication Network); asymmetrical trade opening, and selective deregulation of the economy. Concomitantly, and according to the inherent logic of the model, substantial changes in the regulation of capital-labor relations were introduced, highly restricting or abolishing the historical rights attained by the working classes. The expectations raised by the NPPs have not been satisfied. Once the initial positive shock in terms of rapid GNP growth due to the entry of capitals and inflation control disappeared, the long recession that started in 1998 turned into a depression in 2001 and is only now being overcome. Simultaneously, NPPs promoted the reprimarization of the economy, deindustrialization, and the generalized regressive restructuring of the remaining segment of the industrial sector, the concentration and general transnationalization of the economy, and capital centralization. Several of these ill effects should be highlighted in relation to the problematic of this essay.

To start with, the institutional shock of the 1990s implied the consolidation of new sector regulatory frameworks leading to 'disarticulated restructuring', the disintegration of subcontracting chains, both between trade and industry, and within industry itself (Kosacoff, 2000). In addition, the specialization profile of the country has become reprimarized. The Argentine profile, based on static sectors, seriously compromises its position in the region and the world, as it has become a country exporting natural resources, energy, and industrial commodities. Technologies that lead world expansion—such as telecommunications (that have been privatized), micro-electronics, computing and new materials, biotechnologies, and specializations which are knowledge-intensive and demand creative labor—are absent from this list.

The above industrial picture is associated with a very low average investment in science and technology, and education during this decade. Public expenditure in science and technology comes close to 0.4 percent of the GNP (Aronskind, 2001). The estimated expenditure in all higher and university education is only 0.83 percent of the GNP. Relating these figures to those referring to the dismantling of the productive linkages (suppliers linkages), it is possible to conclude with Nochteff (2001), that science and technology policies in Argentina cannot be regarded as genuine State policies.

Not surprisingly, this absence of State policies in the crucial areas of education, science and technology, and knowledge-intensive industrial growth has resulted in failure to advance towards information-communication-based development. The lack of initiatives to construct a National Society of Information shows a technological determinism which was rejected by the HLEG Report (1997). Finally, it must also be stressed that the neo-Liberal model of growth has been unable to generate positive impacts upon wages and employment (with extremely high rates of unemployment and sub-employment) while at the same time it consolidated a distribution profile that became one of the most unequal in the world, and pushed more than half the population of the country below the poverty line. This evolution is even more devastating considering that following the devaluation of the Peso in 2002, the balance of trade improved (due to increased agricultural exports), but neither the economic model nor the subordination to supranational institutions (IMF in particular) changed.

Towards a Regional Information Society?

How is the above construction reflected at the regional level, MERCOSUR? What are the implications of these processes in terms of engendered informational labor in the Argentine case? Regionally, the neo-Liberal model of growth was expressed through the acceleration of the de-and re-regulation of MERCOSUR, under the assumption that trade liberalization emerging from the agreement would encourage Foreign Direct Investment (FDI), intra-firm trade, and productive specialization. According to the Asunción Treaty of 1991, MERCOSUR may be considered a project to develop a common market. During the decade of the 1990s, the progressive shaping of the automotive region (market) of MERCOSUR, through a new regulatory framework reconstructed the conditions for the sector's growth after the crisis of the 1980s. In other texts, I have referred to the historical linkages between domestic and regional (and/or bilateral) regulation that increasingly constructed the definition of that automotive region, culminating in the New Bilateral Automotive Regime, between Argentina and Brazil in March 2000, modified again in July 2002.

WORK ORGANIZATION AND GENDER DYNAMICS IN MERCOSUR

Car Assemblers Level

Local recession, subsidies, and the Brazilian devaluation attracted the greatest part of investments in the assembler industry. Production was adjusted to the international market strategies of MNCs on the basis of 'global' profit forecasts and intra-firm trade flows. Assemblers located in Argentina import complete vehicles and autoparts from external sources (outside the MERCOSUR area), and decide the production mix of cars and components, that is which 'interlinked' firms do enter or do not enter the intra- MNC circle, and the features of regional subcontracting, with negative effects on the balance of trade, of payments, employment, and wages. 'Containers' carrying autoparts, parts, and pieces imported from Brazil or from the extra zone common to the areas close to the assembly firms and to the same plant, also bear witness to the absence of that systemic search for time economies in the Argentine case and the consequent absence of innovation strategies on the part of firms located in the country. To this, in Argentina, is added the absence of effective Customs control, and prosecution of MNCs that violate present norms.

Technological Transfer and Local Innovations

Lax legislation, high import content, and level of vertical integration conspire against any virtuous dynamics. In the first place, MNCs practices do not comprise genuine R&D or the adaptation of technologies originating at headquarters, as was the practice in previous phases of automotive growth. Whole engineering departments and previous advances in training and know-how have been dismantled, negatively affecting crucial technical and social resources (Roldán, 2000).

In the second place, virtuous dynamics had to be promoted by subcontracting networks connecting specialized suppliers (external JIT). However, car MNC (assembler) networks do not behave according to Argentine expectations but, rather, further shape new center/periphery relations. The 'network' firm notion implies a learning circuit that stimulates endogenous positive externalities specific to the system of relations and, in this sense, they typically exhibit mechanisms promoting innovations and a higher speed of intra network diffusion of newly generated knowledge (Vispo, 1999).

That notion, however, only applies to the center of the network, located outside the MERCOSUR area. The result is the extension of the productive chain with a concentration of creative labor at the center and redundant (routine) labor at the periphery. The fate of the local branches of the car assemblers and subcontracting firms is associated either with the partial transformation of those creations into material products, or with the delivery of imported products to the final market with minimum, if any, local value added according to each firm's 'global' strategies, that is, in activities which are typical to the periphery of the network.

Thus, the possibility of positioning the country on a development path, with dynamic competitive advantages supported by domestic engineering capacities, has been relegated to the field of fairy tales. If no creative activities are assigned to Argentina, the call for engendering nonexistent engineering and design practices does not constitute a feasible feminist goal, even if, occasionally, a few women university engineers could be found in charge of TQC (total quality control).

Assembly Work Organization and Gender Hierarchies at
Car Assembler Level

Assemblers' strategies do not need to attain the high efficiency
of zero stocks and JIT production to satisfy the requirements of
the national markets where the branch is located. It is true that de-
territoriality of production exists, but creative activities which are
conducive to inventions take place at headquarters where important investments in R&D are located, and these operations predefine
the limits of the right to communicate (Dantas, 2001).

Hence, in broad terms, it is plausible to argue the continuity of
patterns detected in the second half of the decade of the 1990s,
that is, the absence of any genuine implementation of the logic of
accumulation proper to the 'Ohnist/JIT' model (Roldán, 2001; Vispo,
1999). The speed of capital rotation is decided upon according to
the 'global' strategies of the MNCs involved, and not by the opti-
mization of production of local (regional) branches. The above-
mentioned transformations at the world, regional, and national
levels help to explain the incompatibility between theory and
practice of the 'Ohnist/JIT' system (including its dimensions bearing on creative informational labor with knowledge 'useful for
production' when applied to a peripheral social formation such
as Argentina).

Let us bear in mind that the goal of attaining an optimum flow
of production by means of an adequate informational organization
means that, under 'normal' circumstances, this model facilitates
the generation of new knowledge and the appropriation of previous know-how by women and men workers. Hence, it simultaneously facilitates communication and interactive learning proper
to the nature of informational labor. However, these expectations
were not fulfilled in the Argentine examples.

The center/periphery divide is logically replicated at this level,
that is, we find labor intensification, minimum 'idle time', very
short work cycle time, team labor coupled to the cycle of production, and based on a 'summing up' conception of workers' skills.
This vicious circle prevents interactive learning, and leads to the
predominance of routine informational labor (rather than to 'intelligent, creative' labor) together with the disfunctionalities proper

of *sui-generis* JIT supplying of parts and components without local productive linkages. The elements of control over labor coincide with those already detected by the literature critical of the 'Japanese model', while the traditional pattern of male gendering of labor employed at the assembly plants continues.

Training carried out in firms which specialize in 'low level decision-making' tends to be restricted to relatively 'redundant' features of the labor process, those in which the personnel in charge of informational labor have not yet been replaced by machinery. There is no available evidence, hence, of instances of labor 'humanization' as was promised by the best publicized representations of 'lean production' in the terminology of Womack, et al. (1991), and the new literature relating knowledge generation, labor organization, learning, and innovation for development. If ICTs and the development of human resources are at the center of the new technological clusters based on these technologies, these clusters are absent from the Argentine landscape.

Autopart Firms Level

The evolution of the autopart industry reflects the same tendencies of transnationalization: low production volumes, high percentage of imported pieces and components, and the drastic reduction in the number, production, and employment offered by small-scale national capital enterprises. This sector was practically eliminated from the market.

Work Organization and Gender Hierarchies in the Autopart Firm Level

Available evidence suggests the replication of the pattern of adaptation found at the level of assembly plants, that is, the *sui-generis* and heterogeneous adaptation of elements of the 'Japanese model' in accordance to the product, market, and national or transnational ownership of the firm. Also absent from this stratum, is the systemic search for time economies proper to that model. In addition, according to Yoguel et al. (2001), technological transference between levels of subcontracting is low due to the high import content.

Although the technological dependence of subcontracting firms vis-à-vis assemblers is a proved fact, yet, it has not been accompanied by in-depth studies exploring the creative-routine dialectics of informational labor at small-scale autoparts firms, whose 'incremental' and hidden innovations may explain the invisibility of creative features not officially registered (Roldán, 2000). The engendering of these processes replicates historical patterns of women's insertion into this industry studied in-depth for the period 1960-90 (ibid.). In other words, women and men are incorporated into (previously invisible) new or old hybrids of the 'Ohnist/JIT' model. An increased process of masculinization in the 'polyvalent' gendering of the 1990s seems plausible in the absence of relevant data.

Considering the labor processes involved in autopart production only, this general observation may be qualified at the level of the type of labor processes involved: (i) whether these are processes previous to assembly, demanding the display of aptitudes pertinent to the broad spectrum of the 'knowing how to do' variety, including those I call 'technical' skills for the operation and/or setting up of qualifying machines, and the 'knowing how to be' variety, be they individual or group ones, according to the level of adaptation of given techniques; or (ii) of assembly itself, which is generally manual assembly, among nationally- owned firms that demands a display of labor 'with knowledge useful for production' in which redundant elements predominate. In addition, we must consider the possible existence of different productive and articulated logics within the same plant. In the example of Roldán (2000), one of them pursued economies of scale, which was based on processes with Taylorist/Fordist dimensions of maximum fragmentation and speed in individual operations. The second and crucial one is a logic of 'hidden *sui generis* Ohnism' pursuing economies of scale and variety in the production of smaller lots, based on team labor organization for the operations of assembly and finishing of the family of filters called 'of nafta type'. This form of organization made possible the attainment of maximum efficiency in a Just-in-Time hybrid that covered two complete work schedules, plus the integration of homework.

In other words, there does not exist one unique relationship between the model that is being hybridized, and its male or female engendering. Among the intervening factors we may mention (a) the product to which it is being applied; (b) the relevant processes involved in its execution; (c) the absence or presence of ICTs, demanding monitoring and problem- solving abilities in real time;

(*d*) which social actors offer needed aptitudes for its production including technical know-how pertaining to the 'knowing how to be' variety, and *tacit* (memory) skills; (*e*) the lowest cost and maximum performance potential; (*f*) the legitimacy of the contract (Collective Agreement) applied; and (*g*) the historical moment and the locality being examined.

Field survey shows that women in production may be incorporated into teams, operate ICTs, and participate in 'up-to-date' teamwork lines. This depends to a large extent on the evaluation each firm carries out of the economic and political (control) advantages and disadvantages of hiring women workers, including the influence of the androcentric trade unions. Within this broad panorama, there are several interplaying elements: the gender composition of the restructuring experience (are these female or male sections); the conditions of the local labor market; the phase of the domestic cycle that potential workers are going through (in the case of women if they are young or mothers who offer 'certainty of responsibility'); factory and trade union experience (or its absence) among others.

In a stage of 'crisis', such as the one in the period under study, the exercise of the diverse aptitudes of the 'knowing how to do' and 'knowing how to be' varieties displayed in teams and the generation and appropriation of tacit skills (memory) of women workers, which in various stages were forbidden or ignored by the Metallurgical Collective Agreement, were made public. Firms can now hire (young, and higher educated) men to display a broad spectrum of aptitudes comprising technical and non-technical skills at no additional cost. To a certain extent, which operations are female and which are male have changed, but the gendering of space has extended.

All men have more responsibilities than before and exercise skills than were previously considered *women's skills*. But, given the present mix of production, it becomes more economic and politically correct to 'bring down' 'men of the trade', who provide the whole spectrum of aptitudes needed, than to 'bring women up.' This would require additional training (that men already possess) at additional cost. Pre-existing gender relations are thus incorporated and re-composed in the capital-labor relation that is being reconstructed.

Concluding Reflections

From the outset, my main concern was the contribution of information-communication-knowledge to capitalist development, and with the 'battle of significations' over, that contribution ingrained in the transition from the information to knowledge societies debate. The debate on 'transitions' implies contending definitions of development and kindred public policies to make it come true. Hence, the terms of the 'battle' had to be clarified from the outset to ascertain their coincidence or divergence from the notion of development adopted in this essay. The theoretical-conceptual recognizance exercise focusing on the neo-Liberal and Liberal (institutional) socio-economic schools had that objective in mind.

Both schools concentrate on the dynamics of 'End of the Century' capitalist development, and highlight its informational, scientific, and technological features that a number of its adherents associate with the construction of information or knowledge societies. Moreover, both schools require a congenial 'global', regional, national, and local regulatory framework deemed to be conducive to that development objective. In this sense, the Bangemann and the HLEG Reports are projects on regional growth that given actors—TNCs, nation-states, and/or supra-national bodies—sustain in their dispute on the future of the world economy with their North American and Asian counterparts. This requires developed regions to produce 'global' legislation to protect telecom industry and operators' business interests, their alliances, and regulate competition the world over. In this sense, neither of the two Reports supports a definition of socio-economic growth leading to development as defined in this essay.

Yet, there are substantial differences between both paradigms, derived from their philosophical underpinnings and conceptions of human nature. The institutional school promotes nation-state and EU Policies based on human resource development that should include those women and men still excluded from highly industrialized European societies. Moreover, the HLEG Liberal emphasis on production, its critique of the technological determinism of the neo-Liberal school, and the privileged position of private-sector interests in the transition are a necessary antidote to the neo-Liberal tenets that characterized the Latin American scene during the 1990s. Both, the European experience and the critiques from Radical political economy, constitute the core of the southern Latin American debate on possible 'transitions' from the mid-1990s to the present.

The Argentine experience is very instructive in this respect. In retrospect, it seems logical that in the absence of State policies in the areas of science and technology, education, and knowledge-intensive industrial growth, there would be no advance towards the construction of information-knowledge-based development. The initiatives concerning the official construction of a national information society reveal a technological determinism rejected in the HLEG Report, and lack of understanding of information-communication as a productive force in its own right: a diffusionist approach along the lines 'if access to ICTs is generalized, an information society will emerge' is seen to have emerged.

The embeddedness of the Argentine Information Society project in a neo-Liberal paradigm, as applied in the periphery, prevented the attainment of even the modest European advances in this field. When applied in the European developed macro-region, the paradigm produced an information economy whose transition to knowledge and eventually to Wise Society is yet to be accomplished. In Argentina, instead, the same project made possible the reaping of record profits by the same (mainly European) MNCs in the newly-privatized telecom industry and services operation sector, amidst the dismantling of the remnants of the former welfare State. If, according to the HLEG Report, many types of Information Societies will exist in the future, Argentina will, without doubt qualify for a peripheral position in that race.

The New Virtual Value-Chain, Work Organization, and Gender Hierarchies

The above finding is replicated by the evidence from case studies, bearing on the construction of a new virtual value-chain through automobile MNCs network in the MERCOSUR area. The concentration of R&D and creative informational labor in the center of the network is a common feature of this trend. After a decade of fieldwork-grounded research, it is an established fact that, be it in the automotive or in other sector, the 'Ohnist/JIT' model will be transferred if it constitutes to support strategies of capital accumulation considered the most appropriate for a given oligopolistic supply, expressed in trajectories of multi- or transregional internationalization. The incorporation of ICTs and the subsequent replacement of human informational labor depend on decisions taken at the center of the network.

Its *engendering* in assembly plants and autopart firms studied, however, follow the hiring criteria and specific strategies of profitability and control adopted by the firms involved. Learning for innovation seems to be seldom in practice in the Argentine case. It is possible to conclude that the models which are hybridized are not the only ones possible and/or desirable, but that the existence or absence of forms of regulation of competition, in accordance with principles of labor 'humanization' (in their signification of growth of the capacities of the personnel and power for its exercise), constitutes a fundamental difference.

In sum, a potentially beneficial informational denouement from FDI in Argentina is neither easily constructed nor foreseeable in the immediate future. The neo-Liberal 'institutional shock' of the 1990s did not implement a Virtuous Circle leading to development, but a non-Virtuous dynamics generating informational underdevelopment. It developed a context that prevented, not promoted, the display of the human and productive potential of a society that would promote a knowledge, and eventually a Wise Society to guarantee the exercise of the economic, social, and cultural rights of women and men workers inherent in the broad definition of development.

Given that the non-Virtuous concatenation itself is the product of a human construction, it is imperative to examine the possibilities of its engendered reversion in southern Latin America. I will stress three dimensions related to national and regional public policies, feminist interventions, and the need for joint engendered informational labor in future theoretical–political endeavors.

In the first place, the reflection on information-knowledge-based capitalist development allows us to detect a crucial focus of new public policies that remains invisible specially under the orthodox approach. This implies a new economic-political agenda placing knowledge-based industry, education, science and technology, the democratization of communication, and the socialization of information, at the center of the debate. That is to say, an agenda for the promotion of all the dimensions and conditions conducive to creative or 'artistic' labor: that labor which valorizes capital, as a necessary condition for the generation of development.

With regard to Active Industrial (Productive) Policies, it is paramount that any society's reservoir of interactive learning and new knowledge generation may be extended along the *productive* chains being developed within the same country or region. Otherwise, in the near future, the only type of informational labor that may be relegated to the (male) periphery could be that of engineers, scientists, and skilled operators trying merely to control machinery reproducing a given foreign model: be it of a car, a tool, or any other product. Let us not forget the useful suggestions given by the HLEG Report regarding the fact that public information services could constitute one new engine of growth in the future information or knowledge societies still to be created in Latin America. Employment creation, mainly in production-related and social/personal services, is not inimical to information-knowledge-based development. The generalized introduction of ICTs need not be a synonym for unemployment. But it certainly involves careful and life-long re-training of the able population and autonomous national and regional regulatory frameworks. These policies could confront the 'brain drain' of students and advanced researchers towards central countries, an exodus that represents a real subsidy to the developed world, which compensates for its shortages in R&D investments.

However, are the above national public policies feasible in southern Latin America? Policy articulation constitutes, in my view, a sine-qua-non condition to ensure the success of a much-needed alternative, human rights-based development project, at the level of each Latin American country concerned, and, simultaneously at the MERCOSUR level as well, provided a new configuration of this regional scheme meets with success.

I have argued that the transition to regional growth in the context of contemporary 'globalization' is a product of complex processes excluding the majority of the world population. These are processes of internationalization of capital that, in spite of their origin in central economies, and in their macro-regional 'developed' expression (NAFTA and the EU in particular), find their 'custom made' space through lax, peripheral MERCOSUR norms. Hence, solutions raised at national and regional levels would remain 'good intentions' only if those causal linkages are ignored. This implies the examination of the world context and the restrictions that this context imposes on the domestic plane of each country involved, as well as on the concomitant regional evolution of the South.

In this sense, public policies related to the construction of Information/Knowledge/ Wise Societies meet special resistance from developed macro-regions. The logic of contemporary capitalism, Brazilian economist María da C. Tavares (2002) argues, comprises an *institutional context* that is undergoing profound reforms in order to make possible the appropriation of information value through processes of privatization that deprive it of its social character. She also shows how inefficient our interventions in these matters have been, as they could not prevent the transformation of telematic networks into new instruments of domination and exclusion. We must make of information a public product, a public resource that cannot be privatized or appropriated, she argues.

In this sense, only a congenial, and alternative international institutional context may provide the appropriate feedback necessary for the designing of alternative macro-economies, the 'natural' frameworks of the Virtuous Circle being promoted. The core of this virtuosity is the recognition that signical production (significative codes) is crucial, and that we are only at the initial stage of understanding how significative codes are generated and communicated in any social relationship, and in economic relations in particular. However, as a consequence of the privatization of information now in progress, indigenous codes (old and new theories and discoveries), are often internationally appropriated, while these same societies frequently lack access to developed societies' new codes. As a result, the human society is being divided into those who have, and those who have not, and this must be resisted. But if new active public policies are required to confront neo-Liberal underdevelopment, these must be 'gender sensitive', a challenge to contemporary feminism.

In the second place, the *raison d'être* of feminism has always been the abolishing of gender asymmetries that, articulated to class and race/ethnic hierarchies, perpetuate themselves in the universe of labor and society in general. In effect, women—albeit in lower numbers than in previous decades in terms of 'formal' employment—continue incorporating themselves into paid, mainly routine informational production, providing special nuances to engendered realities of hierarchical organization of work.

To reverse this trend, predominant southern Latin American feminist thinking on development ought to be revised. In effect, while rightly criticizing the WID (Women in Development) approach, the neo-Liberal GAD (Gender and Development) literature sponsored by international donors has often proved even more limited, if not dangerous, for poor women's survival. If WID was criticized because it represented modernism, GAD postmodernism has done even worse, by replacing the limitations of the nation-state with a voluntaristic logic of individual women's empowerment, a politics that can only result in unheard of levels of deprivation for the vast majority of working women in the South.

Moreover, the role of ethics in feminism and particularly in economics, practices, and ideologies diffused by 'feminist' NGOs that sponsor a false dichotomy between market and the State, must urgently be re-examined. This dichotomy has been found to be false, manufactured to get governments 'off the hook', and particularly suited for consumption in the South, at times when it had already been corrected in the North. The intricacies involved in constructing an alternative agenda based on the effective implementation of the ICESCR were incisively discussed by the feminist contributors to WIDE (Women in Development in Europe) as early as 1998. Unfortunately, no comparable discussion has taken place within southern Latin American feminism.

It is necessary, therefore, that feminists in this area have information-knowledge-based development considerations in mind when approaching these issues, taking into consideration pertinent national, regional, and also international regulations. How are those issues related to world capitalist development dynamics, network enterprises, the new virtual value chain, R&D investments, and its work and learning organization implications? The engendering may be local, but the contexts that allow or do not allow the possible practices to be 'appropriately engendered' are not created locally, and the active solidarity of our sisters (and brothers) in the North is urgently needed to change them.

To act otherwise would mean to resign ourselves to struggles over redundant, routine labor that men are already resisting. Unfortunately, institutionalized southern Latin American feminism, has often assimilated 'the salvation' of a few women, to the accomplishment of gender equity in development. It is imperative, then, to be very careful about what public and private policies we are engendering. Are they, by any chance, policies to enhance the business interests of industrialized, advanced macro-regions, that are simultaneously preventing sound, genuine, development policies in the periphery?

The often-promoted insertion of women into the last fragment of the new virtual value chain, does not contribute to structural development in the area, and also prevents the exercise of women's human rights. The incorporation of young women into *sui-generis* versions of 'Ohnist/JIT' practices taking place in industry, in services, in supermarkets, and subcontracting chains, and presently considered legitimate and made public because of changes in labor laws, cannot be considered a triumph of the women's liberation movement from a perspective of development. On the one hand, the Japanese model does not bring the long promised 'humanization' of work practices. On the other, as the model is hybridized in contexts associated with polarizations, exclusions, increasing unemployment, and trade union vulnerability, its negative features are exacerbated.

As Marta Fontenla and Magui Bellotti's (1999) critical Latin American Feminist Manifesto has stated, it is important to stress that the mobilization needed to redress such practices is not exhausted by 'lobbying' before international agencies such as the IMF, the WTO, and the World Bank. Neither can it just be limited to local level mobilization. The articulation of levels of mobilization—including women's and men's agency exercised at the local level—for the vindication of human rights to development comprises joint solidarity action of women and men in the North and the South. Of course this means that without a generalized awareness of the indivisibility of human rights in the North, actions in the South will not be sufficient. Facing the challenges posed by possible transitions from Information to Knowledge/Wise Societies remains a major task for southern Latin American feminism.

In the third place, there exists the urgent need to acknowledge that a series of theoretical-political development themes has not yet been (sufficiently) elaborated through the lenses of Information Theory. In my view, top priority should be given to the analysis of the immediate social and communicative dimensions of women's and men's labor, particularly in contemporary capitalist societies. A new perspective, integrating Information Theory insights is, thus, urgently needed to confront neo-Liberal and Liberal *usines* of significations. This is because, only through alternative theorizations (codes) can the restrictions and biases imposed by those approaches be effectively overcome.

Towards Development Based on Abundance?

If countries of the periphery forget the lessons of history, they might find that the informational subordination now in progress could be much more difficult to break than any other merely economic-productive, or simply political-colonial linkage, had proved in the past (Smith, 1980).

This leads to the question: is economics the science of scarcity or abundance? This is a question that institutional and critical social scientists have raised, and which is still awaiting a suitable scientific reply. Neo-Liberalism, although tempered in some places, is still predominant. But a theory based on the conception of final equilibrium cannot lead to neguentropic work, or disequilibrium. It will lead instead to entropy, chaos, death. This does not mean that, ultimately, the laws of thermodynamics might not prevail (Dantas, 2002a). However, in the meantime, information as a productive force can open an enormous field for the production of wealth, progress, and the general improvement of humankind, which is now being hampered by capitalist surplus appropriation.

Nobel Laureate, Ilya Prigogine (1993) has written extensively on the needed interdisciplinarity of science at a time when a new dialogue between men and nature is being born. I suggest, therefore, that before men dominate this dialogue, both women and men scientists should accept Prigogine's invitation to examine theoretical, methodological, and political paths. These paths would open if relations among 'noises', uncertainties, growth, and informational labor (neguentropy) are basic economic factors, embedded in the very origin of the evolution and history of humankind, and perhaps also the definition of its future fate (Dantas, 2002d).

This is an urgent demand because human rights to development continue to be violated worldwide. I would argue that this is, perhaps, the greatest and most urgent challenge that the still evolving region of the South must face. Yet, is it feasible to establish macro Virtuous Circles leading to development in countries that do not control the regulation of their own accumulation? So far, however, voices of dissent, are few in number, and are not organized. The emergence of new forms of mobilization, integrating international and local forms of agency and struggle, is crucial. I will finally argue that theory and scientific research—as sources of significations of development based on the vindication of women's and men's indivisible human rights—have a fundamental role to play in these liberation struggles, given that theoretical frameworks, as significative codes, not only give meaning to reality, but actively shape its very construction.

NOTES

1. I am referring to the rights upheld by two International Covenants. These are the International Covenant on Civil and Political Rights, General Assembly Res. 2200A (XXI) adopted for signature and ratification on 16 December 1966 and the International Covenant on Economic, Social and Cultural Rights, General Assembly Res. 2200A (XXI) adopted for signature and ratification on 6 December 1966. The former Covenant was to enter into force on 23 March 1976 and the second on 3 June 1976. See Mariama Williams (1998) for an illuminating account on the politics and economics involved in the different fate accrued to both Covenants (the first one on civil and political rights is applied, but the ICESCR was forgotten) and on the challenges and problems involved in the elaboration, and measurement/monitoring issues of the Economic and Social Rights.

   I am stressing the importance of the ICESCR because it refers specifically to a number of rights that bear directly on the subject of this essay: the right to work (article 6), the right to the highest attainable standard of physical and mental health (article 12), the right to education (article 13), the right to participate in cultural life, to enjoy the benefits of scientific progress and its applications, to benefit from the moral and material protection of authorship interests due to scientific, literary or artistic productions (article 15, para 1, Items a, b, and c) among others, are essential dimensions of the economic, social, and cultural rights. Hence, the multifarious search for information-cum-knowledge development paths necessarily involves the design and enactment of 'humane' forms of work organization, that is those able to meet the demands of the human right to mental, emotional, and physical capability growth and the power to exercise this enhanced capability including the right to inform-communicate (Roldán, 2000, 2003) or agency of workers in the production of knowledge and information and control over both. This is the signification I give to the articles 6, 12, 13 and 15 of the ICESCR (1966), quoted above.

2. See Brenner, 1998 and Chesnais, 1996 among others, and statistics from a diversity of international sources such as the World Bank and the UN. See in particular ECLAC (Economic Commission for Latin America and the Caribbean) Reports for this area.

3. The significant term 'information' originates from the Latin *infomatio, -onis*, and refers to 'the action of forming', hence the verb *informare*, meaning 'to shape or to model' (Dantas, 2001, Part I, Chapter 1). However, he reminds us, it was from the Middle Ages onwards, that the value of this type of information was acknowledged in the discourse and practices of economists, employers, investors, and bankers who paid handsomely to those that provided them with 'news' of what was happening in different regions in Europe and the Mediterranean.

4. In the neo-Liberal management conceptual framework devised by Womack, Jones, and Roos, 1991, 'mass' production is superseded by the 'lean' Japanese-born model of production organization, a transition that the liberal literature terms from Taylorism/Fordism to Ohnist/JIT (Just-in-time) production system. As elaborated in my other texts, both models (Fordist and Ohnist/JIT) have in common 'the search for time economies in the use of circulating capital and machinery and in the application of labor, and the search for dynamic economies as product and process evolve' (Sayer and Walker, 1994: pp.163-164). Briefly stated, both models are based on assembly line production in which the structures of the process, the speed of the line, the machine cycle, and the zero stocks principle in the case of the Ohnist model, determine the work rhythm. The differences between them derive from their own logic of time economies—and, consequently, related skills requirements, communicating abilities (or type of informational labor 'with knowledge useful for production' demands) and 'typical' mechanisms of labor control—and from the specific regulatory context that legitimates their successful implementation. Let us remember that the JIT system pursues a goal of increasing the flow of production, but this is a perfected or much improved flow, since it also includes circulation time before and after production. JIT deliveries and distribution and subcontracting linkages become, as a result, crucial elements of the 'Ohnist' model (See Roldán, 2000 for a detailed elaboration of this topic).

   Notice here that neither model requires the utilization of ICTs per se. Yet, the generalized incorporation of these technologies in the advanced capitalist economies, since the 1980s and 1990s in particular, certainly influences the potential productivity increases and control mechanisms implicit in both models, while also implying changes in the construction of labor skills and related learning practices.

5. With regard to skills, that spectrum comprises a continuum of skills ranging from the 'knowing how to work' to the 'knowing how to be' ('right behavior') varieties. The exercise of aptitudes proper to the function I called 'Delegated Management of Production Flows'—comprising the 'administration of production cycle time, of space, and of materials'; 'reprogramming of production and communication'; 'self-control of defects', and 'problem solving' types of skills constitutes a crucial dimension of Ohnist design. Several features also contribute to this same effect; of communication and interactive learning 'on the job training', the use of *kan ban* cards (as elements of a labor code and as a

mechanism for the decentralization of informational labor and, hence, as a means of communication, within a totally centralized planned system); the 'continuous improvement' principle, Quality Circles, the enforced duty to 'volunteer' improvement suggestions, among others. Finally, let us not forget the mobilization of the knowing *pulsión* of the personnel, through the stimulation of 'creative thinking'. These are all mechanisms that influence the processing of the creative elements of the same labor process.

6. See Chesnais, 1996 for examples of the Critical Political Economy tradition, based on Marxian development thinking (also called 'radical' economic thinking in the USA). Brenner, 1998, and some of Boyer's (1996) texts can also be considered among those pertaining to this School. See other texts by Chesnais for an elaboration of the concept of Regime of Accumulation with Financial Domination that would be prevailing in the USA and the UK. For this tradition, human nature derives from historical *praxis*, and human beings are one of the other biological species. Human biology and human society are thus dialectically related. See Jaggar (1983) for a useful feminist critique of the androcentric features of this school.

7. The following *Mondialisation* features are directly relevant to the shaping of the context within which our problematic is embedded: the hyper mobility of financial capital; the increasing importance of FDI instead of foreign trade as the main axis of internationalization trends; the emergence of intra-sector and intra MNCs or TNCs (Multinational or Transnational Corporations) trade as dominant forms of foreign trade; and the concentration of monetary, FDI and commercial flows in the central economies, among other trends. These processes are commonly associated with the restructuring dynamics of industrial MNCs on the basis of 'network' enterprises combining the centralization of capital and the decentralization of activities; through new forms of management and control; modes of subcontracting; and the possibilities offered by the incorporation of ICTs, particularly if they are accompanied by the adaptation of the 'Japanese' and other flexible models of work organization.

8. Chesnais et al., 2001 argues with reference to Science and Technology in the USA that a financially dominated Regime of Accumulation does not produce Science and Technology. Its goals are very short-run and seek immediate profits. Financial domination also implies that investments in R&D previously undertaken by MNCs are no longer sufficient. In the case of developed economies, such as the US, the most important mechanism to counteract this trend is the intense and continuous in- flows of students and advanced researchers that have benefited that country during the decade of the 1990s. The inverse situation is found in the peripheral countries which suffer the brain drain, deemed to be higher than the financial drain, and the payment of the services of the external debt.

9. Of the 12 ECLAC documents and publications on the theme 'Information Technologies' written between June 2000 and January 2003, only one is engendered. This document, from the Women and Development Unit, focuses on Women and ICTs, and does not deal with the information and/or knowledge societies debate or with development issues. The Women and Development Unit of ECLAC (Women and Development Series) produced 44 texts between September 1989 and February 2003. Of these, only two bear any connection to

the information society debate. The first one on Women and ICTs, was written in 1991 and is not available online; the second one is the one mentioned above.
10. See Becerra, 2003 for a useful account of the history of 'Information Society' projects in Argentina as well as for Science and Technology legislation bearing on this topic. See Azpiazu, Basualdo, and Schorr, 2000 on the changes of the Argentine industrial Establishment, and its association with financial capital; the evolution of the fractions of the power bloc, of the industrial 'top' enterprises (cúpula), and external trade of the same cúpula.

References

Aronskind, Ricardo. (2001) *Más cerca o más lejos del desarrollo? Transformaciones económicas en los 90s*, (Closer to or further from development? Economic transformations in the 90s), Libros del Rojas, 2da serie extramuros, Buenos Aires.

Azpiazu, D., Basualdo, E., and Schorr, M. (2000) *La restructuración y el redimensuionamiento de la producción industrial argentina durante las últimas décadas* (The restructuring and new dimensions of Argentina industrial production during the last decades), Institute of Social Studies and Professional Training of the CTA, Buenos Aires, Argentina.

Becerra, Martin. (2003) *Sociedad de la información: proyecto, convergencia, divergencia* (The Information Society: Project, Convergence, Divergence), Norma, Buenos Aires.

Boyer, R. (1996) 'La globalisation: mythes et realites' (The Globalization: Myths and Realities), *Actes du Gerpisa*, n. 18, Paris.

Brenner, Robert. (1998) 'The Economics of Global Turbulence: A Special Report on the World Economy, 1950–98,' *New Left Review*, 229(41): 251–62.

Castells, Manuel. (2000) *The Rise of the Network Society*, Second Edition, Blackwell Publishers, Oxford.

Chesnais, François. (1996) *A. Mundializaçao do Capital*. (The 'Mondialisation' of Capital), Xama, Sao Paulo.

Chesnais, François, Serfati, F., and Udruy, A. (2001) 'El Futuro del Movemiento anti-mundialización, algunas reflexiones para una consolidación de sus fundamentos teóricos', (The Future of the Anti-globalization Movement: Some Reflections for a Consolidation of its Theoretical Foundations), *Cadermos Em Tempo* (Notebooks of Our Time), n. 320, February–March.

Chudnovsky, Daniel and López, Adres. (1995) *Política Tecnológica en la Argentina. ¿Hay algo más que laissez-faire?* (Technological Policy in Argentina: Is There Anything Beyond Laissez-faire?), Documento de Trabajo 20, Cenit, Buenos Aires.

Comisión Europea. (1994) *Europa y la sociedad global de la información* (Informe Bangemann) *Recomendaciones al Consejo Europeo* (Europe and the Global Information Society: The Bangemann Report, Recommendations to the European Council), Comisión Europea, Brussels.

Cowan, R. and Foray, D. (1998) 'Économie de la codification et de la diffusion de conaissances' (The Economics of the Codification and the Diffusion of Competences) in P. Petit (org.) *L' économie de l'information; les enseignement des théories économiques* (The Economics of Information: The Learning of Economic Theories), La Découverte, Paris.

Dantas, Marcos. (2001) Os significados do trabalho: Uma investigaçao semiótica no processo de produçao. (The Meanings of Work: A Semiotic Research on the Process of Production), Ph.D. Thesis on Production Engineering Sciences, defended before the academic panel in charge of the Coordination of the Postgraduate Programs in Engineering at the Federal University of Río de Janeiro, Brazil (UFRJ).

———. (2002a) *A lógica do capital-informaçäo. A fragmentaçao dos monopolios e a monopolizaçao dos fragmentos num mundo de comunicaçoes globais. (The Logic of Information-capital: The Fragmentation of Monopolies and the Monopolization of the Fragments in a World of Global Communications)*, Contraponto, Rio de Janeiro.

———. (2002b) 'A difícil apropriaçao da informaçao, um valor que só é valor quando compartilhado por todos'. *(The Difficult Appropriation of Information, A Value That is a Value Only When it is Shared by All)*, Text for publication at the FSM, P. Alegre.

———. (2002c) 'Do capitalismo industrial ao capital-informaçao; as novas (e as antigas) dimensoes produtivas das comunicaçoes'. (From Industrial Capitalism to Information-capital: The New (and the Old) Productive Dimensions of Communications), Text presented at the Oficina 'Información, capitalismo, y control de la esfera pública' (Information, Capitalism and Public Sphere Control) during the II Foro Social Mundial (Porto Alegre, RS, Febrero 3).

———. (2002d) 'Informaçao, Capital e Trabalho. Valorizaçao e apropiaçao no ciclo de comunicaçao produtiva' (Information, Capital and Labor: Valorization and Appropriation in the Production-communication Cycle), Paper presented to the II Meeting on the Political Economy of MERCOSUR, Brasilia, 26-28 May.

Dosi, Giovanni. (1996) 'The Contribution of Economic Theory to the Understanding of a Knowledge-based Economy' in OECD (ed.), *Employment and Growth in the Knowledge-based Economy*, OECD, Paris.

Ebert, T.L. (1996) *Ludic Feminism and After: Postmodernism, Desire, and Labour in Late Capitalism*, The University of Michigan Press, Ann Arbor, USA.

ECLAC (Economic Commission for Latin America and the Caribbean). 'Road Maps towards an Information Society in Latin American and the Caribbean' (Consulted at http://www.eclac.cl/publicaciones/DesarrolloProductivo/1/LCG2195Rev1PI/lcg2195i.pdf).

Fontenla, Martha and Bellotti, Magui. (1999) *"ONGs, Financiamiento y Feminismo". (NGOs, Financing and Feminism)*, Anuario de Hojas de WARMI (Yearly Journal Pages of WARMI) Volume 10, pp. 29–40, University of Barcelona, Spain.

HLEG. (1997) *Building the European Information Society for Us All*, Final policy report of the High-level expert group of the Employment, Industrial Relations and Social Affairs Unit, Brussels.

ICESCR. (1966) International Covenant on Economic, Social, and Cultural Rights, General Assembly Res. 2200 A (XXI) adopted for signature and ratification on 6 December 1966.

Jaggar, Alison. (1983) *Feminist Politics and Human Nature*, Rowman and Allanheld, Brighton.

Jürgens, U., Malsch, T., and Dohse, K. (1993) *Breaking from Taylorism: Changing Forms of Work in the Automobile Industry*, Cambridge University Press, Cambridge.

Kosacoff, Bernardo (ed.). (2000) *Corporate Strategies under Structural Adjustment in Argentina*, Macmillan, London.

Lastres, H. and Ferraz, j.C. (1999) 'Economia da Informaçao, do Conhecimento e do Aprendizado' (The Economics of Information, Knowledge and Learning) in Lastres, H. and Albagli, S. (Orgs.), *Informaçao, e Globalizaçao na Era do Conhecimento, (Information and Globalization in the Era of Knowledge)*, Editora Campus, Sao Paulo.

Lojkine, Jean. (1995) *A Revoluçao Informacional. (The Informational Revolution)*, Third edition, Cortez Editora, Sâo Paulo.

Lundvall, A. (2000) 'The Challenge of the Learning Economy and the Need for a New Type of Policy Coordination at the European Level,' in International hearing for the Portuguese presidency of the European Union, The prime minister's office, Lisboa.

Nochteff, H. (2001) Ponencia Inaugural: *'Las políticas y actividades de ciencia y tecnología. Un enfoque desde la economía política'*. (Main Paper 'Policies and Activities in Science and Technology: A Political Economy Approach') IX. Jornadas de Jóvenes Investigadores de la Asociación de Universidades 'Grupo Montevideo' (A.U.G. M) (IXth Session of Young Researchers of the Universities of the 'Montevideo Group') Rosario, 12–14 September.

Prigogine, Ilya. (1993) *¿Tan solo una ilusión? Una exploración del caos al orden. (An Illusion Only? An Exploration from Chaos to Order)*, Tusquets Editores, Barcelona.

Roldán, Martha. (2000) ¿Globalización o Mundialización? Teoría y Práctica de Procesos Productivos y Asimetrías de Género. (Globalization or Mondialisation? Theory and Practice of Production Processes and Gender Asymmetries), UNP (SJB) Delegación Zonal Trelew Flacso, Eudeba, Buenos Aires.

———. (2001) 'Desarrollo, construcción de regiones, y regulación privada: algunas implicaciones para la dinámica productiva y del trabajo' (Development, Region Construction and Private Regulation: Some Implications for Production and Work Dynamics) in Costa Lima, M. (Org.), *O Lugar da América do Sul na Ncva Ordem Mundial, (The Place of South America in the New World Order)*, Cortez Editora, Sao Paulo.

———. (2003). 'Information, Knowledge, Work Organization and Development: Towards a New Virtuous Circle in 21st Century Information Society? A Synthesis of the Theoretical "State of the Art" in Argentina (1990s–2000s)' Discussion Paper 1, Göteborgs Universitet, Department of Education, Sweden.

Sayer, Andrew and Walker, Richard. (1994) *The New Social Economy: Reworking the Division of Labor*, Blackwell, Cambridge.

SCANS Report (The Secretary's Commission on Achieving Necessary Skills). (1991) *What Work Requires of Schools: A SCANS Report for America 2000*, US Department of Labor, June.

Smith, Anthony. (1980) *The Geopolitics of Information: How the Western Culture Dominates the World*, Oxford University Press, New York.

Tauile, Jose Ricardo. (2001) *Para (re) construir o Brasil contemporáneo. Trabalho, tecnologia e acumulaçao. (To (Re)construct Contemporary Brazil: Work, Technology and Accumulation)*, Contraponto, Rio de Janeiro.

Tavares, M.C. (2002) 'Prologue', in Dantas (2002a), *A lógica do capital-informaçäo. A fragmentaçao dos monopolios e a monopolizaçao dos fragmentos num mundo de comunicaçoes globais. (The Logic of Information-capital: The Fragmentation of Monopolies and the Monopolization of the Fragments in a World of Global Communications)*, Contraponto, Rio de Janeiro.

Vispo, A. (1999) 'Reservas de mercado, cuasi rentas de privilegio y deficiencias regulatorias: el régimen automotriz argentino (Market Reserves, Privileged Quasi Rents and Regulatory Deficiencies in the Argentine Automotive Regime)' in Azpiazu, D. (Comp.), *La desregulación de los mercados. Paradigmas e inequidades de las políticas del neoliberalismo, (Market De-regulation, Paradigms and Inequities in Neo-liberal Policies)*, Grupo Editorial Norma/FLACSO, Buenos Aires.

Williams, Mariama. (1998) a) "What are Economic and Social Rights?", b) "Economic Rights and Economic Justice in Economic Theory" in Jo Brew (ed.) *Women's Economic and Social Rights*, WIDE (Women in Development in Europe) Bulletin, Brussels.

Womack, J.P., Jones, D., and Roos, D. (1991) *The Machine That Changed the World*, Harper Perennial, New York.

Yoguel, M., Novick, M., and Marín, A. (2001) 'Tramas produtivas, processos de inovaçao e tecnologias de Gestao social:uma aproximaçao metodológica aplicada ao complexo automotor argentino, (Productive Networks, Innovation Processes and Social Management Technologies: A Methodological Approximation Applied to the Automotive Complex in Argentina)' in Araujo Guimaraes, N. and Martin, S. (Orgs.), *Competitividade e Desenvolvimento, Atores e Instituiçoes Locais, (Competitiveness and Development, Actors and Local Institutions)*, Editoria SENAC, Sao Paulo.

PART II

Gendered Spaces
in the Digital Economy

4   FEMALE SPACES IN THE PHILIPPINES' ICT INDUSTRY

CZARINA SALOMA-AKPEDONU

One way of taking account of technological work in so-called developing countries is to complement studies on dependent technological development with an examination of work requiring knowledge and expertise. A focus on knowledge and expertise in developing countries brings to view some changes in the global and gender division of labor which are not fully observable in global economic terms. These changes are to be seen in the context of technological areas requiring knowledge and expertise in these countries, and in the presence of women in such areas. Using the case of the Philippine information and communication technology (ICT) industry, I demonstrate, that discussions within the framework of the 'new international division of labor' (Fröbel et al., 1980) and feminization of labor (Standing, 1989) have lost their explanatory power vis-à-vis these changes.

The chapter consists of three main sections. The first develops a framework based on Alfred Schutz and Thomas Luckmann's (1973) notion of a social distribution of knowledge, and Gudrun Lachenmann's (1997) concept of female spaces, to examine practices, and relations within the Philippine ICT industry. The second describes the context for ICT work in the Philippines, focusing on gender relations within Philippine society, and the nature and structure of ICTs and ICT work, which are conducive to the emergence of female spaces. The third section examines the creation of female spaces in some fields of the ICT industry and discusses its implications on issues of feminization of labor and invisibility of women in technological production.

UNDERSTANDING GENDERED HIGH-SKILL TECHNOLOGICAL WORK

The global division of labor has changed since the late 1970s and 1980s, and some forms and organization of knowledge, and expertise in so-called developing countries have rendered some theorizing about gender relations, and the global division of labor, obsolete. Likewise, the examination of technological work will yield richer insights, by taking account of the social shaping of technology, particularly the practices and relations of technological actors as they pursue practical work. Thus, the current gendered global division of labor in the Philippine ICT industry is examined in terms of:

1. Variety of individuals who possess knowledge and expertise which are distributed unevenly in space, and
2. Female spaces wherein women participate actively in high-skill technological work.

Social Distribution of Knowledge and the Technological Elite

The Philippine ICT industry is inhabited by different groups which possess different kinds of knowledge: groups of individuals who possess basic knowledge needed in routine back office services coexist with groups of individuals who possess knowledge needed in the modification and adaptation of standard technological products. The variety of fields in the information technology industry, and the variation within it, implies that activities vary from relatively low-end customer services provision to high-end designing of hardware and software technologies (see Mitter, 2004). Within customer service centers are higher-end activities of technical customer support engineers, application developers, and network security engineers. To further make a distinction among these many groups, the notion of a social distribution of knowledge is adopted. A social distribution of knowledge, manifested as distinctions between the knowledge possessed by the layperson, the well-informed, and the specialist or expert (Schutz and Luckmann, 1973: 306–318), implies that members of any society possess dissimilar knowledge. Specialists or experts are individuals who possess the relevant special knowledge needed to solve particular problems. This means that in relation to a particular problem of type A, there are specialists and everyone else, laypersons. Moreover, this means that there are specialists for problems of type B, in relation to which everyone else, including the specialists of the problems of type A, are laypersons (Schutz and Luckmann, 1973: 323). In this formulation, special knowledge is knowledge that is relevant only for problems linked with specific social roles and is routinely transmitted only to the 'role-holder'. In contrast, general knowledge is knowledge that is relevant for 'everyone' and is routinely transmitted to 'everyone'. This is the knowledge possessed by laypersons.

In my analysis of ICT work, I refer to knowledge that is neither specialist in terms of technical scientific knowledge, nor lay as informed knowledge. Possessors of informed knowledge have an analytical overview; they possess more than general knowledge but not the theoretical and practical details that characterize specialist knowledge. Individuals who possess rare, specialist, technical scientific knowledge and individuals who possess informed knowledge comprise the 'technological elite'. This group includes, but is not limited to, hardware developers, software developers, web content developers, and technopreneurs who possess difficult-to-find skill sets (e.g., skill sets in Java, C++ programming, Oracle, XML and MS.Net development, third generation mobile communications, and web security), and extensive experience in project management, software programming and quality assurance, mobile communications, and web security. They consume, process, and repurpose global, standard ICT products[1] for local consumers, and in doing so, engage in a new mode of knowledge production (Gibbons et al., 1994) where the producer and the user of knowledge are one and the same. This is so, for example, in the case of a programmer who uses C++, a computer language that is used for high-end applications for back-end processes (e.g., databases) and front-end processes (e.g., spreadsheet applications) in order to create business applications software for an insurance company.

Female Spaces

Aside from changes within the global division of labor, another important aspect in the analysis of the Philippine ICT industry are changes within the gender division of labor. In an analysis of the 'gendered embeddedness of the economy', an approach that looks at contexts of women's activities and the gendered structuration of economic fields, Gudrun Lachenmann (1997: 52) introduces the concept of 'female spaces'. Developed from the idea of a public sphere that usually segregates women from men, female spaces are spaces in the public sphere wherein women take part in public life. This notion of female spaces as part of the public sphere finds resonance in the structures and social construction of technology. Technology started out as an arena that puts much value on physical strength and hence, an arena that, even at present in certain fields, practices gender segregation. The idea of a female space is therefore very much in the sense of women's presence in hitherto 'male spaces'. For example, in the field of programming, the President of a Filipino software development company recalls that, 'in the old, old days of computing, there were only programmers', and mostly these were men. When, over decades, software developers recognized a process of software development that involved requirements analysis, systems design, coding and testing, programming ceased to be the only job description in the industry. As user expectations and technologies developed, software development began to include the process of ascertaining users' needs and interests. Hence, systems analysis became part of the software development process along with programming. The job of 'systems analyst' would offer women an entry point into the software development sector of the Philippine ICT industry. At present, three patterns are notable in the female spaces within the Philippine ICT industry: one, there are more men in hardware development and web designing; two, there are more or less equal number of women and men in software development and technical support services; and three, there are no fields where women are predominant in number, and there are also no fields that are exclusively male spaces.

The modification and adaptation of global, standard technological practices, and knowledge to the needs of local end-users, and the involvement of women in these activities indicate that there are fields in the ICT industry which contradict patterns set by the 'new international division of labor'. In the 1970s and 1980s, the division of labor saw the start of a transfer of a significant portion of low-skill industrial activities from the developed world to select developing countries (Fröbel et al., 1980). In the production of semiconductors, for example, the new international division of labor is manifested in the designing and fabrication of products taking place in developed countries, where they are done mostly by men, and in developing countries where the final assembly of these product is performed by women (see, for example, Webster, 1996: 85-86).[2] In contrast, the barriers to entry in the development of business applications based on global standard ICTs are not as high, compared to those in the development of semi-conductors and standard proprietary hardware and software.

CREATING FEMALE SPACES

Underlying the emergence of the technological elite in the Philippine ICT industry are user-friendly technologies, horizontal knowledge structures, and 'hybrid practices' in some fields of the ICT industry.

User-friendly Technology

Connie, who was among the first batch of programmers hired by NCR Philippines in 1966, narrates how the shift from mainframe computers to minicomputers to personal computers reduced the complexity of ICT work:

> In terms of the mainframe...education and training, the people who were involved in these, really had intensive training. And unlike now, where the computers are very user-friendly, there were no user-friendly computers before. You had to understand the intricacies of the computer inside and out.... You had to be able to visualize how the computer is working inside, because programming was dependent on that. Unlike now, when you say user-friendly, you are just taught to press a few buttons. There are software programs and you can go.... In the 1960s, no software was ready-made. We had to develop everything. That meant people were more careful with details, with logic.... Like you got a flair for it, some skills, like an eye for details, like if you put a comma instead of a period, everything goes berserk. Now, there is so much room for error. (Author's interview with Connie, Chief Executive Officer of an IT consultancy firm, 22 June 2000)

Innovations such as personal computers, interactive computing, and off-the-shelf software programs correspond to the diversification of the activities of the technological elite. This diversification suggests that in addition to the programming activities attendant to the mainframes, there are activities in the ICT industry that do not require programming skills. The move from monolithic mainframes to smaller personal computers, implies an increasing ability by end-users without any technological backgrounds, to use their own systems in their own ways. While some web designers started out designing by codes, various software programs with graphic user interfaces are making the job less complicated.

Horizontal Knowledge Structures

As a means of transmitting information and knowledge, the Internet results in the creation of horizontal, proactive structures of knowledge that broaden the traditional, vertical hierarchies of information and knowledge transmission such as the state, national media, religious institutions, and multinational corporations (Youngs, 2000: 117). In horizontal knowledge structures such as those found in online communities, there is no one true source or dispenser of knowledge as the emphasis is on one's ability to respond to the current need and less on the individual's social position. A Filipino software architect in the US describes these horizontal knowledge structures in online communities as:

> The total (or almost total) absence of hierarchy. Attempts of companies to monopolize the discussion in the communities they sponsor usually fail....Individuals could not flaunt titles, peerage or attitude (or could only do so in a very limited way) lest they get booted out of the community (Author's email correspondence with Ruben, 26 February 2000).

There is no formula as to how one learns information and communication technologies: some are learned by studying an existing web page or online tutorials, others are learned by taking jobs at multinational companies, and still others are learned by enrolling in short-term programming courses. But, all means of learning exhibit similar patterns: learning ICT skills is facilitated by access to technologies and information (e.g., online information and online-user groups). The possibility of learning on one's own is a prerequisite to the creation of new technologies and knowledge. Feminist writers (see, for example, Cockburn, 1987; Schwartz Cowan, 1987; Wajcman, 1991, 1995) point out that technology is the privileged possession of certain social groups. One source of this understanding is Jörgen Nissen (1996) who explains why hacking of computer games in Sweden involves boys/men. Hacking, which is about mastery and control of technology, is connected to earlier activities and contexts that are considered masculine. For example, computer games first appeared as arcade games which eventually became a masculine domain, computer clubs are dominated by men, and computer magazines are placed in shelves aimed at men (Nissen, 1996: 243–244). Horizontal and proactive structures of learning have widened access, not only to information and knowledge, but more importantly to the tools and know-how of information and communication technologies. As noted by Youngs (2000: 112), horizontal and proactive structures of learning have an empowering effect on social groups which have their own ways of dealing with technologies.

Hybrid Fields

The technological elite also traffics in some fields in the ICT industry that are characterized by mixtures of practices. One of these mixtures is characterized by disciplinary hybridity, or the amalgamation of disciplines such as computer science, business and industrial management, communication arts, etc. Disciplinary hybridity means the linking of so-called ICT skills with non-ICT skills, as well as the interface between technical and non-technical skills. In the context of a company selling accounting software, 'technical' implies familiarity with the hardware and computer network, while 'non-technical' refers to familiarity with accounting processes. The cumulative nature of knowledge and practices to be learned on the job requires familiarity with computers but not necessarily a degree in computer science. Indeed, there is an increasing preference for a business background over a technical one.

Disciplinary hybridity also explains the role of ICT technopreneurs who have specialist knowledge of markets and audiences for ICT products, but not specialist knowledge in ICT. Having only informed knowledge of ICTs (e.g., what ICT tools are needed to create new ICT products), these technopreneurs cannot do tasks related to hardware and software. Since they cannot do programming they cannot tell the programmers 'this is what you need to do'. However, they can ask, 'why is a program not working?' and understand when programmers reply that, 'the software is not suitable or because it is not compliant'. Spaces for business skills and other forms of non-technical knowledge prevent the creation of a homogenized ICT industry that requires specific technical skills.

Philippine Gender Relations and the ICT Industry

The examination of female spaces in the Philippine ICT industry must also take into account the so-called 'gender egalitarianism' in the Philippines. This perception of a gender-fair system is generated by a variety of accounts that show the relatively high status of Filipino women vis-à-vis Filipino men,[3] and vis-à-vis women of many Asian countries. The perception of the relatively high position of Filipino women in comparison to the women of many Asian countries appears to especially derive credence from United Nations Human Development Reports.[4]

In some fields of the ICT industry, 'Filipino gender egalitarianism' is confirmed by the relatively high rate of female labor force participation. A survey of the Philippine ICT industry conducted in 1999-2000 showed that 40 percent of the workforce (excluding data encoders) is composed of women.[5] This figure is the highest in the Southeast Asian region, while the lowest, 8 percent, was recorded in Japan (Formoso, 2000). The survey also reported that in 2000, women comprised more than 30 percent of the membership of the Philippine Computer Society. To provide some form of comparison: women comprised only 10 percent of the membership of the British Computer Society (Webster, 1996: 81).

The concept of gender egalitarianism must however be treated critically as it may suggest that the momentum towards gender equality in the ICT industry is a momentum that male colleagues should approve of and contribute to. While gender egalitarianism provides the context for women's entry into the industry, the presence of women in the Philippine ICT industry is largely based on notions of technical competence and professional dedication.

> The more I travel, especially in Asia, the more I appreciate being a Filipina. This is because here in the Philippines ... the only objection to employing women would be the maternity leave which takes the woman away from work for a long time. But, there are companies which do not mind this. If you really exhibit a lot of skills, especially

when you combine technical with people-skills, the company will take you. When you are in sales, you've got to be good technically and you've got to have people-skills. And this combination is very difficult to find. Moreover, shift work is also no longer an issue now as women are now willing to work on the graveyard shift, unlike in the past where it was mostly men who did that. (Author's interview with Connie, Chief Executive Officer of an IT consultancy firm, 22 June 2000)

FEMALE SPACES AND THE FEMINIZATION OF LABOR

Why are women likely to be in software development and technical support services? What are the implications of female spaces in the ICT industry on issues of feminization of labor and the invisibility of women in production?

Feminization of Labor and Other Related Issues

In the analyses of gender and technology relations which focused mostly on semi-skilled assembly functions and production processes in free-trade zones of Southeast Asia, Latin America, China, India, and in countries that comprised the 'East and Southeast Asian Miracle', two issues may be considered central. The first is the feminization of labor which corresponds to the creation of a working class of women. Women's entry into the formal economy did not result in an increased status as most women found themselves doing low-status and low-waged work. Consequently, certain jobs and job attributes such as low-wage, flexibility, and deregulation became associated with women's work. Over time, the feminization of labor was not only being felt by women in the routine and badly-paid character of their own jobs but also in the loss of the male wage as certain attributes formerly reserved for female jobs were being associated with male jobs (Haraway, 1991: 166; Pearson, 1998: 176; Standing, 1989: 1079). A development closely related to the feminization of labor is 'deskilling'. Braverman (1974) describes deskilling as the fragmentation of work into smaller, simpler, and unskilled tasks and the consequent displacement of skilled labor by unskilled labor, which chiefly consisted of women and untrained young people.[6]

The second issue is the invisibility of women in production. Doing low-status and low-waged work means that women also have an 'invisible' status in the production process. The invisibility of women in the production process is due to the fact that the components assembled by women (e.g., integrated circuits) are usually not visible as end products. It is also a result of studies that focus on areas such as development and design where women are scarcely present. While such studies examine the shaping of technology in the hands of its creators, these studies failed to see women since most of the creators of technology are men.[7]

Related to the issue of the invisibility of women is the question as to whether women, when in control of technology, would design technologies differently and on account of their own female interests or not. Gill and Grint (1995: 12–14) refer to this phenomenon as the 'dilemma of ideology'. One part of this question is rooted to the view that men create technologies on account of their own (male) interests which, in itself, implies that women would design different technologies. Completing the dilemma, however, is the historically and culturally masculine construction of technology, which ensures that the presence of more women designers would not result in fundamental changes in the nature of technology. The dilemma of ideology is played out in rationalization which requires that social characteristics (e.g., gender, ethnic background, political beliefs) do not appear in the performance of one's work.

Why is Feminization of Labor not Happening in the Philippine ICT Industry?

Three features of the Philippine ICT industry explain the patterns of the creation of female spaces in the ICT industry and why women's presence in certain ICT fields such as software development, web design, and technical support services has not resulted in the devaluation of female labor in these fields. These three features are:

1. Presence of fields in the ICT industry that require a business background;
2. Absence of gender tracking in the compensation structure of some fields in the ICT industry; and
3. Recognition of women's epistemic privilege and standpoint.

First, some fields in the ICT industry require a combination of disciplinary skills in computer science, business and industrial management, and communication arts. This counters the gender tracking that exists in the Philippine educational system. Selected statistics (Illo, 1997) show that the gender tracking at the tertiary level of education in the Philippines is one where more women than men go to tertiary school. The highest percentage of women enrollees are in business education. Business education, which includes commerce and accounting courses, has the third highest ratio of women to men students, after education and health-related courses. The existence of ICT fields that require a business background, a 'feminine' track in tertiary education, and fields that do not specify 'masculine' backgrounds (e.g., computer engineering) means that the gender tracking in education is not reproduced in occupational fields.

Second, disciplinary hybridity also prevents gender tracking in the compensation structure. The literature documents ways in which the gender division of society has affected technological change through the different wages paid to women and men (MacKenzie and Wajcman, 1987: 22). The common view is that women are in low-paid occupations because they are unskilled, but as Wajcman (1991: 37) points out, definitions of skill can have 'more to do with ideological and social constructions than with technical competencies that are possessed by men and not by women'.

In some fields in the Philippine ICT industry such as software development, the compensation structure prevents the feminization of these very fields. To manage the number of people involved in systems development, software development companies rely on methodologies or standard ways of systems development. In one Filipino software company, software development involves requirements analysis, systems analysis/design, and coding and testing (programming), and is being done by a team comprising a project manager, systems analysts/designers, business analysts, and programmers. In this software development company, programmers, and systems analysts have computer science backgrounds and normally share the same salary scale. The business analyst may, however, get a higher pay, depending on whether this person has a Masters in Business Administration or not.

Individuals get promoted within job categories suggesting the absence of a ladder-type structure. This means that a programmer does not have to become a systems analyst or vice versa in order to have a higher pay.

In software development, men are considered to be good programmers (e.g., good at working with rigid, technical entities) and women to be good systems analysts (e.g., good at working with ambiguous entities such as assessing customer's needs). When gender tracking in the occupational structure does exist, the job that is associated with women professionals has a higher level of compensation. In the 1999 Occupational Wages Survey, systems analysts and designers, a category associated with women ICT professionals, are rated as the highest paid in the computer industry, while computer programmers, a category associated with men, earn about 30 percent less than systems analysts and designers (Bureau of Labor and Employment Statistics, Philippines, 1999).

Third, gender differences are seen as advantageous in some fields of ICT. Take as an instance, e-commerce and e-business. In such applications, the design of the user interface (that is, what people see on screen) matters, because what sells is premised on the intimacy between the seller and the client or audience. It is therefore important, that the generalized target audience is able to find some identification in the interface. In this regard, two of the most important factors in the design of interfaces are the age and gender of the web designers and programmers. The owner of a free email service company explains what kind of skills and perspectives are necessary in the designing of the company's website:

> I want to have female programmers because our product is being developed by programmers. For whatever, I want to have everything. It is very important to know what visuals work with women. A 'true blue' woman will really tell me what clicks with women. It is really hard to find women programmers. Knowing the gender composition of your audience is very important. Generational, too, but mostly we have young people with us.... Maybe, I don't know, it could just be one interface. (Author's interview with Dom, founder of a free e-mail service company, 10 April 2000)

Here, social perceptions of feminine qualities are not phrased in utilitarian terms but rather as 'epistemic privilege' (e.g., it takes one to know one) on so-called 'feminine tastes and preferences'. Dom's point of view acknowledges a basic tenet common to the view of 'epistemic privilege', and feminist standpoint theory: that one's position as a woman is a factor in gaining knowledge and understanding of other women. Knowing what his women clients want and finding women programmers are, however, not the only problems faced by Dom. His intention of creating products from the standpoint of women's experiences must also contend with the awareness that there is no single privileged position from which to view women's social experiences (Harding, 1986: 18ff). Thus, Dom takes the notion of 'epistemic privilege' (e.g., women web programmers gain insights into other women that may not be achieved by men programmers) one step further with his admission that 'for whatever, I want to have everything'. The recognition of the diversity of women's social positions and experiences, and the corresponding diversity of women's points of view (both as clients and programmers) acknowledges the social situatedness of knowledge and not just 'epistemic privilege'. In this sense, Dom's intentions are a compelling case for multiple perspectives, in that every programmer brings 'highly specific visual possibilities, each with a wonderfully detailed, active, partial way of organizing worlds' (Haraway, 1991: 190).

The new international division of labor literature in the 1970s showed that the end-result of the process of a feminization of labor was the creation of jobs for Filipino women but mostly because of the lesser cost of women's labor (see, for example, Chant and MacIlwaine, 1995). Thus, while the feminization of labor thesis might predict the devaluation of fields that require the soft or nontechnical skills associated with women workers, this development is preempted by interdisciplinary requirements in some ICT fields that recognize the contribution of such skills. The 'ideology dilemma' that prevents women from creating technology differently is likewise resolved by the recognition of women's epistemic privileges as well as multiple perspectives. It would seem that although these are related phenomena, how to facilitate the entry of more women into hitherto male spaces is currently a more important question than the question of the feminization of labor in the ICT industry.

Concluding Remarks

In global economic terms of gross domestic product, foreign direct investment, production share in the global division of labor in the ICT industry, and others, certain categories seem unperturbed. The USA, the countries of the EU, Japan, Singapore, and Taiwan, among others are ahead of other countries. Yet, there are changes in the global division of labor which are characterized by the broadening and diversification of technological activities and actors.

Changes in the global division of labor are observable in the development of non-assembly work and female spaces in the Philippine ICT industry. Vital to the development of non-assembly activities is the technological elite, a group of ICT professionals who consume, process, and repurpose standard products for local consumers. Factors that are crucial to the emergence of the technological elite in the Philippine ICT industry are the introduction of user-friendly technologies, the presence of horizontal ways of knowledge diffusion, and the mixed practices in the ICT industry (e.g., skill sets that require both technical and non-technical skills). These factors, which support the development of the technological elite, also provide the context conducive to the creation of female spaces—spaces where women participate actively in public life—in the Philippine ICT industry. Fields in the ICT industry that require a non-technical background; the absence of gender tracking in the compensation structure; and the recognition of women's epistemic privilege and standpoint have so far ensured that the emergence of female spaces in the Philippine ICT industry does not result in the feminization of labor. However, with the scope of the diversification of technological actors and activities still being contested, it is up to women to seek out and maximize changes in the technological structures and in the meaning strata, and to resolve to venture into socially constructed technological male spaces. Broadening the inquiry to include women who are doing non-assembly work does not mean taking attention away from the issues of assembly work. Rather, it implies the creation of female spaces and the entry of more women into hitherto male technological spaces.

NOTES

1. The ICT industry is one arena where globalization strongly manifests itself as a homogenizing process and condition. For example, about ten companies such as IBM, Microsoft and Oracle dominate 90 percent of the global standard software market (Schwanitz, 2001: 1).

2. Semiconductor companies in Europe, which are concentrated in Scotland and Ireland, also let women carry out semi- and unskilled production operations. However, these companies carry out complex product manufacture on a batch production basis, unlike the assembly and mass production being done in Southeast Asian offshore companies (Webster, 1996: 87). To illustrate, wafer and slider development and fabrication, considered to be the highest form of technology in the disk drive production process, are mostly done in the USA, Europe, and Japan.

3. Jeanne Illo (1997: 5) however notes, that in a country with 111 linguistic, cultural and ethnic groups, some with gender systems that are more egalitarian than others, ethnicity has a differentiating effect on the status of different groups of women. For a discussion of the debate concerning gender egalitarianism in the Philippines, see Chant and MacIlwaine (1995).

4. Based on the Gender Empowerment Measure (GEM), a composite index measuring gender inequality in three basic dimensions of empowerment—economic participation and decision-making, political participation and decision-making and power over economic resources (UNDP, 2004). In 2004, the country has a Gender Empowerment rank of 37. This index put the Philippines ahead of Japan (ranked 38), South Korea (ranked 68), Malaysia (ranked 44) and Thailand (ranked 57), Asian countries which have higher Human Development Indices than the Philippines.

5. The survey was done on high-end labor force employees such as analysts, consultants, managers, database administrators, multimedia artists, and CAD (computer-aided design)/CAM (computer-aided manufacturing) experts. Excluded in the survey, were low-end ICT workers such as encoders, data entry people, and call center operators who perform basic, routine work.

6. Studies on the computerization of office work, however, point out that while some women working at the lower levels may have lost jobs as certain skilled occupations disappeared, others at the middle level experience skills upgrading and new job opportunities (see, for example, Ng, 1994).

7. Some studies of technology have addressed the issue of the invisible woman by examining how users or consumers (who are mostly women) are shaping technology not only through their feedback but also through their use of technologies in ways that are sometimes unintended by their creators. Cynthia Cockburn and Susan Ormrod (1993: 9) demonstrate, in a study of microwave ovens, how a study can make women come into view as creators of technology by extending the scope of technology from design to production where women are preeminent in the assembly line; to distribution, where women are the sales staff and the shoppers; and to the household, where women are the main users of domestic technology.

REFERENCES

Braverman, Harry. (1974) *Labor and Monopoly Capital: The Degradation of Work in the Twentieth Century*, Monthly Review Press, New York.

Bureau of Labor and Employment Statistics, Philippines. (1999) 'Occupational Wages', Survey, www.manila-online.net (Accessed 3 March 2002).

Chant, Sylvia and MacIlwaine, Cathy. (1995) *Women of a Lesser Cost: Female Labor, Foreign Exchange and Philippine Development*, Pluto, London.

Cockburn, Cynthia. (1987) 'The Material of Male Power' in MacKenzie, D. and Wajcman, J. (eds), *The Social Shaping of Technology*, Open University Press, Milton Keynes and Philadelphia, pp. 125–46.

Cockburn, Cynthia and Ormrod, Susan. (1993) *Gender and Technology in the Making*, Sage Publications, London.

Formoso, Dittas. (2000) 'Report on the Regional ICT Manpower and Skills Survey Year 1999–2000', www.cait.jipdec.or.jp/research/kokusai/pdf/h12/h12k-f.pdf (Last accessed 25 January 2005).

Fröbel, Folker, Heinrich, Jürgen, and Kreye, Otto. (1980) *The New International Division of Labor*, Cambridge University Press, Cambridge.

Gibbons, Michael, Limoges, C., Nowotny, H., Schwartzman, S., Scott, P., and Trow, M. (1994) *The New Production of Knowledge*, Sage Publications, London.

Gill, Rosalind and Grint, Keith. (1995) 'The Gender-Technology Relation: Contemporary Theory and Research', in Gill, R. and Grint, K. (eds), *The Gender Technology Relation*, Taylor and Francis, London, pp. 1–28.

Haraway, Donna. (1991) *Simians, Cyborgs, and Women: The Reinvention of Nature*, Routledge, New York.

Harding, Sandra. (1986) *The Science Question in Feminism*, Cornell University Press, New York.

Illo, Jeanne Frances. (1997) *Women in the Philippines*, Asian Development Bank, Manila, Philippines.

Lachenmann, Gudrun. (1997) 'Frauen and Globalisierung: aktuelle Entwicklungen and kritische Diskurse (Women and Globalization: Current Developments and Critical Discourses)', Working Paper 282, Sociology of Development Research Center, University of Bielefeld, Germany.

MacKenzie, Donald and Wajcman, Judy. (1987) 'Introductory Essay: The Social Shaping of Technology', in MacKenzie, D. and Wajcman, J. (eds), *The Social Shaping of Technology*, Open University Press, Milton Keynes and Philadelphia, pp. 2–25.

Mitter, Swasti. (2004) 'Globalization, ICTs and Empowerment: A Feminist Critique', *Gender, Technology and Development*, 8(1): 5–30.

Nissen, Jörgen. (1996) 'The Hacker Culture and Masculinity,' in Frissen, Valerie (ed.), *Gender, ICTs and Everyday Life*, Office for Official Publications of the European Communities, Luxembourg, pp. 230–49.

Ng, Cecilia. (1994) 'The Descent of New Technology' in Ng, Cecilia and Munro-Kua, Anne (eds), *Keying into the Future: The Impact of Computerization on Office Workers*, Women's Development Collective and Universiti Pertanian Malaysia, Kuala Lumpur, pp. 25–46.

Pearson, Ruth. (1998) '"Nimble Fingers" Revisited: Reflections on Women and Third World Industrialization in the Late Twentieth Century', in Jackson, C. and Pearson, R. (eds), *Feminist Visions of Development: Gender, Analysis and Policy*, Routledge, London and New York, pp. 171–88.

Schutz, Alfred and Luckmann, Thomas. (1973) *The Structures of the Life-World, Vol. 1*, Northwestern University Press, Evanston.

Schwanitz, Simone. (2001) *Die Softwarebranche in Rußland (The Software Industry in Russia)*, Deutsches Institut für Entwicklungspolitik (German Institute for Development), Bonn, Germany.

Schwartz Cowan, Ruth. (1987) 'Gender and Technological Change' in MacKenzie, D. and Wajcman, J. (eds), *The Social Shaping of Technology*, Open University Press, Milton Keynes and Philadelphia, pp. 53–54.

Standing, Guy. (1989) 'Global Feminization Through Flexible Labor', *World Development*, 17(7): 1077–95.

United Nations Development Program. (2004) 'Human Development Reports', http://hdr.undp.org/statistics/data/indic/indic_228_1_1.html (Last accessed 25 January 2005).

Wajcman, Judy. (1991) *Feminism Confronts Technology*, Polity Press, Cambridge.

———. (1995) 'Feminist Theories of Technology,' in Jasanoff, Shiela, Mackle, Gerald, Petersen, James, and Pinch, Trevor (eds), *Handbook of Science and Technology Studies*, Sage, Thousand Oaks, CA, pp. 189–204.

Webster, Juliet. (1996) 'Gendering Information Technologies: Lessons from Feminist Research' in Frissen, V. (ed.), *Gender, ICTs and Everyday Life*, Office for Official Publications of the European Communities, Luxembourg, pp. 81–111.

Youngs, Gillian. (2000) 'Questions of Agency and the Internet', Paper presented at the International Roundtable Discussion: Developing Creative and Inclusive Partnerships for Fostering a Lifelong Learning Center, UNESCO Institute for Education, Hamburg, Germany, 27–29 November.

5

WOMEN'S AGENCY
AND THE IT INDUSTRY IN INDIA

GOVIND KELKAR, GIRIJA SHRESTHA, AND VEENA N.

The Indian Information Technology (IT) industry in 2003–04 is a US$15.9 billion enterprise that has developed from scratch in less than three decades (NASSCOM, 2003). The software industry in India which started in the early 1970s has grown at a phenomenal rate since 1980 due to software services such as coding, custom software development, and Year 2000 (Y2K) work (Heeks, 1998). In the beginning, much of this work was carried out at the client's facility 'onsite' rather than offshore in India (Heeks, 1998; Millar, 2000; Rajghatta, 2001). The Y2K scare of the 1990s and the building of the India Inc. brand helped the software industry develop an annual export growth rate of 42 percent from 1990 to 2000 (Heeks, 2001). At the same time, IT-enabled services (ITES) such as call centers, customer interaction, back office operations, insurance claims processing, medical transcription, database management, digital content, and online education also developed in the country. In all, the Indian IT industry employed over 813,000 people in 2003–04. Of these, more than 568,000 people were in the software sector and about 245,000 in ITES/Business Process Outsourcing (BPO) sector (NASSCOM, 2003).

The exact number or percentage of women at various levels in the Indian IT industry is not available due to the lack of gender disaggregated data in existing literature, including the National Association of Software and Service Companies (NASSCOM). It is estimated that women constitute 21 percent of the total IT workforce which is higher than their participation in the national economy as a whole, at 13 percent (NASSCOM, 2001). In a recent study undertaken for UNDP (2004) of nine Asian countries (China, India,

Indonesia, Malaysia, Mongolia, Pakistan, Sri Lanka, Thailand, and Vietnam), the authors noted that despite the absence of gender disaggregated data at national levels, the role of IT industry in promoting gender equality was positive. On an average, of the IT professionals, there is one woman employee for every seven men employed in the IT industry in India. Women professionals constitute 12.5 percent of the IT industry, with NIIT having the highest proportion of women employees (29 percent), and Rolta the lowest (4 percent). Nearly 20 percent of TCS employees, 19 percent of Wipro employees and, 17 percent of Infosys employees are women (Rani and Mahalingam, 2003) (Figure 5.1).

Figure 5.1
Women to men ratio among IT professionals in India

Company	Women: Men Ratio
Rolta	1:24
HCL Infosystem	1:12
Sun Microsystems	1:6
HP	1:5
Infosys	1:5
Wipro	1:4
TCS	1:4
Philips	1:3
Cognizant Technology	1:3
NIIT	1:2

Source: IDC, 2002 as cited in Rani and Mahalingam, 2003.
Note: Figures have been rounded off.

The development of IT in Asia has had a clear impact on women. Studies of 'Village Pay Phones' in rural Bangladesh (Richardson, Ramirez and Haq, 2000), and computer aided technologies and teleworking in Malaysia and India (Ng, 1999; Mitter, 2000; Mitter and Sen, 2000; Gothoskar, 2000a, 2000b) have observed that household income has increased, and women have more mobility and more say in household matters. But the gender-based division of labor at home has been maintained, and in some cases even magnified despite women's involvement in paid work in the IT industry. Therefore, with the introduction of new Information and Communication Technologies (ICTs) most women's daily workload has multiplied, because they have to do unpaid housework as before, in addition to paid work in the IT industry. Technology itself is gendered and strongly shaped by patriarchal yardsticks of class and gender, as Veena N. and Kusakabe (2004) have shown in the case of the gendered nature of the Internet.

It is not simply a question of access to information technology, but of restoring and carrying forward a creative and empowered participation of women in technology development and enhancing women's agency through increased knowledge, skills, and education (Omvedt and Kelkar, 1995). Information Technology is, however, characterized by a production system of networking, outsourcing, and subcontracting which requires individualization of capacities. The nature of work in the IT industry is different as compared to other industries. In the IT industry, labor loses its collective identity and individualizes the capacities of workers. The positions of owners, producers, managers, and workers are increasingly blurred in a production system of variable geometry of teamwork, networking, outsourcing, and subcontracting (Castells, 2000a). The networking capacities required by information technology increase women's capabilities to take decisions on their own and construct greater space to enhance their agency, though within the limited terms of socially sanctioned structural inequalities.

Women's agency is understood as the capacity for autonomous action in the face of constricting social sanctions and structural inequalities. This, in turn, offers a framework in which constraint is seen as constitutive of gender norms and relations between women and men, which are entrenched and durable, but not unchanging. Enhancing women's agency requires public/social action on a number of fronts: access to technology education, control over property and assets, participation in household and community decision-making, measures to halt domestic and other violence against women, tackling discrimination against girls and women in building basic capabilities—health care, education, self-esteem, mobility, social visibility, and dignity. All these are crucial aspects of transforming gender relations.

Few would disagree with Castells' analysis in *The Rise of the Network Society*, that social changes are just as dramatic as economic and technological transformation. Interestingly, with the development of the IT industry in India, patriarchal relations within the home and outside have become 'a contested domain, rather than a sphere of cultural reproduction, leading to a fundamental redefinition of gender relations, family and sexuality' (Castells, 2000a: 2–3). Seen in this context, our basic questions are: How are women affecting and being affected by these wide-ranging changes of the IT age and technological advances? How can IT enhance women's agency and further change patriarchal conditions which limit women's participation in production and technological transformation?

In recent years, newspapers, NASSCOM reports, and a team of researchers and scholars have produced some baseline, quantitative data on the growth and expansion of the IT industry, giving rise to the popular perception that India is an 'ICT superpower' (Ekdahl and Trojer, 2002). However, in order to be able to understand some human gender-specific aspects of this IT phenomenon, it may be important to look at some aspects qualitatively as well, particularly through the perceptions of workers and managers in the IT industry. These perceptions are likely to offer further insights that large-scale quantitative studies may miss, or at best treat as peripheral in understanding the complexities of new technological change in India. This Study is an attempt to draw attention to the social and gender-specific consequences of the growth of the IT industry in India.

Methodology: To assess women's roles and contributions to the IT industry in India and the consequent change in women's situation, we interviewed a total of 64 persons in two cities: 30 women and five men in Bangalore and 25 women and four men in Delhi/ New Delhi during August–November 2000. The majority of our interviewees were women employed in teleworking centers, call centers, medical transcription centers, computer training centers, cyber cafés, web designing centers, software companies, and NASSCOM. Based on their positions in the industry, the respondents were divided into three categories: those engaged in management, those engaged in technical decision-making, and those who were involved in data entry in ITES. The research took account of the experiences of both married and single women and men in all three sectors to understand changes in gender relations in the family and community. Based on a prepared checklist of relevant questions, the four focal points of discussions were: Is there any change in the gender division of labor based on cultural assumptions, family-assigned work allocations, acknowledgements, and rewards as a result of their employment in the IT industry? Is there any change in women's social mobility and time used in housework and childcare? Is there any change in the attitudes of family members and co-workers in the industry towards women employed in the IT industry? What was needed to improve the situation of women and gender relations in the future?

Inclusion of Women

Software Industry: Interviews conducted in some of the top 20 IT companies in India—Satyam, Infosys, Wipro, NIIT (National Institute of Information Technology), IBM—as well as other smaller companies showed that women contribute significantly to the generation of revenue of Indian software and services industry. However, their benefits from the industry are not in any way equitable with the benefits men draw; though the number of women employees has increased significantly during the last 10 years. There are a number of women in the positions of software and senior software engineers. The number of women varied depending on the company's reputation (job security), location (travel), timings (flexi-time, part-time, virtual office), and policies (accommodating or strict).

The median age of software professionals is about 27.5 years. The skills in high demand include software analysis, domain specialist, information security, database administrators, integration specialist, network specialist, communication engineers, data warehousing, and semiconductor designers (NASSCOM, 2003). A DQ-JobsAhead study conducted among 150,000 Indian IT professionals found that women constitute over 19 percent of the total workforce at lower levels (up to three years experience). The percentage drops to 6 in the senior workforce (10 years experience) (Kalghatgi and Seth, 2003). A common factor across all the workplaces we studied was the large number of women at lower levels and the gradually decreasing presence of women at higher levels, especially in decision-making positions. Our study, however, noted a number of women in human resource management, marketing, quality control, finance, and training departments.

The human resource management sector has a larger number of women, and this is common across many industries in India. Credit is normally given to women's better interpersonal skills, ability to relate to people, communication skills, high interpersonal relations, and capacity to handle people better. However, the importance of a human resource manager in the information technology industry is itself in question. Evidently, all that matters is the technical qualification. A 27-year-old woman who was a Human resource manager in Bangalore said, 'We only have to match the resume to the technical profile given by the technical head. We recruit heads and resumes, not people.' In other places, the human resource manager only collects and passes on resumes to the technical heads (mostly men), who decide whether the person is suitable.

Importantly, women's presence in decision-making positions as partners or entrepreneurs makes a difference to the recruitment and promotions of women in higher positions. One woman, a partner in a growing IT company, said her physical presence at the interviews led to the recruitment of more women. Otherwise, even sensitive men (her partners, who have discussed this issue) do not look for alternatives, solutions, or other ways of recruiting women. The attitude of the people in charge of recruitment plays an important role in the number of women and their positions.

> For one year, I was away in the US, and when I came back, I found that the number of women in our company had fallen. The men are aware of the problems, but when I am not around to participate in the decisions, they do not try to accommodate the needs of the women (Authors' Field Survey, 2000).

The high visibility of women in marketing is because women are considered better at building a rapport with a client, to possess pleasing voices, better communication skills, more sincere, thorough, and so on. To quote a woman deputy general manager in IBM: Women are typically left out of the team-building, drinking camaraderie, because they would prefer to go back home, especially, if they have a child. (Authors' Field Survey, 2000)

Many women in quality control departments said that they preferred this career because they felt that the pressures were less when compared to technology development divisions. The position was not inferior in any way, they insisted, because they made up the last line of control before the product goes out. Over a period of time, they can even contribute to the development of technology through suggestions to engineers. However, these contributions to technology are mediated through engineers who are mostly men.

Finance is another sector with a large number of women as they were viewed as more honest, less demanding, cheaper, and hard working. The senior management in most cases felt that men with the same qualifications demand a lot more remuneration. Women tend to accept less remuneration because they have to balance responsibilities at home and in the office.

Time is a big problem for women at all levels. The work in the IT industry is very demanding, requiring 12–14 hours a day. It normally stretches to 18, even 20 hours, including phone calls and emails from home at night. Work-life balance is a part of the human resource management jargon in most IT companies, but in reality, it is only IT work. There is no such balance between work and family in the industry. Meetings are typically scheduled from 8 A.M. to 9 P.M., but nobody complains as it is seen as an essential part of the IT culture.

IT-Enabled Services: In many ways, the spread of ITES has been immensely beneficial to both women and men, especially those who have limited skills and lack the resources to invest in higher education. Minimum wage in India is just over Rs 1,000 per month (US$1 = approximately Rs 45 towards the end of 2004); in the ITES industry, however, monthly wages range from Rs 5,000–Rs 15,000. The ITES industry in India includes medical transcription, call centers, and data entry centers.

There is a proliferation of small medical transcription centers in garages and basements, which typically employ people on training for 3–6 months and then close shop overnight if they do not get any contracts. Most of these centers close down because of the need for high investment including traveling to the US to maintain contacts and build business. These employees do not receive any benefits despite Employees State Insurance and Provident Fund contributions being cut from their pay.[1] There are no unions, no tenure and therefore, no job security or protection for women and men workers in this industry. In medical transcription centers, the minimum qualification required is a Bachelors' degree, however there are Masters' graduates working in such centers. Many feel the job offers no challenges, no scope for growth, and very little satisfaction.

Women working in the medical transcription centers stated their problems. There is no benefit-sharing in the business. The client in the US typically pays about Rs 3 per line, of which the transcriptionist gets Rs 0.18/line. The job has little prestige and the woman has no decision-making powers in the workplace. Promotions are only up to a certain level (team leader). As a consequence, people feel their career has stagnated. They need better technology as some recordings (voice data downloaded over the internet) are not clear, and so the repo.ts are not good. Productivity suffers.

In a study in Mumbai, Gothoskar (2000b) quotes a worker in the back office of an airline company: 'But to tell you the truth, the work itself is very boring. There is nothing creative or challenging in the work itself. Sometimes, we wonder what we are doing here' (p. 2295). Our discussions repeatedly revealed that women and men who join the ITES sector, do so because they are unable to enter the more competitive areas of the industry like MNCs or large Indian firms. Therefore, as soon as they get openings in the mainstream, they move on for challenging and better paying jobs. Interviewees working in call centers in Bangalore and Delhi said the work is repetitive, boring, and also quite stressful. However, women were happy to be away from the everyday drudgery of housework at least for few hours. It gave them new energy to tackle responsibilities at home, and their relationships with their husbands and other family members had improved. When they stayed at home all the time, they were perpetually tense which led to many quarrels with their husbands. Further, employment in night shifts helps women to gain some freedom from domestic restrictions on their mobility.

In call centers, a 'good' (American) accent, and good communication skills are considered important qualifications and women educated in convents (12th grade) are preferred, though those with English medium schooling are also recruited. Call centers in Bangalore employ highly qualified professionals, like engineers and chartered accountants to clarify and answer questions for people living in the US and Canada. Most of the women and men did not seem to be explicitly conscious of the gender dimensions of their workplace. However, when asked to reflect on this, women in particular discussed the unfair burden of work they have to shoulder.

According to a DQ-IDC India Survey on 'BPO employee satisfaction' (2003): (a) Call center/BPO professionals have better job
satisfaction than their IT counterparts, but satisfaction decreases
rapidly with time and was found lowest among those with more
than five years experience. (b) Job stress and occupational ailments,
including sleeping disorders, digestive system disorders, eye, and
throat problems are common. ITES in India is expected to grow
five times to an approximate US$57 billion employing four million
people by 2008 (Kripalani and Emgardio, 2003). What is needed,
therefore, is to be pro-active to support women in their demand
for better working conditions and to ensure that women have an
equitable share of employment in this era of technological change.

The Dilemma of Domestic Work

A major concern of feminist scholarship has been the impact of
new technologies on women's lives, particularly on women's work
(Cockburn and Furst-Dilic, 1994; Folbre, 1994; Kelkar and Nathan,
2000, 2002; Omvedt and Kelkar, 1995; Mitter 2000; Ng, 2001;
Shrestha, 2001; Wajcman, 1991, 2003). While employment in the
IT industry has decreased the time available to women for domestic work, their responsibility for these tasks has not diminished.
Women are expected to balance both home and work. Most women
have mothers/in-laws/housekeepers to count on. Men do help in
the housework, though this help mainly manifests itself in childcare or when the woman is traveling. The housework remains the
woman's responsibility and is unshared or minimally shared, with
the exception of one or two cases, where it is equally shared.

The primacy of domestic work has several consequences for
women who seek wage employment. Given the patriarchal structure of the Indian family, women are swamped in never-ending
demands of caring for the homes, husbands, children, and the aged.
We found women agitated by the culturally defined gender-based
division of labor, which they felt is unfair to them. A 30-year-old
woman employed in a call center in Delhi reported: 'I am frus-
trated when my unmarried junior colleagues are promoted.
However, because of my household responsibilities, I cannot work
long hours and therefore cannot expect to progress at work.'

A number of other call center employees, however, saw nothing wrong with the existing state of affairs. Women professionals too were influenced by the ideology of gender roles and relations. To quote a 31-year-old woman employed as a software development manager in an MNC in Bangalore: 'Cooking and cleaning are women's jobs. How can a man do the housework?' In the same breath, she added, 'However, my husband helps me everyday, so my workload is lighter.' Further discussion revealed that the only activity the husband was involved in was childcare, and that too, only when she was cooking or involved in other household chores. Some married and single women said that they would quit the job after they have a child. 'It is a woman's duty to do the housework and take care of the children,' a data entry operator in the banking sector stated proving that 'received ideas frequently acquire the status of unshakable truths' (Nabar, 1995: x).

Women's participation in the IT industry does not fundamentally challenge the concept of gender-based division of labor at home. It is likely to change only with an increased awareness about women's autonomy and equality, and the dismantling of gender roles and relations. Of course, these issues have been taken up by the Indian women's movements and individual feminist scholars and activists but are yet to be translated into practice among masses of women. We learnt from the management that the majority of women in the IT industry are in the 20–30 age cohort and very few are above 35 years. Most of the women interviewees in management positions were single women. Single women do not feel the constraints of gender-based division of labor as they usually live in their parental homes, where the mother assumes the responsibilities of childcare and domestic work.

Married women, particularly those with children, felt disadvantaged and at odds with the industry, largely a result of their socially-defined responsibilities in childcare and housework. Employers, of course, have adapted their human resource strategies to provide appropriate support to women employees. For example, Infosys has a company-run creche for women employees, while 'Novell Software and Wipro are experimenting with telecommuting in order to maintain the skill-levels of female workers for short periods when family commitments require their presence at home' (Millar, 2000: 2259). However, this does not bring about much change in women's assigned responsibilities for home and childcare. Portals which cater to Indian women have channels focusing on careers, education, and finances, but women are encouraged to manage both home and office with a total absence of any sharing of domestic work/responsibilities on the part of men (Asmita, 2000).

There are, however, some innovative examples of attempts to introduce a change in the gender-based division of labor. NIIT, with a large proportion of women employees, has instituted part-time and flexi-time schemes for both women and men as some men were found to be involved in childcare. Paternity leave and part-time/flexi-time work for men are also being instituted in some companies. Women's entry into the labor market and the changing socio-economic structure of the family may help change the gender division of labor. Some women and men reported sharing of domestic work in Delhi and Bangalore. This was especially common among nuclear families and couples who had worked abroad together. A 38-year-old woman, associate project manager, employed in Infosys told us:

> I have forgotten my home. I am free to focus on my career as my husband has taken charge of the house. We have a very efficient housekeeper who does all the domestic chores. When she is away, it is my husband who takes charge, not me. He is also totally dedicated to our son and takes care of all the related activities like parent-teacher meetings, exams, homework and shopping. (Authors' Field Survey, 2000)

Other studies have found that, 'New technologies do disrupt established patterns of sex-typing and thereby open up opportunities for changing the sexual division of labor', (Wajcman, 1991: 34) and widening the scope for expressing women's agency. Our field research revealed that women's status in the family and society was directly related to their status in the workplace—women employed in ITES like call centers and back office work had limited prospects of rising in their careers and felt little change in their social status, while women in management noted a rise in their familial status. Women in higher management in the IT industry reported less unequal gender relations at home and more decision-making power. However, they recalled that when they joined the industry, they faced opposition both at home and at work. Husbands and in-laws asked them to prioritize their familial duties while the atmosphere in office was equally traditional.

One of the indicators of the status of a woman's autonomy or agency is her decision-making power in the household and society. Two contradictory trends were found in the household decision-making process. While most of the women said they play a larger role in household decision-making after becoming financially independent, others said they were too busy at work to take charge of the home. Therefore, decision-making was handed over to other household members. 'I hand over all my salary to my mother-in-law and get housekeeping money from her. All financial decisions are taken by my husband and in-laws. Of course, they keep me informed about them' (Authors' Field Survey, 2000).

However, most women noted that their control only extended over their own earnings. Major decisions regarding property and family income were still taken in consultation with, and approval of, men. Some women have managed to save or use the money as leverage to secure a good position within the household. In traditional settings, the woman's job is not considered crucial and she has little negotiating power. In families which would like to have a higher standard of living or comfort, the woman's income is needed, her job is more respected, and she becomes a member of the decision-making team at home.

MOBILITY

We looked at the mobility of women in the IT industry at two levels: the emergence of women from seclusion at home; and the mobility of women to advance their careers. Seclusion norms and controls on mobility effectively cut women off from many spheres of knowledge, interaction and activity, thereby curbing their agency. However, this has been changing in India as a consequence of women's entry into the IT industry. Restrictions on women's mobility have loosened over the years since such mobility has a direct bearing on their ability to take up employment outside the house (Kalpagam, 1992). A large number of single young women now live in the cities away from their families and male relatives.

While single women seem to find a significant change in their mobility enabling them to take up jobs and advance their careers, a large number of married women are still bound by domestic and childcare responsibilities, and are still not as mobile as men. A DQ-JobsAhead survey in 2003 found that 52 percent of the women (and 28 percent of the men) were 'not open to relocation' (Kalghatgi and Seth, 2003). As a senior woman manager in a software company in Delhi reflected:

> To further advance in my career, I have to go abroad, but due to my responsibilities towards the kids and household, I cannot take a job abroad even if I get one. There is no such restriction on my husband. (Authors' Field Survey, 2000)

During the last 10 years, women's participation in ITES has been increasing. Many women have moved from the hotel industry, sales, fashion designing, teaching, and so on to ITES. They view IT as an emerging phenomenon, an ideal working environment for women. Gender differences operate in how women and men are differentially placed in availing these opportunities. Men, for example, move from one company to another as they find better opportunities. However, the percentage of women who move from one company to another for better opportunities is very small. Restrictions on women's mobility due to household responsibility and societal barriers make it difficult for them to change jobs frequently. Women have less locational choices than men do. This makes them less competitive in terms of exploiting the opportunities. Married women cannot spend a lot of time on commuting to work, unlike single women and men, who can. So, they negotiate for lower positions in companies located near to their houses. One woman in a call center in Delhi said: 'Although the work is monotonous, I do not want to quit this job, because it is close to my house.'

Strangely enough, women's lower mobility has influenced the recruitment policies in the industry in their favor. Hence, employers prefer married women with children as they are not too mobile and would be willing to stay in 'a boring job' for domestic reasons. Women were viewed as 'efficient in the work and do not leave the company as soon as they get better opportunities' (Authors' Field Survey, 2000). In a study of ITES in India and

Malaysia, Mitter (2001) notes, 'Employers often feel that women work better in repetitive jobs such as those related to data processing' (11).

These jobs, nevertheless, offer women a major opportunity for economic empowerment. 'I decide what I want to do with my money,' a woman working in a medical transcription center in Bangalore said. Several women also stressed that the money they earned, gave them a voice in the decision-making process within the family. 'Because I am earning, I can go out and spend my money whenever I want. I do not have to ask my husband for permission or for money,' a woman call center employee in Delhi said. As Mitter succinctly summarizes: 'This is one of the cases where it is possible to say with confidence that globalization has yielded gains for some developing countries and women in them' (2004: 3).

GLASS CEILING

There is a definite male preference in hiring and promotions at the senior levels of management in the IT industry. There are few women in the high echelons of the IT industry. The higher the position in the corporate ranks, the more serious is the gender divide. 'Even within the same hierarchy, female executives earn much less than their male counterparts,' says Ranjit Shahani, CEO, Novartis India Ltd. (*Financial Express*, 2001). While human resource managers of all companies insist that the pay scales are equal for women and men, this is not the case in reality. In an industry where demand outstrips supply, the pay scales are vastly variable. The pay scale for a post is only the starting point, the final remuneration depends on the negotiating capacity of the employee. A lot of perks and stock options are also negotiable. In such cases, women tend to negotiate for less pay, as compared to men. Women also take other factors into consideration (distance from home, their household and childcare responsibilities. company reputation, job security, and other benefits), thereby reducing the number of choices. On the other hand, men have a wider choice of possible jobs and are able to negotiate for higher salaries.

There are comparatively more women in middle-level positions as technology managers. They handle a few clients, and it is their responsibility to build up the portfolio by building a better relationship with the client. Human resource managers interviewed in the field told us that about 20–25 percent of the project leaders and team leaders were women. Typically, a person needs 8–10 years experience to be in this position, though younger people are increasingly being promoted. People who shift jobs faster, rise faster and women, largely because of their domestic responsibilities, typically stay longer in each job as compared to men. While this works in women's favor during recruitment, it also delays their promotion. So women with eight years experience find themselves in positions and pay scales similar to men with just five years experience. As a woman Manager in Satyam explained:

> I wanted to ensure that I had enough time for my kids, so I opted for a job with less pay, even though they offered me a higher position. However, now I find myself with less pay, I still do all the work that a senior person would normally do. I have no time, and I have made a bad career move by opting for a lower position. (Authors' Field Survey, 2000)

Notwithstanding these problems, there are a noticeable number of women in management, in the non-technology sectors of the IT industry. However, as the number of women in a sector increases, the prestige attached to it decreases. The highest prestige is now attached to core technology development where very few women are found at the top or at decision-making levels. There were three women in Bangalore in the position of head of technology division, which needs 15–20 years experience. (These women joined the industry in 1980–85 when few women studied engineering and most of them opted for teaching.) Those who have risen to this position remember the days when the only other women in their office were the secretaries. 'I was often mistaken for the secretary by new engineers, even though I was their boss,' says a woman entrepreneur who resigned from an Indian MNC to begin her own venture. For these women, it is lonely at the top, more so because they are women. They feel the absence of a network of women in similar positions and male resistance to their authority.

Lack of networking plays a crucial role in making women invisible in senior managements in the IT industry. Two factors continue as major obstacles to women's networking: old boys network, and male colleagues' wives or girlfriends. A woman Senior Manager at Intel says, 'I did find networking to be a major problem. I cannot have the same informal "outside work" relationship with my peers and senior executives that my male "competitors" could have without spouses being concerned and some people's tongue wagging' (Kandaswamy, 2003).

But this has been slowly changing over the past few years. Revathi Kasturi of Tarang, Infosys Women Inclusivity Network, and Women of Wipro have been organizing and mentoring other women to (a) talk more openly among themselves; (b) network within the organization (the need for a social group to hang out with) and reverse mentoring sessions along with initiating policies, benefits, and training; (c) set up a common platform to share and learn from each other with a mandate, 'unless you aspire, you will not get anywhere in this competitive world' (Sathya Mithra Ashok, 2003).

Women managers in the IT industry also reported that some men are unwilling to accept women managers. In one case, a man refused to report a problem to his manager, a woman, and instead went to her boss, who was a man. 'I called the man who went to my boss and told him that if he has any problem with the work, he should approach me.' Her boss supported her and the man had to accept the situation, albeit grudgingly. Culturally, men have felt superior to women, so accepting a woman's authority in the workplace was problematic. There is a socially-sanctioned double standard in dealing with women in the workplace. As a very senior woman manager from Wipro in Bangalore put it, 'If you complain, it is seen as a sign of weakness. If you are aggressive, you are a bully. If you have a mentor or friend in office, you are having an affair. Some of these perceptions are changing now, but only marginally' (Authors' Field Survey, 2000).

Women are seen in significant numbers in training departments. Reasons for choosing this department vary. According to a training manager in Bangalore, 'There is better job satisfaction. We can meet more people and interaction is not restricted to machines. Work pressure is not sustained and so I do not have to work late every evening. But I can still keep in touch with the latest technology' (Authors' Field Survey, 2000). This seems like an ideal way of being 'in' technology, while at the same time not being restricted only to technology.

ENHANCING WOMEN'S AGENCY

There has been an undeniable improvement in the social mobility and work participation rate of women in the IT industry. The nature of work (such as flexi-time, teleworking, and working from home), the tools (such as email and Internet), and the individualization of capacities required by information technology make women more capable to take decisions on their own and construct greater scope to enhance their agency.

We discussed four aspects of women's participation in the IT industry: Inclusion of women, the dilemma of domestic work, mobility, and glass ceiling. The presence of a large number of women in the IT industry broke some traditional concepts, including that of women as only homemakers and men as only breadwinners. As financial contributors to the domestic economy, women's bargaining power within the home has increased. The performance of women's autonomy and agency are, however, subject to variations, depending on the way in which work, relations of power and hierarchy, and resources are shared in the household. In a large number of households in Bangalore and Delhi, we observed that domestic work was/is still considered women's responsibility. However, many women within the industry have managed to displace this responsibility by employing other women (and some men) to do the domestic work. While not denying the existence of the glass ceiling and discrimination against women in the IT industry, we noted that a number of women have broken through these barriers to reach management positions.

IT does constitute the basis of the redefinition of traditional gender norms and supports a media of information, understanding, and knowledge in which women's interests, opinions, and rights are taken into account. Nevertheless, they function within the dominant interests of the family and patriarchy. This provides a non-threatening mobilization of women's labor for the benefit of their families and communities. It has not yet been possible for women in the IT sector to challenge and transform structural inequalities and gender relations.

Gender inequality is embedded in the history and political economy of the Asian region, including India. Yet, women are not silent observers of the male appropriation of traditional and technological knowledge, power, and resources. There are women (as evident through women's movements, women's writings, NGOs) who speak publicly against the growing male dominance and control over resources. Others, who do not, would speak if power and resource inequality did not create obstacles. There are also women who remain silent and seemingly choose to comply with male dominance due to fear of insult and assault on the body. Despite the power and gender inequality in the market, many women prefer to work outside the home, in an attempt to improve their social position, rather than be subject to family-based dependency and coercion.

The gender-equitable answer lies in working out systems, whereby society, industry, and government institutions share the cost of social services required to keep women working on a regular basis like other employees. Currently, women work multiple shifts at home and in the office—being entirely responsible for childcare, housework, and their official duties.[2] This triple workload is a result of culturally embedded notions of womanhood, women's work, and women's place—which are now being challenged. Cultures do play a major role in interpreting human values. But, cultures are not static, nor something given for all time. The factors that lead to cultural change are varied, and include inter-cultural exchanges and communications, where ICTs can play a major role. The cultural ceiling that effectively debars women from contributing to creating new technologies needs to be overcome in order to increase the potential of human society.

Information Technology has furthered the networking of women and broken the monopoly of tradition over modernization, and technology projects. Women's groups in various parts of Asia are able to keep in touch with each other and with groups in other parts of the world through email and other such communication systems. The resulting networks of such organizations are able to work in close coordination in conducting campaigns on various issues affecting women. Indigenous women's groups, indigenous people's organizations, organizations protesting against large dams—all such groups are now networking in a manner, made possible by the new communications technologies. The transformation of information technology does not end power inequality, but it does allow women and disadvantaged groups more scope to project themselves.

A recent example includes an innovative program for Village Knowledge Centers set up by M.S. Swaminathan Research Foundation in a group of six villages in Pondicherry in India in 1998. Two major features of the project were the development of local language Tamil Software, and gender sensitivity (for example, considering the health needs of impoverished rural women) in the assessment of the information needs of the local people (MSSRF, 2002). Another example from Thailand involves the struggle against the forced relocation of Akha villagers in Huay Mahk village in northern Thailand in 2000. The Internet was used to communicate the problems of an isolated people and mobilize support from others around the world. In a breakthrough for community rights, the villagers were able to retain their homes, lands, and forests and thereby avoid the drugs, crime, and poverty cycle that has hit other relocated communities in the region (Cholthira Satyawadhana, 2001). There is an emerging 'global civil society' which exists in different locations but agrees on the value systems, and development goals of education, health care, and gender equality.

The software industry as well as the ITES have provided further scope for the achievement of these goals and for the expression of women's agency. While a large number of women continue to work in gendered homes and paid work sites, there is an ongoing struggle on their part to challenge the embedded patriarchal relations and existing structural inequalities even as they constantly seek to balance work and domestic responsibilities. The effects of transforming gender relations, however, go far beyond benefiting women alone. Enhancing women's agency will enable an increase in production and productivity of new technology, which in turn challenges existing structural gender inequalities. Thus, gender-responsive new technologies, as a tool, will assist and facilitate the creation of an egalitarian society. The ripple effects will spread across all spheres of human existence and create new dynamics in transforming the nature of information society.

Notes

1. ESI and PF are employee benefits where the employer deposits a small percentage of each employee's salary with the government. ESI benefits include

health care for the employee and family, while the PF amount is returned to the employee on retirement.
2. Castells (2000b) discusses the four shifts for women workers—paid work in the office, house chores, child care and night shift for the husband's sexual needs.

REFERENCES

Asmita, M.J. (2000) 'Report on Women's Portals in India,' submitted to Gender and Development Studies, Asian Institute of Technology, Bangkok, unpublished.

Castells, Manuel. (2000a) *The Rise of the Network Society*, Blackwell Publishers, Oxford, UK and Maden, USA.

———. (2000b) 'The End of Patriarchalism: Social Movements, Family and Sexuality in the Information Age', *The Power of Identity*, Blackwell Publishers, Oxford, UK and Maden, USA, pp. 134–242.

Cholthira Satyawadhana. (2001) 'The Akha Struggle for Natural Resources and Forest Conservation in Thailand', *Gender, Technology and Development*, 5(2): 323–29.

Cockburn, Cynthia and Ruza Furst-Dilic. (1994) *Bringing Technology Home: Gender and Technology in a Changing Europe*, Open University Press, Philadelphia.

Ekdahl, Peter and Lena Trojer. (2002) 'Digital Divide: Catch up for What?' *Gender, Technology and Development*, 6(1): 1–20.

Financial Express. (2001) 'Retaining Women in the Workforce: Panel for "realistic action strategy"', 16 October (Available at http://www.ciionline.org/news/ciiinnews/2001/Oct/16oct2.htm, accessed on 19 October 2001).

Folbre, Nancy. (1994) *Who Pays for the Kids?*, Routledge, London.

Gothoskar, Sujata (ed.). (2000a) 'Nature of Teleworking in Key Sectors: Case Studies of Financial, Media and Software Sectors in Mumbai,' *Economic and Political Weekly*, 35(26): 2277–92.

———. (2000b) 'Teleworking and Gender,' *Economic and Political Weekly*, 35(26): 2293–98.

Heeks, Richard. (1998) 'The Uneven Profile of Indian Software Exports.' Development Informatics Working Paper Series, Working Paper 3 (Available at http://www.sed.manchester.ac.uk/idpm/publications/wp/di/di_wp03. htm, accessed on 20 October 2004).

———. (2001) 'Indian Software Export Figures,' IDPM, University of Manchester, Manchester, UK (Available at http://idpm.man.ac.uk/idpm/isiexpt. htm, accessed on 9 October 2001).

Kalghatgi, Manjiri and Seth, Rishi. (2003) 'Why Just a Few Women on Top?', *DataQuest*, 30 June (Available at http://www.dqindia.com/content/strategy/hrd/103063001.asp).

Kalpagam, U. (1992) 'Women and the Household: What the Indian Data Sources have to Offer' in Saradamoni, K. (ed.) *Finding the Household: Conceptual and Methodological Issues*, Sage Publications, New Delhi, pp. 75–116.

Kandaswamy, Deepa. (2003) 'Talibanism in Technology', *Dataquest*, February 26 (Available at http://www.dqindia.com/content/special/103022602.asp).

Kelkar, Govind and Nathan, Dev. (2000) 'Technological Change in Asia: Women's Need of Life-long Learning', Paper presented at the International Roundtable Discussion: Developing Creative and Inclusive Partnerships for Fostering a Lifelong Learning Center, UNESCO Institute for Education, Hamburg, Germany, 27–29 November.

———. (2002) 'Gender Relations and Technological Change in Asia', *Current Sociology*, 50(3): 427–41.

Kripalani, Manjeet and Emgardio, Pete. (2003) 'The Rise of India', *Business Week Online*, 8 December, http://www.businessweek.com/magazine/content/03_49/b3861001_mz001.htm.

Millar, Jane. (2000) 'Sustaining Software Teletrade in Bangalore: Fostering Market Agility through Economic Competence,' *Economic and Political Weekly*, 35(26): 2253–62.

Mitter, Swasti. (2000) 'Teleworking and Teletrade in India: Combining Diverse Perspectives and Visions,' *Economic and Political Weekly*, 35(26): 2241–52.

———. (2001) *Asian Women in the Digital Economy: Policies for Participation*, UNDP, Malaysia.

———. (2004) 'Offshore Outsourcing of Information Processing Work and Economic Empowerment of Women', Paper presented at the World Bank Digital Divide Seminar Series, 2 June (Available at http://www.worldbank.org/gender/digitaldivide/offshore.stm, accessed on 29 August 2004).

Mitter, Swasti and Sen, Asish. (2000) 'Can Calcutta Become Another Bangalore? Looking for Windows of Opportunity in International Telework', *Economic and Political Weekly*, 35(26): 2263–68.

MSSRF. (2002) 'Village Knowledge Centers', *Gender, Technology and Development*, 6 (1): 147–52.

Nabar, Vrinda. (1995) *Caste as Woman*, Penguin Books, New Delhi.

NASSCOM. (2001) 'First Ever Workshop on IT-Enabled Services for Women Entrepreneurs, Jointly organised by NASSCOM and Government of NCT of Delhi,' NASSCOM Press Release, Delhi, 22 February 2001.

———. (2003) *Indian Software and Services Industry: Nasscom Analysis*, Indian IT Industry—Fact Sheet, NASSCOM, New Delhi, India (Available at http://www.nasscom.org/download/IndianITIndustryFactsheet.pdf, accessed on 20 October 2004).

Ng Choon Sim, Cecilia. (1999) 'Making Women's Voices Heard: Technological Change and Women's Employment in Malaysia', *Gender, Technology and Development*, 3(1): 19–42.

———. (2001) *Teleworking and Development in Malaysia*, UNDP and Southbound, Penang, Malaysia.

Omvedt, Gail and Kelkar, Govind. (1995) *Gender and Technology: Emerging Visions from Asia*, Gender Studies Monograph 4, Asian Institute of Technology, Bangkok.

Rajghatta, Chidanand. (2001) *The Horse that Flew: How India's Silicon Gurus Spread Their Wings*, HarperCollins India, New Delhi.

Rani, Sarita and Mahalingam, T.V. (2003) 'A DQ-IDC INDIA SURVEY: BPO Employee Satisfaction Survey 2003', *DataQuest*, 21 October, http://dqindia.ciol.commakesections.asp/02101701.asp.

Richardson, Don, Ramirez, Ricardo, and Haq, Moinul. (2000) *Grameen Telecom's Village Phone Programme: A Multi-Media Case Study*, TeleCommons Development Group, Canada (Available at http://www.telecommons.com/villagephone/index.html, accessed on 20 October 2004).

Sathya Mitra Ashok. (2003) 'Superwomen', *Dataquest*, (Available at http://dqindia.ciol.com/04060510.asp, accessed on 11 October 2004).

Shrestha, Girija. (2001) *Gender Relations and Housing Design: A Study in Kathmandu Valley, Nepal*, Gender Studies Monograph 10, Asian Institute of Technology, Bangkok.

Veena N. and Kusakabe, Kyoko. (2004) 'Use of the Internet in the Context of Sexual Exploitation of Women and Children', Research report, Asian Institute of Technology, Thailand, unpublished.

Wajcman, Judy. (1991) *Feminism Confronts Technology*, Allen and Unwin, Australia
———. (2003) *Technofeminism*, Polity Press, Cambridge, UK and Malden, USA.

6

VALUING WOMEN'S VOICES: CALL CENTER WORKERS IN MALAYSIA AND INDIA

CECILIA NG AND SWASTI MITTER[1]

With the shift towards a more competitive ICT-based services industry, call centers are fast becoming characteristic institutions of today's information economy. These novel institutions, which provide enhanced services to their customers, represent distant or external sites of corporate entities and respond to an increasingly sophisticated and discerning clientele. Within the 'customer services and care' industry, two simultaneous trends are apparent. The first is the establishment of call centers within countries which are key players in the digital economy; the second is the phenomenal growth of such centers in the developing world, where Information Technology Enabled Services (ITES) are increasingly outsourced to low-waged, multilingual countries with relatively low overhead costs.[2]

India and the Philippines have seen a mushrooming of out-sourced call centers, providing white-collar employment to many who would have found it difficult to obtain employment after secondary and tertiary education. On the other hand, in Malaysia, the contact center business is geared primarily towards the local market, but with projected regional and global ventures in the pipeline.[3] Multinational companies have started setting up in-house call centers that serve the region, providing the much-needed push to upgrade the industry.

Interestingly, an increasing number of workers in these call centers are women, giving rise to debates whether the relocation of these service sector jobs mirrors the experience of the 'runaway' manufacturing jobs of the global assembly line in the 1970s.[4] Indeed, recent literature on the gendered aspects of call centers, particularly outsourced call centers, points out their adverse and overwhelmingly negative impact on the working conditions of the women workers.[5] A recurring refrain is that women's work tends to be low-end, low-skilled, repetitive, and with little opportunities of career advancement 'recreating the pattern already observed in export-oriented manufacturing production' (Ghosh, 2004; Gothoskar, 2000). Others point to the feminization of these institutions, an undervaluation and exploitation of women's labor giving rise to terms such as 'cyber coolies' and 'off-shore proletariat', undertaking work that is 'mind-numbing and de-skilling' (Gaerlan, 2004; Gurumurthy, 2004; Stanworth, 1998). The transient nature of these jobs is also noted as rapid technological changes might erode the relevance of the skills that women have acquired in these centers. Moreover, off-shore jobs are particularly vulnerable due to the growing protectionist lobby in the North against the outsourcing of customer services and other ITES work to the South.

Recent debates on export-oriented industrialization have critiqued the simplistic and overgeneralized 'oppressed and marginalized' thesis of women workers. Similar critiques have been raised about the totalizing negative portrayal of women call center workers, offering a viewpoint that employment in these industries could 'liberate and empower' women workers.[6] Analysing both, the exploitative, and empowering aspects of women's employment, and the socio-cultural context of how women negotiate and reconstitute their positions and spaces, some authors have raised the issue of women's agency. They point out how women call center workers have learnt new skills, are reshaping and remaking their work and lives, and even re-territorializing public spaces (Pearson, 1998; Basi, 2005; Kelkar, Shrestha, and Veena, 2002).

This chapter addresses these debates and assesses the opportunities and threats of these new institutions by examining the situations in Malaysia and India, two countries whose governments are pushing towards the provision of such customer care services in the context of the Knowledge economy. It discusses the challenges encountered by women in the face of changing employment patterns and relations brought forth by these new technologies, particularly in the face of rapid technological advancements and neo-Liberal globalization. By producing new empirical data and privileging the voices of women workers themselves, this chapter hopes to contribute to the debates about whether new and stable opportunities are being provided for women or whether these jobs follow the earlier paths of labor flexibilization and informalization.

The first section looks at the global ITES industry with a focus on call centers in the Asian region. This is followed by a discussion on the enabling ICTs environments in Malaysia and India respectively, after which the chapter turns to specific case studies of call centers in these two countries. Drawing from these cases and highlighting the voices of the women, the final part takes on the above debates on the gendered nature of call centers and the issues related to changing employment conditions in the industry before looking at the future prospects and challenges in the region.

The Global ITES Industry: The International Story

In the 1980s and 1990s, the introduction of computer technology led to an effective fragmentation of production processes, and facilitated the outsourcing of manufacturing jobs from high-waged countries to low-waged ones. Young women in developing countries, within and outside export processing zones, were the major recipients of these jobs. Today, similar and perhaps more dramatic changes are now taking place in the relocation of service sector jobs, again involving women of the developing world.

The current relocation of service sector jobs is a consequence of global business strategies as well as technological advances. The convergence of communications and networking technologies has made it possible to digitize a vast amount of information that can be transported, processed, and retrieved to and from a distant location at little cost. From a technical and productivity standpoint, an information-processing worker sitting 6,000 miles away might as well be in the next cubicle and on the local area network. In this scenario, with the cost of telephony steadily falling, the advantages of relocating ICT-related and ICT-enabled jobs from USA or UK to India, Malaysia, or Ghana are obvious.

It would cost a company US$13,000 to hire a fresh graduate with combined IT, engineering, and business skills from the Indian Institute of Management in India, while a Stanford University graduate in the US with similar qualifications will be paid about US$95,000. But the cost differentials are equally noticeable in the relatively low-skilled end of the information processing sector, such as customer care services, medical transcription, processing of airline tickets, accounting, and tax return forms. The average annual wage of an employee in a call center in the UK is £12,500 compared to the £1,200 average annual wage of a similar employee in India (BBC NEWS Online, 15 December 2003).

The worldwide market for such ITES is set to grow at a rate of 66 percent per annum in the coming years, and is forecast to be worth well over US$500 billion in 2004 (Bhattacharya et al., 2003). These services are a very important part of the Business-to-Business (B2B) component of e-commerce arising out of what is described as the off-shoring of business process outsourcing (BPO) (Mitter, 2004).

Countries in the Asia Pacific are also competing with each other to attract western companies to relocate or outsource their call centers within the region. For example, the cost per transaction is US$2.03 in Hong Kong and US$1.15 in Singapore, but these countries lose out to cheaper places like Malaysia (54 cents), China (52 cents), Philippines (37 cents), and of course India (29 cents). In this context, the Philippines is expected to double its seat count from 20,000 in 2003 to 40,000 in 2004, while seats in India will increase to about 160,000 in 2004, up 65 percent from 96,000 in 2003.[7] Apparently, out of the 38,000 seats coming to the ASEAN region from the US or Europe, 80 percent will be taken up by the Philippines (Raslan Sharif, 2004).

Globalization now offers women in some developing countries, opportunities on an unprecedented scale to find employment in information technology-enabled service sector jobs, arising from offshore outsourcing by global corporations. The next few sections examine the situation in Malaysia and India and evaluate to what extent these ITES jobs, particularly call centers, have brought benefits or new challenges to women workers in the two countries.

RESEARCH METHODOLOGY

The research for the Malaysian case studies was conducted from July to December 2004, during which period, the first author visited two companies and interviewed the workers there. A cross-section of employees were interviewed, including agents, supervisors, and management personnel, with discussions evolving around the experiences of contact center employees. Information was also gleaned from the management about the training and supervision of agents, and about business strategies in the Malaysian and regional contexts. The research in India was conducted in 2003 as part of a wider Survey on the ITES sector.[8] Due to the predominantly transnational nature of the business in India, and the somewhat anxious publicity the phenomenon was getting in the West, it was difficult to obtain company level information. Hence, interviews with women workers took place outside their offices. Nonetheless, in both field research and in the writing of this chapter, the voices of the women themselves are prioritized—how they experience and perceive their work and lives, and how they engage with the challenges in these new workplaces.

THE MALAYSIAN K-ECONOMY STORY

As noted in the Knowledge-Based Economy Master Plan, the rationale for the shift from manufacturing towards a K-economy is underscored by the erosion of Malaysia's global competitiveness and low labor cost (ISIS Malaysia, 2002). Some of the key initiatives that have been taken were, the launch of the National Information Technology Agenda (NITA), and the highly publicized Multimedia Super Corridor (MSC) in the late 1990s. The Malaysian government has also ploughed substantial investments in K-economy projects, putting aside RM5 billion[9] to fund ICT-related programs as well as allocating RM23 billion to education and training for the 2002-2005 period (Turner, 2003). In this context, as early as 1997, call centers were seen within the focus area of borderless marketing and the Call Center Association of Malaysia (CCAM) was registered in March 1999 in the Multimedia Development Corporation (the body entrusted to spearhead the MSC). Since then, CCAM has expanded its scope to become the industry association for contact centers and customer relations management, and recently changed its name to the Contact Center Association of Malaysia (Han, 2004).

The Malaysian Contact Center Industry

A.T. Kearney's 2004 Offshore Location Attractiveness Index ranked Malaysia third globally, behind India and China. A well-developed, low-cost infrastructure and strong governmental support were cited as its strengths. However, it is widely acknowledged that Malaysia's business processing outsourcing prospects still have a long way to go. Currently, Malaysia has 320 contact centers with 12,000 employees clustered around the financial services, telecommunications, and IT sectors. Nonetheless, there has been tremendous growth in the industry. The total revenue of these centers grew from RM28.5 million in 1999 to RM43.4 million in 2004, and is projected to increase to RM185.5 million by 2007 (Lim, 2004).

The burgeoning of the industry can be seen in a recent prominent half-page advertisement by an MNC asking English-speaking graduates or diploma holders to apply as global support executives to 'provide high quality service to a diverse range of customer telephone enquiries.' Since the Service Center serves the group in the West and parts of Asia Pacific, the job requirements include excellent oral and written skills in English, ability to understand and interpret numeric data, and the flexibility to work non-standard hours in line with business requirements (*Star Recruitment,* 2004).

The first survey of the Malaysian contact center industry provides a glimpse of the nature of this emerging industry (Han, 2004). The survey found that only 30 percent of contact center companies have been in operation for more than six years. The majority of those polled have 50 seats or less, and only 21 percent have more than 100 seats. Most of these currently service only Malaysia or the ASEAN region. The average monthly wages of contact center agents, mostly women with college or university education, are between RM1,001 to RM2,000. Retention of skilled personnel is a key problem for contact centers due to the lack of a career path, the lack of accreditation for workers' skills, and the perception that this is a temporary employment option. As such, most agents stay in a job only 1–2 years, on an average.

While the industry caters mostly to domestic demand, the government's drive to boost contact center outsourcing capabilities is expected both, to stimulate domestic demand and attract foreign clientele. Currently, there is no exclusively third party international call center in Malaysia. There are fewer than 10 companies catering simultaneously to both domestic and foreign clients. However, Malaysia recently received a boost when some big multinationals, including Shell and HSBC, set up their regional in-house call centers in Malaysia, some of them moving into Cyberjaya, the hub of the MSC.

Company A: An in-house Contact Center

Company A, which started its operations in 1995, is currently a leading mobile communications operator in Malaysia with about 2,700 employees in its various departments. Remote customer services are dealt with by three contact centers—two in-house centers handle post-paid customers for the consumer and corporate sector respectively, while the third center, which serves pre-paid customers, was outsourced to a third party company in 2001. The centers were launched at the end of 1995 with less than 20 staff members. The figure had reached 380 by 2004.

This research focused on the contact center serving the consumer market. The agents, customer care consultants, work in teams of 10–12 each. 55 percent of them are women and 65 percent are single. The teams are supervised by their own supervisory executives, 56 percent of whom are women. Of the women executives, 80 percent are married. Many of these executives were promoted from the ranks, and have been with the Company since it started. Most of the senior management personnel are also women. Salaries for the consultants start at RM1,500 a month, while the executives earn more than RM 2,500 a month. Educational qualifications range from graduates to people with 11 years of schooling and at least three years experience. Shift work is practiced, as agents are on call 24 hours a day. Why are more women hired? According to the Planning Manager this could be:

> Because they are more pleasant to hear on the phone. They must have patience, which is the basic necessity to be call center agents. Perhaps female voices release some enzymes or hormones to soothe the customers. Women prefer to apply. The churn rate for the males is higher.

Originally the consultants were all permanent employees. Currently, under the new business strategy, the agents are hired on an annual contract basis. Interestingly, since mid-2004, new workers are being contracted in from another company, when needed.

The skills set needed in this industry is divided into soft skills (communications skills), and product knowledge. The preference is to hire graduates who have computer and technology skills as 'they have to handle a lot of systems'. These two types of skills are scored separately, as employees are evaluated based on targets and goals, that is efficiency and quality of their work. Efficiency is based on the average handling time (AHT)—180 seconds per finished call.[10] There are occasional campaigns to increase the efficiency rate to 160 seconds per call.

Quality assessment is based on transaction monitoring by the quality assurance team on the basis of soft skills and product knowledge of the consultants. Five calls are randomly recorded per month, and these are evaluated based on a set of monitoring tools measuring the Key Performance Indicators (KPI), which disclose the fatal and non-fatal errors of the consultant. Out of the total KPI score, each consultant is not supposed to make more than five percent fatal errors per month; these consist of giving incomplete and inaccurate information, not providing a solution, and not showing respect to the customer. As for non-fatal errors, no more than 10 percent of such errors are allowed. These include courtesy and etiquette, professionalism as in positive language, troubleshooting, and procedural efficiency. Those consultants who cannot make the required scores are coached by the team leader and the quality assurance team to improve their scores. Those who underscore consistently or are unable to take the pressure and the discipline imposed on them have no choice but to leave. Incentives, monetary and non-monetary, are given to the best team.

Company B: A Third Party Contact Center

Company B is a regional third party telemarketing call center company with headquarters in Singapore; its other centers are in Bangkok, Hong Kong, Manila, and Taipei. The Malaysian contact center began operations in October 2001 with 10 employees and is geared towards a seat expansion of 300 by end 2004. Plans are underway to make the Malaysian subsidiary a regional hub. The Malaysian center serves mainly the Malaysian market conducting outbound calls selling the products of financial institutions, IT sector, and telecommunication companies. Recently, it contracted with a multinational IT company to undertake both inbound and outbound calls to sell its IT products to about 20 countries in the Asia Pacific.

Employees in Company B work on a full-time basis; 65 percent are permanent and 35 percent are on a contract basis. The attrition rate is quite high with more than 40 staff members leaving annually, mainly in the first few months. Employees appear more likely to stay when they are working with inbound calls, as there is less pressure. The staff is predominantly single women in their mid-20s. Out of total of 188 agents, 65 percent are women. Of these, only 10 women are married. However, there is gender parity among the team leaders, with 11 women and 12 men; and in management, with 13 women and 11 men senior executives and managers. According to the management, women agents or telesales executives (or TSEs) have the right profile, with qualities such as patience, and pleasant voices. Their clients are mainly men, and apparently women agents are able to sell more to men clients. As observed by one Senior Manager,

Women neutralize the situation. Women, because of their characteristics are more attentive compared to men, who are more detached. They have a better edge over men. Women can humanize their communication better and their voice quality is better, superior. The top sales agents are women, while the end customers are predominantly men.

TSEs start with a base salary of RM1, 500, plus commission, and performance incentives. The company is moving towards a grading system in which salaries will be paid by the hour. Agents are monitored daily based on four types of compliance—information, professional conduct, verification, and technical compliance. Those who do not meet these requirements are coached by their team leaders who obtain their scores from a select team of auditors who listen in to 30 calls per day. As in Company A, remuneration is closely connected to performance, and commissions increase if more sales are closed leading to relatively high levels of stress in this fast-paced work environment.

Nevertheless, with the shift towards an hourly-based salary, a two track occupational structure is emerging. Newly appointed TSEs are paid on an hourly basis, unlike the IT graduates working in the multinational IT products campaign, who receive a monthly salary of RM2,200. The majority of the TSEs are women, while the IT staff comprises women and men equally. According to the Program Director 'gender is not important—it is the knowledge and the skills which are more important in this type of position'. In fact, due to the need for multilingual skills, the company is in the process of hiring Thai, Vietnamese, and Korean staff to serve the specific needs of the region. They are paid much higher salaries than local staff, with additional perks such as housing, and transport allowances.[11]

The Company's aim is to become the provider of the best-customized solutions and teleconsulting services in Asia, thereby positioning itself as a 'people management company.' Nonetheless, several human resource challenges were noted by the Operations Director. These include the need to reduce attrition and absenteeism through various initiatives such as organizing sports and recreation events, acknowledging staff through employee of the month and year awards, and rotating staff with different products and under different team leaders. The idea is to make the workplace a second home for young employees where they should have fun while on the job. There are plans to introduce a profit-sharing scheme, and bonuses and remuneration based on a combination of individual and team performance.

Women's Voices

Prema, a 31-year-old woman, has been working in Company A for the past five years and would like to look for a career in the Company. As a permanent employee, her salary is now RM1,755, with another RM100 as hardship allowance. There is also a meal allowance of RM7.50 per day, with two days flexi leave a week. Prema has been working the night shift for the past four and a half years. Most of those on the night shift are single. Prema says she prefers working at night as she likes her team: 'We work well together—like a family,' moreover, she gets to do more things during the daytime.

She likes talking, has interesting customers, and learns from them as well. She cannot face customers, so she is happy talking with them over the phone. There is more tolerance and one can control one's emotions. She has developed new skills, particularly in customer service relations. She feels most satisfied when she can solve customer problems because she goes 'haywire,' and feels guilty if she cannot respond adequately to complaints. However, she feels stressed especially when calls are 'overflowing'. There is no space to breathe. It is particularly bad when there are irate customers. She also feels pressured by some customers who are 'sexual perverts,' and is hard pressed to release such calls as in the company, one has to 'entertain' the customers—there is a clause.

Work and goals are set by the department and she sometimes feels pressured by the demands for efficiency and productivity. Earlier, there had been no time 'quota'—the average call handling time was 240 seconds. This was reduced to 180 seconds, and presently it is 160 seconds. One is also pressured by team performance. There are campaigns every three months where one has to be productive and reach the quotas set by the company. Prema pointed out that there is a SMILE campaign now. Everyone has a mirror in front of them. If you win there is a RM100 one-off reward. She thinks this is 'fun' as it encourages them to be good workers—and it is a material incentive. This is a good company to work for—it is prestigious'.

Hari, a 27-year-old woman, joined Company A in February 2001 as a contract worker, with the contract renewable annually. She studied banking at a local college, and finished her Diploma in 1998. She sees the call center job as a stepping stone to a better position in the company. She started at a salary of RM1,400, but now receives RM1,600 with a few benefits: flexi benefits up to RM380 per year, hand phone claims up to RM500 once in two years and RM100 as a hardship allowance. Transport home is provided when she is on night shift.

She is married and her husband, who joined the same company in 2000, is also a call center employee. They used to work on the same shift, but now they have different shifts so she does not see her husband so much. There is no solution so she is looking for another job—in banking or management. Despite this, she feels the company is a good place to work in.

Hari reveals that the computer evaluates the employees, for example, your tardiness or punctuality, because one has to log in. Another evaluation procedure is a customer survey called VIEW

CAST whereby customers are asked to rate you after their call. There is also an SMS survey—after the call the customers will be asked to rate the consultant via SMS on a score of 1–5.

Hari's AHT is 160 seconds, with no more than five percent of calls abandoned. She receives between 100 and 140 calls per day. She feels stressed to complete the calls within the stated time. Earlier, it was more relaxing but now she feels pressured with the new AHT. The staff has complained, but nothing has been done. Many workers have left. She has migraine headaches on a regular basis and her shoulders ache. So she just goes home, lies down, and refuses to take calls. And now that she has a son, she has no time to rest.

Mimi, a 31-year-old woman, joined company A in March 2004 but is hired by another company. In other words, she is an out-sourced contract worker. She enjoys being in the customer relations line as she likes talking to people. Her pay is RM1,800, with an RM100 hardship allowance. She is quite happy with her work, and does not mind the shifts, as she says this gives her time to go to the bank or run errands.

However, she feels stressed, as she has been unable to make the AHT quota for the past three months. Sometimes her team leader picks the wrong call to monitor her work, which can be quite de-moralizing. She feels insecure as the company can terminate her with only two weeks notice. The company, she says, demands too much from the workers, only noticing when employees slack. She feels harassed regarding talk time, holding time, or when her team leader asks her to cut her talk time. She feels especially stressed when there are a lot of calls. 'Even when the bladder is bursting—you have to take the calls. And as I am a smoker, I am all the more stressed!'

Mimi feels that she will not be working in call centers forever. However, she feels there is potential in the industry and would like one day to oversee the call center flow floor of a multinational company. She prefers working in telecommunication contact centers to bank contact centers as the work is more interesting.

Sue, 24, was studying accounting part-time, but applied for the job of a Telesales Executive in Company B seven months ago to earn some money. She has stopped her studies for a while. She is now working full-time as a permanent employee. Sue sells credit card insurance and finds the work challenging. Every morning, the team gets a briefing on targets. She proudly says that she was the top Sales Executive in an insurance campaign where all TSEs were asked to sell at least 10 policies per day. She is paid hourly at RM9 per hour and can earn an income as high as RM2,300 a month, commission included. According to Sue,

Once you reach the 11th sale, you get commission at $1.50 per sale. If you make 10 sales and below, the commission is forfeited. Once you reach 16 sales, the commission will be higher at $2.50 per sale, then it goes up to $3.50 per sale. I can sell 40 policies a day; my personal best is 48 a day. I sell more to men in the 20-30 age range, it is easier to sell to them. I speak English, Malay, and Mandarin. Our Malay colleagues pass on Chinese customers to us, so we have an advantage.

Sue says that for this credit card insurance campaign, the talk-time is very short—no more than 10 minutes. She has a step-by-step script to follow. She says she is happy in the job. She feels more confident in handling people and their different attitudes, and has learnt a lot about people and their attitudes. In fact, since she joined she has been the top sales person in her team and says that she can still handle it. But she smokes more now, given the tension to meet targets. However, it is tense for her colleagues who cannot make the target required.

Her career path, she says, is still okay at the moment: 'I don't think of leaving yet.' She is not aiming to be promoted, as a team leader does not earn commission. Even though Sue can earn actual money, she does not see any future in this area, as she wishes to be an accountant. Nonetheless, she says that it is good for girls to work in call centers because they do not need to go out to get customers and work is safer.

Connie, 23, is single and hails from Kuala Lumpur. She just graduated with an IT degree from a local college. Her title is Telesales Executive, a permanent position in Company B. As a telemarketer, Connie handles outbound calls selling 10-year term life insurance for credit card holders. She talks to the customers, explains the benefits of the plan, and convinces them to get (another) life protection plan. She calls four customers every hour, and spends on an average 15 minutes with each customer. Executives are encouraged not to talk more than 15 minutes, Connie says. 'It's productivity sales and controlled time.'

The daily sales target is at least five sales per agent per day. Most of the time, the team can reach the target, and can even sell more than seven policies per day. Connie is paid on an hourly basis at RM9 per hour. However, she is paid a commission for every sale at the rate of RM1.50 for the first three sales, RM5 for the fourth and fifth sales; RM8 for the next three sales; RM10 for the ninth to 11th sales; and RM12 for above 12 sales. Insurance is hard to sell, and 11 policies per day are her maximum sales. In terms of skills, she says that telemarketers

must have listening skills, care for what the customer is concerned about, show that we care, like a consultant answering their questions and solving their problems, be nice to them, courteous, polite and they can feel our smile, be in a happy mood. It's a challenging job. Everyday we start at zero sales and work up. I push myself to move up. I enjoy the work, the colleagues are nice and there's challenge in getting sales. The job has changed me. I can make faster responses to answer questions that people ask. I like talking. It's an energetic job. I have become more aggressive. If there are no sales, then we make ourselves cheerful. It depends on luck. We have group activities, we sing, encourage one another, it's fun.

She has to follow the script as every call is recorded and monitored by the QA department. If one says something wrong, it will affect the whole team's KPI. She says she will work here for as long as she can. She sees a career path for herself and aims to become a team leader.

It's a good job, I enjoy it. It has a good future. I am satisfied with the campaign. I earn about RM 2,000 plus monthly. We can take MCs from panel doctors and still get paid. There are 14 days of unpaid leave. If I have any problems, I can go to the team leader or project leader or HR. It's a fun working environment, we are quite close to each other. Every month there's a birthday celebration, we play games, have an annual dinner, and employee of the month.

Call Centers in India

India's Comparative Advantage

In spite of competition from other developing countries and the difficulties that global companies face in operating in the country, India is still the most popular site of ITES sourcing by US- and UK-based companies, particularly for call centers. India's large English-speaking, highly educated, and low-wage talent pool has helped to establish it as one of the fastest-growing outsourcing service markets in the world. A virtual 12-hour time zone difference with the US and other markets is also in India's favor, especially for data processing.

An article in McKinsey quarterly in the year 2001 rated India as the most preferred offshore service location. A recent survey by the Indian National Association of Software and Service Companies (NASSCOM) found that almost two out of five Fortune 500 companies currently outsource some of their software requirements to India. Unions in the UK have predicted that up to 200,000 jobs in the finance sector would leave, mostly to India, as companies take advantage of India's cheaper labor cost.

The cheaper labor cost is only one consideration for choosing India as a desired site for relocation of work. There are more IT engineers in Bangalore (150,000) than in Silicon Valley (120,000), creating an enabling cyber culture. India now produces two million college graduates a year (a number which is expected to double by 2010), 80 percent of whom are English-speaking (*The Economist*, 2003).

Government policies have been supportive as well, in providing an enabling framework for the industry. By the late 1990s, recognition of the potential of the Information Communication Technology (ICT) industry led to establishment of the National Task Force on IT and Software Development, and the Ministry of Information Technology. In March 2003, the Union Cabinet approved a proposal to ratify the ILO Night-Work (Women) Convention to provide flexibility in the employment of women during night shifts.

There are already more than 160,000 employees on the payrolls of call centers in India; approximately 45 percent of them women.

In some companies, the figure can be as high as 70 percent. One major challenge is the attrition rate, which is lower than that in the US or UK but at 30–35 percent is still high, apparently due to stress and the low level of job commitment. The staff working at call centers tends to be young and aspires to further study and other professions. Most women leave the job after marriage—and most Indian women marry young. Companies are now scouring the towns and countryside away from the big cities to locate employees who can be trained for jobs in these centers. If the trend continues, women in India are likely to benefit, at least in terms of the number of available white-collar jobs.

This study of two typical call center companies in India—one a subcontractor, the other a subsidiary of an overseas company—gives some indication of the call center business and the impact of such growth on the career paths of women.

Company X: Case Study of a Local Subcontractor

A New Delhi-based company, Company X is owned by one of the software giants of India, which holds 96 percent of its shares. The other four percent is with the management of Company X. This company claims to be the first third party outsourcing company in India and also one of the main BPO companies in the country, with six centers in different cities. The Company undertakes a large number of outsourcing jobs assigned to them by various companies located in different parts of the world, mainly UK and US. The assignments include services at the lower end of the value chain, such as medical transcription from dictaphones as well as those at the higher end, such as providing technical support and marketing products through inbound and outbound calls.

The company opened in 2000 with around 320 employees. Today, there are 10,000 employees working in the five centers, with 3,000 employees in the Delhi center alone. The ratio of women to men employees in Delhi is 45:55 at lower levels, and around 37:63 at higher levels. All the employees are at least graduates. Recruitment is followed by two months of rigorous training in voice, accent, grammar, and culture of the client country. The company prefers young people who are expected to be more efficient and have better computer skills.

Company Y: Case Study of a Subsidiary
The Bangalore-based Company B is a subsidiary of a leading US-based remote e-services company. It was one of the first companies to establish a fully operational international call center from India. There are two operation centers, one in Bangalore and the other in Pune. The Company claims to provide high quality, value-added contact center services, and BPO services to Fortune 500 companies. The main area of work is customer service which includes in-bound and out-bound voice services; transaction processing and web-based services to many clients including a US-based financial house and credit card company.

Company Y started in 2000 with a staff of only 30, which has grown to 3,200 in three years. More than 90 percent of the employees are graduates, while the others are postgraduates who come from educated, and socially and economically well-off families. There are graduates and software professional women employed here, and men who have been educated as lawyers, dentists, engineers, and software professionals. Most of the staff members are unmarried, and in their early 20s. The majority of the employees are women, though only a few women work at the managerial level. Most often, the employees work for up to two years and then look for better prospects. Most of the women workers leave the job after their marriage.

Women's Voices

Ashima has a degree in hotel management and joined the call center through campus placement in May 2003. She currently earns about Rs 8,000 per month with some incentives.[12] While she sees chances of promotion within the Company as low, she nonetheless views her job as a welcome break from study and also as an opportunity to earn some quick money. Although trained in hotel management, she is not keen on a hotel career. While she does not see the call center as a 'career' and would like to study further, she is nevertheless enjoying the freedom and the money, and may not leave the job in a hurry.

Ashima sees little challenge in the job because of its repetitive nature. While there is no clear link, she feels the irregular meal timings may have aggravated a low blood pressure problem, and the deterioration of her eyesight. In her opinion, the job is not compatible with marriage because of its irregular timing.

The Company hosts a late night party every month which is compulsory for all employees to attend. Ashima has not attended any of these parties as she is not very comfortable at them. If any employee does not attend the party, he/she faces the consequence of being singled out, which has happened to Ashima on several occasions. This also affects the employee's promotion prospects. The party is part of a process of acclimatization to a different culture. According to Ashima, this job induces a completely different life style, attitude to life, and values.

Sanjana has been working in a call center for the last two years. She is currently earning around Rs 12–13,000 a month, with the benefits of provident fund and reimbursement of medical expenses. She was previously working with a commercial bank but found the job too stressful. The call center, with its college-like atmosphere, has a very relaxed atmosphere. She likes the culture of using first names for all, irrespective of position. She disagrees that the job is incompatible with marriage. She has married friends working in the call center, and argues that it is the understanding between husband and wife that matters.

Sanjana was attracted to the job because of the salary. She likes the job, finds it challenging, and feels that this industry has given the younger generation, especially girls, a welcome opportunity to know about the world, and earn well after graduation. She is comfortable with the timing of the job, and says she has ample time to spend with friends and family. A native of Delhi, she has no hesitation in working nights, which ensures her safety. Even her family members do not have any problem with this. The job has given her a sense of freedom, especially in terms of money, and the training has given her a lot of self-confidence.

Deepika joined the call center in October 2003 as it offered better remuneration, and there were more opportunities for growth in a new company. Deepika has been trained in hotel management and finds call center work less stressful than the hotel industry. Shifts are shorter and timings are fixed. In fact, she feels she has more time to herself with this job than she would have anywhere else. According to her, call center companies value graduates from hotel management courses because of their work discipline, and the training in people management that they are given during their course.

Deepika says that the call center training has helped her in developing her communication skills. It has helped her grow mentally. She feels that the training helps to make one more alert and to acquire a sixth sense. As far as the western culture of the centers is concerned, she said the training makes one familiar with the accent and the western culture. She said that in every set up or culture, there are negative and positive aspects, which one should understand and accept.

As the call centers provide transport and a good atmosphere for women to work, more women are joining the industry. Deepika feels that women have benefited considerably due to the increase in the outsourcing business in India. She is planning to pursue a career in this field, as she likes the job and does not plan to leave the job after marriage.

Priya has been working in a call center for the past year and a half. She had previously worked for two other private companies—working for more than eight hours for a meager salary of Rs 3,500 a month and no other benefits. In her present call center job, she works from 8 pm to midnight and is paid Rs 4,000 a month including two days of paid leave. She took up this job because of its pay and the prevailing friendly atmosphere. Though she has no plans of further studies, the company encourages its employees to study further. Internal job postings are made and vacancy notices are displayed on the notice board. Though there are different designations, there is little hierarchy, employees address each other by their first names, and are free to meet and discuss any problem anytime.

She feels that employees learn a lot about banking, marketing including information about other countries—their culture, their accent, and their economic status. Indeed they have gained a lot of worldly knowledge, self-confidence, and courage. To be competitive, they have to keep themselves updated about news of other countries and talking to global customers really improves their knowledge. She feels the job is a platform for many youngsters to prove their potential. According to Priya, the negative side of this industry is that exposure to western culture and a free flow of cash in their hands is resulting in an increasing number of girls visiting pubs, smoking, and trying to imitate the west.

Rekha said she was a reserved and shy person before starting this job, but after the training she gained so much self-confidence and knowledge that she can face anybody and talk boldly. She gives full credit to the company for that. Rekha mentioned that she had faced health problems such as weight loss, and throat and back pains. Lack of proper sleep and food did affect her health in the beginning. But after some time she got used to the work, and she has been working there for the past 20 months.

The job is very stressful, she added, and sometimes it becomes monotonous and boring. She mentioned that there is no insecurity in this job as long as the employees are capable of satisfying their clients. This job has not affected her social life as she is not used to going out and meeting friends. The company arranges for activities such as team outings, weekend picnics, cultural get-togethers, and competitions, which are fun and encouraging for employees.

Each employee is provided with a cubicle, a personal computer, a comfortable chair, and a table with drawers to keep their personal belongings. The whole office is centrally air-conditioned with music piped in through the system. Priya said that the annual get-together which the company organizes and to which family members and relatives are invited is very good to clear the doubts of family members about the company. This has really helped to change the misconceptions of parents who are against their daughters working in the night shifts.

GENDER AND CALL CENTERS: EXPANDING THE DISCOURSE

Defining Call Centers: Beyond Stereotypes

Originally a call center was a facility set up specifically to handle calls from the public or businesses. It was a structured environment in which a group of agents handled only incoming telephone calls. However, what were previously termed call centers are now increasingly becoming Contact Centers, which deal with email, fax, video, text-chat, and voice over IP.

Through the years, the nature of call centers has been changing and it would be prudent not to stereotype these institutions. It is now clear that there are different types of contact centers that vary in terms of organization, function, services, and working conditions. Some contact centers are in-house; others focus on companies wishing to outsource their non-core business processes. Some concentrate either on in-bound or out-bound customer services, and others deliver both. Some focus on the domestic market, while others are offshore locations serving companies or multinationals based in the North. India is currently positioned as a key player as an offshore location for BPO. On the other hand, Malaysia's contact center industry primarily serves the domestic market, although the government wants the industry to complete with India as an offshore location for BPO in coming years. Working conditions and benefits in call centers vary according to the type of services provided. In-house call centers that provide only in-bound services, are less stressful than out-bound third-party call centers. The former are most often part of a larger company, such as a telecommunications company or a financial institution, and hence there are opportunities to be transferred, re-deployed, or upgraded to other departments within the main company.

They have a variety of job titles, including customer service representatives or consultants, telephone sales, and service executives, and occupy a range of positions including operators, technicians, engineers, account executives, and software analysts. As such, they are a very diverse group with a heterogeneity of skills, an issue which will be discussed later.

WORKING CONDITIONS: EXPLOITATION OR AGENCY?

The findings show that there are several similarities between Malaysia and India, particularly in relation to employment patterns and conditions of work. The bottom line of this industry is 'least cost for greater customer value' or plainly speaking 'do more but charge less'. To achieve this goal, various strategies are employed to obtain increasingly high value at lower costs. Our research shows that young, single women, mainly fresh graduates, are the preferred workforce in this industry, as a certain type of dynamism, communication skills, and IT skills are required to 'care' for the customers, who in some sectors are predominantly men.[13] This trend towards the feminization of work not only reflects the gender bias in society, but also shows signs of labor market fragmentation by caste and class. For example, in India, those employed come from the urban upper caste English-speaking elite of Indian society, thus reinforcing existing socio-economic inequities (Ghosh, 2004). Yet, the data also shows that in the Malaysian case, increasing skill levels lead to a more equal gender division of labor, reflecting and simultaneously challenging the gendered hierarchy of skills in back office services.[14]

The intensification of the labor process by measuring the quantitative (AHT) and qualitative productivity of the workers; the constant monitoring, surveillance, and disciplinary-based supervision; the fast-paced work structure; competition among teams for monetary incentives; and performance-linked remuneration, all lead to high levels of stress. In addition, the physical stress of continuous work with few breaks and night shifts—are all reasons for the high attrition rate, particularly in third party, out-bound call centers.[15] Other reasons for the transient nature of this workforce include the mundane nature of the work, the perceived lack of opportunities for advancement in the industry, and the low status of call center work.

Despite these problems, interviews revealed the contradictory voices of these women employees, reflecting the tensions between work and self fulfillment. The women workers in both Malaysia and India seem to be relatively satisfied, stating that they enjoy their work. Especially in India, women have found that the wages they earn enable them to experience a new found freedom and autonomy. In India, women's mobility and spending power have traditionally been controlled by men, even in the case of highly educated, working women. Although their wages are lower than those of their counterparts in the North, call center workers are paid at par with, if not more, than other graduates in the market in Malaysia, and receive much higher salaries than graduate teachers and nurses in India. Women in both countries point out that they have learnt new skills and some have even become more assertive persons. The acquired skills, ranging from so-called soft-skills like communication, listening, and inter-personal skills to product knowledge and technical competency, have given the women a sense of confidence in dealing, both with their customers and with society at large. While some women are in it for a short period, others plan to pursue careers in the call center industry.

Women's interpersonal skills are now being recognized and valued economically. In the workplace, these skills are used by women who work in diverse fields, such as human resources, public relations, and training, but these skills are hardly ever given an overt value. They are considered 'intrinsic', if not invisible skills of women. However, in call centers, a premium is attached to women's voices and their interpersonal skills, as these are closely connected to the quality of customer care, and ultimately, will ensure the profitability of the company. Research in the 1980s and early 1990s on computerization and women office workers, pointed out how these interpersonal, cognitive, and experiential skills remain hidden and invisible because they are associated with 'women's jobs'. Recommendations were then put forth to recognize and reward these skills (Pullman and Szymanski, 1988; Ng, 1994).

Aware that call center work can become routine and boring, managements offer facilities like reading rooms, Internet browsing centers, gymnasia, free transportation after night shifts, and recreational and cultural activities for the staff. As a training manager in Malaysia noted, part of his job is to de-stress the agents and 'make them enjoy their work even if it sucks'. In India, where middle class families still shelter their daughters, family days, and sports activities are organized. Family members are invited to interact with the management and clarify their apprehensions. Parents need to be reassured that their daughters may be working unconventional hours, including night shifts, but are engaged in perfectly safe, decent, and socially-accepted work. To reduce attrition, employees enjoy monetary perks, are assured of career advancement in Malaysia, and encouraged to pursue further education in India.

Even in these rather tense times over the issue of offshoring, and uncertainties over future trends, women's voices show that there are reasons to be hopeful about the benefits that export-oriented ITES jobs have brought to women. Regrettably, there seems to be a trend towards the informalization of call center work, as discussed below.

LOOKING AHEAD

The debates about the gendered nature of call centers in developing countries will continue, particularly in the context of the feminization of labor, a defining attribute of this era of neo-Liberal globalization. The conditions of work and potential informalization of export-oriented ITES jobs, including those call centers serving domestic needs, warrant caution and action. Reasons for this apprehension lie in the current pattern of work as well as in the potential non-sustainability of these jobs. Although located in the formal sector, the newly created jobs in both Malaysia and India display characteristics that suggest informalization.[16] In Malaysia, insecurity in employment arises from the current conditions and contracts of employment. In the case of in-house call centers, there is a trend to outsource these jobs on a contract basis. In India, the business is controlled by global companies that could leave the country without facing any significant resistance either from employees or from the national government. Shift work, a non-permanent workforce, high attrition rate, and the difficulties of organizing labor in both countries, all point in the direction of informalization.

It is possible that employment in export-oriented services sectors, including that in call centers, may be highly volatile, as it depends on the economic and political climate of the client countries. India is already at the center of the recent concern in the US, where politicians are starting to blame offshore outsourcing for the jobless recovery in technology and services sectors. An outcry in Indiana recently, prompted that state to cancel a US$ 15 million IT contract with Tata Consultancy Services. The telecom workers' union is up in arms, and the US Congress is probing whether the security of financial and medical records is at risk. The state legislature in New Jersey is proposing to make it compulsory for every call center to identify its location, and give callers the right to insist that their calls be re-routed to a call center in the USA. Similar pressures for protectionism are heard in the UK and Europe as well.

Thus the euphoria of limitless outsourced jobs may not last long in the face of technological changes, and a protectionist global trading environment, an irony in today's free trade liberalization rhetoric. However, unlike the manufacturing sector which can easily relocate to cheaper sites in other countries, it may not be so easy to do so in the case of call centers which rely on language, communication skills, cultural knowledge, and IT infrastructure to ensure quality customer services. To further strengthen these features, national governments and the ITES industry have to ensure that jobs in call centers are stable, and become accredited and professionalized so that a career track is ensured.

To ensure the sustainability of the industry, an important strategy would be to use the current boom in outsourced work to create a climate of cyber culture where skills and expertise gained in providing services to overseas companies could be used to meet local needs. The spread of e-governance in India and Malaysia and the drive towards a knowledge economy open up possibilities for improving productivity, increased access to information, and employment opportunities for poorer women and men in information processing work. After all, in the New Economy, the questions of gender and class inequalities remain just as valid in assessing sustainability, replicability, and indigenization of best practices, as they were in the Old Economy.

NOTES

1. The Survey in India was carried out by Grace Fernandez and Shaiby Varghese of the Institute of Social Studies Trust (ISST) under the guidance of Swasti Mitter. Part of the information on India has also been published in an article by Mitter, Fernandez, and Varghese (2004).
2. The Information Technology Enabled Services (ITES) industry refers to services delivered over telecom networks or the Internet to a wide range of business areas. Most of the functions are labor intensive, in which the technology is used as a tool to provide these services. Because of their labor-intensive nature, these processes and services can be outsourced to achieve cost advantage without giving up quality. ITES covers mainly back office operations like accounts, financial services, call centers, data processing, geographical information services, human resource processing, insurance claim processing, legal database processing, payroll processing, and the like.
3. In Malaysia, the nomenclature 'contact center' is now used, as the tasks have expanded beyond responding to queries from customers. In this chapter, the terms call center and contact centers will be used interchangeably.
4. The proportion of women call center workers is yet to match that in the manufacturing sector. In fact, the predominance of women in the latter, which used to reach rates as high as 80–90 percent of the total workforce, has now reached a plateau, and may even be decreasing in aggregate terms (Ghosh, 2004).
5. Because call centers are a relatively new phenomenon, there has not been much grounded research on its implications on the working lives of women workers there. Much of the literature has been anecdotal and journalistic and sometimes sensationalized, depending on which perspective one takes.

6. See the article by Habiba Zaman (1999) which has summarized these contradictory positions. Ng and Mohamad (1997) and Chhachhi (1999) locate this debate in the context of the implications of technological changes on the situation of electronics workers in Malaysia and India.
7. The call center industry calculates the size and potential of the industry by the number of seats available in the workplace.
8. The basis of the research in India is different from that in Malaysia.
9. Since 1998, the Malaysian Ringgit has been pegged at RM3.80 to the US Dollar.
10. This is further broken down to 'talk', 'call hold', and 'after call' work time.
11. The researcher could only interview the team leaders and the manager due to the security issues of this contract.
12. In 2003, 1 US Dollar was equal to about 50 Rupees.
13. For example, in the Malaysian cases, campaigns aimed at credit card holders and the provision of customer services to telecommunication and IT dealers, who are mainly men.
14. See Chapter 2 of this volume. Nonetheless, the Malaysian case shows that women are entering a specialized skills arena that requires specific expertise and managerial authority.
15. Even so, the attrition rate is not as high as in the West, where it is about 40 percent. The national survey in Malaysia actually disclosed a relatively low attrition rate of about 10 percent while in the two companies researched, wherein the initial drop-out rate, employees tended to stay for a few years, particularly those in the more highly skilled categories.
16. While this is not new in the manufacturing sector, the process of informalization is now creeping into the office environment, which traditionally has been more 'formal'.

REFERENCES

Basi, Tina. (2005) 'Faces and Places: Women Working in Delhi's Call Center Industry', *Conference Proceedings on Gender, Development and Public Policy in an Era of Globalization*, Bangkok, Asian Institute of Technology.

BBC News Online. (2003) 'Call Centres are Bad for India', 15 December, http://news.bbc.co.uk/2/hi/south_asia/3292619.stm.

Bhattacharya, Somnath, Behara, Ravi S. and Gundersen, David E. (2003) 'Business Risk Perspectives on Information Systems Outsourcing', *International Journal of Accounting Information Systems*, 4: 75–93.

Chhachhi, Amrita. (1999) 'Gender, Flexibility, Skill and Industrial Restructuring: The Electronics Industry in India', *Gender, Technology and Development*, 3(3): 329–60.

Gaerlan, Kristina. (2004) 'IT in India: Social Revolution or Approaching Implosion', *Women in Action*, No. 1: 14–17.

Ghosh, Jayati. (2004) 'Globalisation and Economic Empowerment of Women: Emerging Issues in Asia', Paper presented at the High-Level Intergovernmental Meeting on the Beijing Platform for Action, UN-ESCAP, 7–10 September

Gothoskar, Sujata. (2000) 'Teleworking and Gender: Emerging Issues', *Economic and Political Weekly*, 35(26): 2293–98.

Gurumurthy, Anita. (2004) 'When Technology, Media and Globalization Conspire: Old Threats, New Prospects', *Women in Action*, No. 1: 18–21.

Habiba Zaman. (1999) 'Labor Rights: Networking and Empowerment: Mobilizing Garment Workers in Bangladesh', in Porter, Marilyn and Judd, Ellen (eds), *Feminists Doing Development*, Zed Press, London and New York, pp. 158–71.

Han Chun Kwong. (2004) 'To Be or Not To Be a Hub?', Paper presented at CCAM National Conference, 25–26 August, Kuala Lumpur, Malaysia.

Institute of Strategic and International Studies. (2002) *Knowledge-Based Economy Master Plan*, ISIS Malaysia, Kuala Lumpur.

Kelkar, Govind, Shrestha, Girija, and N., Veena. (2002) 'IT Industry and Women's Agency: Explorations in Bangalore and Delhi, India', *Gender, Technology and Development*, 6(1): 63–84.

Lim Keng Yaik. (2004) Speech by Y.B. Dato' Seri Dr. Lim Keng Yaik, Minister of Energy, Water and Communications at the CCAM National Conference and Exhibition, Kuala Lumpur, 24–25 August.

Mitter, Swasti. (2004) 'Globalization, ICTs and Economic Empowerment: A Feminist Critique', *Gender, Technology and Development*, 8(1): 4–29.

Mitter, Swasti, Fernandez, Grace, and Varghese, Shaiby. (2004) 'On the Threshold of Informalization: Women Call Centres in India', in Carr, Marilyn (ed.), *Chains of Fortune: Linking Women Producers and Workers with Global Markets*, Commonwealth Secretariat, London, pp. 165–83.

Ng, Cecilia. (1994) 'The Descent of New Technology: Computerization and Employment in Malaysia', in Ng, Cecilia and Munro-Kua, Anne (eds), *Keying into the Future: The Impact of Computerization on Office Workers*, Women's Development Collective and Universiti Pertanian Malaysia, Kajang, pp. 25–46.

Ng, Cecilia and Mohamad, Maznah. (1997) 'The Management of Technology and Women in Two Electronics Firms in Malaysia', *Gender, Technology and Development*, 1(2): 178–203.

Pearson, Ruth. (1998) '"Nimble Fingers" Revisited: Reflections on Women and Third World Industrialization in the late Twentieth Century', in Jackson, C. and Pearson, R. (eds), *Feminist Visions of Development: Gender, Analysis and Policy*, Routledge, London, pp. 171–86.

Pullman, C. and Szymanski. S. (1988) 'The Impact of Office Technology on Clerical Worker Skills in the Banking, Insurance and Legal Industries in New York City: Implications for Training', in Tijdens, Kea, Jennings, Mary, Wagnar, Ina, and Weggelar, Margaret (eds), *Women, Work and Computerization: Forming New Alliances*, North Holland, Amsterdam, pp. 225–33.

Raslan Sharif. (2004) 'Malaysia Calling: Local Callcentre Aspirations Beset by Fierce Competition', *The Star-Intech*, 9 September.

Stanworth, Celia. (1998) 'Teleworking and the Information Age', *New Technology, Work and Employment*, 13(1): 51–62.

Star Recruitment. (2004) 'Talk to the World', 4 December, p. 1.

The Economist. (2003) 'Relocating the Back Office', 13 December, pp. 65–67.

Turner, Donna. (2003) *The K-Economy Transition and the Politics of Labour Reform in Malaysia: Some Socio-Political Implications for Labor*, Occasional Paper Series, Institute of Malaysian and International Studies, Universiti Kebangsaan Malaysia, Bangi.

7 WOMEN WEAVERS ONLINE: RURAL MOROCCAN WOMEN ON THE INTERNET

SUSAN SCHAEFER DAVIS

This chapter presents a case study of how gender functions in the information society at two sites in rural Morocco. At both sites, mostly illiterate rural women sell the rugs and other textiles they weave, by using the Internet. Even in western societies, where both women and men have the advantages of a high level of education and easy access to infrastructure and technology, one often hears about gender disparities in access to and use of information technology. Rice found that for American students in primary and high school, 'Both the literature and the fieldwork ... reveal deeply-rooted obstacles to involving girls with computer technology ...' and added that this is complicated because most teachers are women and may have problems with technology themselves (1995: 69). Pollock and Sutton (2003) describe a large variety of obstacles to the use of the Internet by Canadian women. Skuse notes that technology has the potential to reduce poverty and en-courage empowerment, but that research is needed to establish its potential and its availability to women and the poor (2001: i). This essay provides some of that information.

In both Morocco and the West, it is women who suffer from these technological disparities, but rural Moroccan women face many more constraints than Western women. First, the educational level of rural women is very low; only 11 percent of rural Moroccan women were literate compared to 39 percent of rural men in 1994 (Royaume du Maroc, 1994). While Morocco is encouraging school enrollment and adult literacy, the generation of weavers at these two sites is mostly illiterate—a serious problem for using the Internet. A second constraint is the cost of the technology: no village women (or men) can afford a computer to access the Internet. A third problem is with various aspects of the infrastructure in these rural Moroccan sites. One village has standard electricity, while the other has it only at night from a shared generator. Neither village has fixed telephone lines, but both benefit from mobile phones. However, the southern village is in the mountains and the network only reaches one site on a high point outside town, so one needs an appointment to call. Therefore, going into a near-by town to use a cyber café is the best way to have access to the Internet. However, that too is a constraint at the southern site, where the trip to town takes about an hour on a dirt road, and public transport is limited—at neither site do people have their own cars. Finally, transfer of funds internationally is possible but expensive, and there can also be problems with fluctuations in the exchange rate of currencies.

Given all these constraints, how do Moroccan women manage to sell their textiles via the Internet? This essay describes that process and the benefits and constraints involved in it.

Selling Textiles on the Internet

Why?

A first question may well be, 'Why deal with all these constraints and try to sell on the Internet? Why not use the traditional means, either selling to middlemen or taking the rugs to dealers in Marrakesh or Fez?' As a development practitioner, I thought the Internet could provide the solution to the perennial problem of marketing the products of isolated rural women. In addition, it could allow women to keep a larger share of the final profit, which often instead goes to middlewomen/men and/or merchants. Having sold Moroccan textiles purchased from dealers on the web since 1994, I know that it works. I implemented this idea as a non-profit experiment with rural women in November 2001 at N'Kob and October 2002 at Ben Smim.

The Sites

N'kob is located in the Anti-Atlas Mountains in southern Morocco, south of Marrakesh and north of Tazenakht. It is part of the Ait

Ouaghrda tribe, famed for its skilled weavers. The village has a population of about 700 people, and nearly all the women over the age of 13 know how to weave. They learn from their mothers and help them at home; there are no factories or commercial workshops. There is a primary school with classes up to sixth grade, and after that students must go to Tazenakht, an hour away by dirt road. There is no regular electricity or telephone lines, and mobile phones work only at one spot in the village. A photo of N'kob is available at http://d2ssd.com/www-source/me_apr02/spring02.1.html.

Ben Smim is located in the Middle Atlas Mountains near the small town of Azrou, not too far from Fez and Meknes. The population is about 1,300. They too have only a primary school. They have regular electricity, and good mobile coverage. Ben Smim is pictured at http://d2ssd.com/www-source/me_nov02bensmim/bensmim1.html. People in both villages speak Berber, the Tashelhit dialect in the South and the Tamazight dialect in the North.

The Process

Selling textiles on the Internet involves many steps: photographing, measuring, and weighing (to calculate postage which is built into the price) the items which remain with the women until sold. The women are also interviewed briefly about their life situation, their work, and the use of their earnings, and photographed if they agree to appear on the Internet (most do). At each site an educated local assistant is trained to eventually replace the author who initiated the projects. The assistant helps with the previous steps, takes orders over the Internet or by telephone, and handles packing and shipping. The two sites provide an interesting gender contrast, since in Ben Smim the assistant is a college-educated young woman, and in N'kob a man who has not finished high school. This mirrors the geographic situation in Morocco, where women reach higher levels of education in the north. At N'kob, the most educated young woman had only studied up to seventh grade and was not skilled enough.

Using the information above, material is prepared for the web, including editing photos, writing text describing the textiles and the women, pricing items, and placing them on web pages. When an item sells, the pages must be updated. Presently, I do this as the assistants lack English and computer skills. Orders are sent to me by email, and I check with my assistants either via telephone or email to see if an ordered piece is available, and inform the client by email. They then pay me, by check or electronically. Payment directly to Morocco is slow and expensive, so this seems the best option at present; it also allows the client to deal with an English-speaker. I then send the payment to Morocco either by fax for bank transfer, by wire transfer, or through friends. I email the shipping address and the financial details to my assistant. Once the local assistant knows the money is available in town, s/he gets the rug from the weaver, packs it, and takes it into town to send it, and picks up the money with which to pay postage and other expenses, and on returning pays the weaver. Paying the weaver when she parted with her rug would be ideal, but would require two trips into town for each rug, one to get the money and the other to ship it. This raises both costs and time invested, so payment is made later the same day.

It is apparent from the above that selling on the Internet can be fairly complex, and for the project to be sustainable, someone in Morocco should be able to handle all the steps. At this point the project assistants can do some and are learning more, but I still do a great deal. An assistant must live in a village to have the trust of villagers and to have daily contact about rug availability, yet, it is very unlikely that a villager would have the fluent English necessary to write web pages. Web skills could be learned but will take training. The most likely solution would be for a Moroccan living outside the village with the requisite skills to handle these aspects of the project. However, they would need to be trustworthy and trusted by the villagers, and would definitely need to be paid either a salary or a commission on sales. At present I volunteer my time and services since I wanted the project to get started in the best possible conditions, including affordable prices to encourage more people to buy. But, the villagers in N'kob and I have been exploring the idea of someone in Morocco taking over much of the web site work to make the project sustainable. At this point, if I were unable to continue, the project would grind to a halt, and that is not acceptable. Once the project is well-established, hopefully customers would not mind the rise in price necessary to hire a person.

CONSTRAINTS OF SELLING ON THE INTERNET

One encounters various constraints when trying to sell items from a developing country on the Internet, especially when the goal is to make local people as self-sufficient as possible, and even more so, when women are to be the main beneficiaries. These include finding an appropriate assistant for the illiterate women, the training and material needs of the assistant, benefits for the assistant, infrastructure requirements, issues related to currency transfer and exchange rates, and visibility of the web site.

Selecting an Assistant
Since the weavers who sell online are illiterate, they needed someone literate to assist them to keep accounts, read and send emails, and have at least basic computer skills. I wanted the project to work with women at all levels, so envisioned having the women sellers work through a woman assistant. Morocco is a Muslim society with varying degrees of gender segregation, so a woman should also have easier access to the women weavers. Since the assistant controls the financial aspect, including paying the women, he/she should also be someone the illiterate women could trust. Initially I thought of an educated relative of a weaver, perhaps a daughter or a niece. The assistant should also live in the village, for familiarity with, and quick access to the weavers.

I was able to meet all these requirements in the assistant at Ben Smim, the village in north central Morocco. Habiba, the assistant, is single, and in her late twenties, has a B.A. in geography, is literate in Arabic, French, and a little English, can keep basic books, and already knows how to use a computer for email. In addition, her sister, mother, and sister-in-law are among the weavers selling on the Ben Smim site. She lives in the village and is respected for her family status, education, and also because she was previously a literacy teacher for women there.

At N'kob, it was more difficult to find the ideal woman assistant. The major constraint was the lower educational level for women in the south. Thus the most likely candidate for assistant there, was a young woman with seven years of education. She had helped me work with women and measure rugs, and was obviously intelligent. Yet, when I asked her to write rug sizes in the notebook while I measured, she said: 'Do you think I'd still be in this village if I could do that?' It was apparent that her level of literacy was below what was required. In that setting, she would also probably have less freedom to go into town to use the Internet than would a man. One sees the regional variation in Morocco in that such trips were no problem for Habiba at Ben Smim.

However, I was able to find a man assistant who had most of the required qualities. Si Brahim is a married man around 40 who resides in the village and is the President of the village development association, a position which demonstrates that he has the trust of the villagers. In addition, he is related to several of the weavers on the site, including his sister, and mother. He did not complete high school, but he is literate in Arabic and to some degree in French, and can keep accounts. Although he is a man, he can contact women weavers either through their male relatives, directly, or with the help of the village women leaders trained by an international organization working in the area, The Near East Foundation. However, he had never used a computer, and would need French or English to communicate with me by email. To deal with this, I communicate with him mainly by telephone in Arabic, and also have worked with another villager, Ahmed, who is part of the development association and knows French, some English, and most importantly, how to use the computer and email. Ahmed lives in a nearby town and has quick access to a computer at the cyber café, while there is none in N'kob. Recently however, Ahmed has left the project and Si Brahim has begun to use email himself.

One sees both traditional gender constraints and a reversal in the selection of project assistants. I wanted women assistants and feared I would have a problem locating village women with enough education. This was true in N'kob in southern Morocco, where education is more limited, especially for women. Yet, in Ben Smim I was able to find a woman assistant with all the desired qualities; ironically, the woman had a higher education and more skills than the man assistant in the south.

Training and Material Needs of the Assistant

The assistants needed training in several areas, some of which I was able to deliver and others that have been delayed. The project also requires them to have access to material equipment like cameras and computers.

Photographing, Measuring, and Weighing

Each of these steps in getting a rug online can involve constraints. First, the assistant needs to be able to use a camera of reasonable quality to photograph the rugs and the weavers. I use a digital camera and download directly onto my computer on which I have editing software. A film camera with good resolution can also be used, and the photos scanned into computer files. Initially I did all photography on visits to the sites. However, Habiba took her own initiative and rented a film camera, took photos of textiles and had them scanned, and emailed them to me. Since she lived near where I taught, she also came to the university and had some basic training and practice with a digital camera. In July 2004, I received her first digital photos, sent by email with the necessary descriptions (in French) and measurements. She is well on her way to doing all the local work herself. Si Brahim has done none of this yet, but his colleague Ahmed has taken and scanned traditional photos of a few rugs and emailed them to me. These differences may be related to gender, to educational level, to access to the materials, or to all three. Both Ahmed and Habiba have more education and better access to materials than does Si Brahim, but Habiba's greater initiative may be related to gender in that Moroccan women are accustomed to working hard to get ahead.

Both assistants have learned how to measure and weigh rugs. They measure width and length twice, once on each end and side, to catch major variations. At both sites we borrowed a scale, a hanging scale used to weigh livestock in N'kob and what we call a simple bathroom scale, used to weigh people, in Ben Smim. We now have a project-owned bathroom scale in N'kob. In Ben Smim, Habiba balances rolled-up rugs on a can on the scale, and in N'kob Si Brahim is weighed himself and then holding the rug. Since airmail from Morocco is expensive, at both sites we add two kilos to the measured weight to calculate postage in order to compensate for packing materials and any inaccuracies.

Pricing Items

While at both sites the assistants know what goes into the price calculation for the rugs, they do not do it themselves. As the project has evolved, so has the rug pricing, and it can be rather complicated. At first there were several unforeseen costs, and pricing has gone through at least four versions. Figure 7.1 below shows the first and last versions at N'kob. At Ben Smim, Habiba gets 15 percent of the weaver's asking price.

Figure 7.1
First and Last Versions of the Pricing of Rugs in N'kob

Item	October 2001	May 2003
Weaver's price	Whatever she asks	Whatever she asks
Mailing price Airmail	Rug weight plus 1 kilo (for packaging)	Rug weight plus 2 kilos (for packaging)
Village Association	5 percent of weaver's price	5 percent of weaver's price
Stamp from Artisan Ministry, via merchant	2.5 percent of Weaver's price	6 dirhams
To School Library	–	2 percent
Transportation from village to cyber café, for 2 visits	100 dirhams (dh)	–
Use of cyber café, 2 × 1 hr	20 dirhams	10 dirhams (one visit)
Transport rug to mail	50 dirhams	110 dirhams
Fax address for mailing	20 dirhams	– (email)
Wash rug	30 dirhams	– (omit)
Return receipt	12.50 dirhams	– (include with insurance)
Postal insurance	–	40 dirhams
Telephone calls from US	–	100 dirhams
Telephone calls from N'kob	–	30 dirhams
Packing box	–	20 dirhams
Packing fee	–	50 dirhams
Online payment fee	–	5 percent of total charges
Allowance for currency fluctuations	–	5 percent of total above
Total fixed charges	232.50 dirhams	366 dirhams

Note: $1 = 10 dirhams in 2001, 9.5 dirhams in 2003, 9 dirhams in 2004, 8.5 dirhams in 2005.

It is clear that charges changed in the two periods, for example replacing transportation from N'kob to the cyber café with telephone calls, and a fee for online payment was added. Another complication is that to add the full current fixed amount of 366 dirhams to a small inexpensive piece, raises its price and lowers the weavers' share dramatically, so I only add 250 dirhams to those pieces by eliminating the costs of packing, boxes, some telephone, and the return receipt. If items are shipped at the same time, the transportation fees for items beyond the first are saved, and these go into a petty cash fund to be used for other unforeseen expenses. Any extra funds at the end of the year will be given to the village association in N'kob, while at Ben Smim, the weavers spend it on a party.

Web Skills

At present, I finish the process of getting rugs onto the Internet. Neither assistant has been trained to edit photos on the computer, or to write web pages or descriptions of the rugs, although Habiba has done the latter a bit without training. When I designed this project, I planned on more computer training for the assistants, but to date have not found funding. Therefore, training on photo editing and web page construction is on hold for the present. Currently I do these steps myself. The descriptions are in English, and it would be very difficult to find an assistant living in a village with high-level English, so I also do that step. Hopefully either the assistants can take over more of these steps in the future, or the project will hire a Moroccan with web skills outside the village.

Although this essay is focused on gender and technology in Morocco, here I would mention that gender also plays a role in my having the web skills to be able to construct and maintain this site. As a development practitioner, I do not have a large budget to spend on web site development and maintenance: I largely do it myself or it does not get done. In fact, I have some degree of the 'techno-phobia' widely attributed to women. But I also have a very helpful 'geek' spouse, who knows, and loves technology. With his assistance I have learned to use the computer, email, take and edit digital photos, and build and maintain a web site. This is not to say that all women need such support, or that the support has to be from a man. But I think it is worth saying that having someone who is approachable and always available can be very helpful in mentoring technological skills in any culture.

Material

Several kinds of equipment are necessary for this project, including a camera, perhaps a scanner, a computer, a scale, a measuring tape, and a telephone. While a low-end digital camera works well for people and close-ups, it cannot capture the detail of a full rug. Thus, one needs access to a good quality digital or film camera to photograph the textiles, weavers, and sites. If using a film camera, one also needs a scanner to digitize images for the computer. At neither site can the project afford to buy a camera, but camera stores or photographers often rent film cameras in Morocco, so this is one alternative. At Ben Smim, Habiba tried this and took the photos to a cyber café and had them scanned. Many cyber cafés and perhaps also photography shops seem to have scanners, so purchase is not necessary. However, the quality was just adequate, so unless better cameras or scanners are available, this is not a good solution. A digital camera has been donated to the Ben Smim site, and Habiba is learning to use it and the associated software. This process began in July 2003, and by July 2004 she was emailing me digital photos (unedited) of rugs and their descriptions in French.

A computer is necessary for email contact, and for processing photos when the assistants get to that stage. Having a computer at each site was considered but rejected later. A major problem was cost, and buying computers was impossible without funding. However, buying them is also probably inadvisable as they are readily and cheaply available in cyber cafés in much of Morocco. In Morocco, computer access in cyber cafés is relatively inexpensive (about US$0.50–1.20 an hour), and the owner repairs and maintains the computer. In addition, connection fees for the Internet are included in the hourly cost.

A scale is necessary to weigh the rugs, so shipping prices can be calculated for the Internet. A hanging scale is probably more accurate, but currently both sites are using simple bathroom scales.

The apparently simplest piece of equipment is something with which to measure rug size. A tape measure is easy to manipulate, transport, and store. One possible problem is that it should contain both English and metric measures, since the former is used in the US and UK and the latter almost everywhere else.

Initially I planned on communicating only via the Internet and not using the telephone, since international calls are quite expensive. However, sometimes one needs an immediate answer. In addition, the isolation of N'kob means that it costs about the same for Si Brahim to travel into town to the cyber café as it does for me to call him. In addition the call saves him the travel time of an hour each way, and he is more comfortable using the telephone than the computer. Thus, both assistants have a mobile telephone, and the costs of using them are built into the pricing structure.

Benefits for the Assistant

Although it may seem odd to include benefits in a section on constraints, the way benefits are allocated, or expected, can form a constraint. It is very important to have a project assistant in order to move toward sustainability, but one must decide how to reward the assistant. In N'kob, the Internet sales project was developed in collaboration with the village development association rather than with an individual. As president of that association, Si Brahim donates his time as project assistant. The association gets five percent of the woman's asking price (this is added to the final price, *not* deducted from the woman) of each piece sold. To date, they have used this income to help build latrines at the village school and to buy paint for the village pump house and a school building. In early 2004, they were making plans to build a multipurpose meeting room to be used for the association meetings, rug displays, and the village preschool. They hoped to finance it partially from Internet rug sales.

In Ben Smim there is no local association to work with the weavers. Habiba, the assistant, works with the women as an individual with individuals. In this case, she is paid a percentage of the women's asking price for each rug, again added to the price and not subtracted from the woman. This reward structure made it difficult to have a second assistant in Ben Smim: how would the second person be paid? Habiba was understandably reluctant to share her commission, and indeed she did a great deal of work to earn it.

The training and material needs of the project are not clearly related to gender: both women and men need training and materials. While Habiba is more comfortable using a computer and digital camera than Si Brahim, that is due to the difference in education rather than gender. This serves to illustrate the point that one cannot assume that because of general gender differences in a society (Moroccan women are on average less educated than men), one gender is incapable of, or worse at, certain activities. In terms of rewards, one might expect a married man to need or want more than a single woman. Yet, in both cases, the Assistants live in extended families, with several people contributing to the family budget. Si Brahim seems satisfied with the prestige his role as association president, including his central role in helping local people sell rugs, affords him. In addition, the main family income probably comes from the rugs his sister and mother weave. Habiba, on the other hand, lives with her father who is a farmer and an irregularly employed married brother, so has a greater need for cash. Again, we see that we cannot generalize on the basis of the most common gender roles.

Infrastructure Requirements

Selling on the Internet would appear to require access to electricity and telephone lines, to run the computer and connect to the Internet. Yet, while neither of these is used at the two sites, the women still manage to sell their rugs. By using a nearby cyber café, villagers without access to electric or phone lines can still sell on the Internet. In fact, both villages have electricity, Ben Smim via regular electric lines and N'kob from a village generator that runs for several hours each night. At both sites they could recharge camera batteries if necessary.

In Ben Smim, I contact the assistant, Habiba, on her mobile phone. Since she may be in town at the cyber café or visiting women with rugs, this is an efficient way to reach her. In N'kob there are no fixed phone lines, although at this site they might be preferable. This is because N'kob is in the mountains and does not have good network coverage, and sometimes one loses contact on the mobile phone. On the other hand, currently this is the only means of contact with Si Brahim. Yet, this is still problematic, since the network only reaches a certain high spot outside the village; if he is anywhere else in the village, the call does not go through. We need to set a time when I will call and then he waits at that point. Recently, he got voice mail service that works even when his phone is out of reach of the network, so I can leave a message about when I will call and he gets it when he checks messages.

The gender difference seems to contradict stereotypes: the woman assistant has better access to mobile telephone technology. However, this is not due to gender but the infrastructure at each site.

Currency Transfer and Exchange Rates

Any site that functions internationally must be able to transfer funds from one country and bank account to another, and to accommodate fluctuations in the exchange rates of various currencies. Since selling on the Internet is designed to open the markets of the world to artisans in developing countries, these are two important areas that must be dealt with.

My site is located in the U.S. and to date most of the clients are American. Prices are listed in dollars and people pay in dollars with personal or cashiers' checks, postal money orders, or online with a service called PayPal. I considered being able to accept credit cards, but there was a large setup fee. PayPal has no such fee, although they charge me about 3 percent of any transaction (the customer does not pay extra). To date most clients use personal checks or PayPal. PayPal can also accept payments from several other countries, saving dealing with currency exchange, although the fee may then be 4 or 5 percent of the transaction.

Transferring payment to Morocco is more complicated. First, the project assistant needs to have a bank account into which funds can be transferred. This has been arranged at both sites, in both cases with the bank in a larger town. Using a bank-to-bank wire transfer or Western Union, cash transfer is probably the most direct, but both are relatively expensive at about US$30 or more and would add substantially to the cost of a small rug. An international postal money order was possible, but took six to eight weeks to arrive so would really delay shipping. Now these money orders do not exist for Morocco, although they still work for a few countries. Currently I have a bank account in Morocco and send a fax directing the bank to transfer a certain amount to the account of one of the assistants (in one of their branches). This costs only the fax fee and funds are sent the same or the next day. When my account is depleted, I can send one large wire transfer, or ask a friend in Morocco to transfer an amount into my account and I repay her in dollars.

In the past the Moroccan dirham—US dollar exchange rate has been very stable. In addition, when I sold items I had purchased outright and sold for a profit, I could absorb rate changes out of my profit. But when working with the women weavers, where they ask a certain amount in dirhams for each rug and the costs of shipping and handling are closely calculated, there is no profit.

Since I donate my services, there is no profit from which I can absorb currency changes. Thus when the dirham began to fluctuate in February of 2003 and eventually fell from about ten to 9.5 to one dollar, prices calculated on the basis of ten fell short by 5 percent. I recalculated prices on the basis of 9.5 dirhams to the dollar, and built in another 5 percent fluctuation factor to cover a further fall in the exchange rate. If the rate stays stable, the excess would be returned to the village association or to the weavers. But by January 2004, the dollar had fallen to 9 dirhams to the dollar, and to 8.5 by late 2004, so another recalculation of prices was necessary.

Site Visibility

To do business on the Internet, the public must be able to find one's site easily. Just having a site does not guarantee that it will be found by search engines, and such searches are the major way of getting new customers. Factors like the use of key words, hits on the site and links from other sites all enter into how a site comes up on a search engine looking for 'Moroccan rugs.' One can also boost visibility and site visits by other means, including the use of mailing lists and publicity.

My Moroccan textile site, www.marrakeshexpress.org, was the first on the Internet with these products, beginning in 1994. Because of its early start and long tenure, many other sites linked to it, thus, boosting its visibility. It came up first on Google (in September 2003) when searching for 'Marrakesh' or 'Moroccan textiles', but later, though still on the first page, when one searches for 'Moroccan rugs.' By August 2004, this had changed somewhat because I had to change web hosts which changed the address. At that time, my site came up first on two of the major search engines, Google and Yahoo, when searching for 'Moroccan textiles,' and in the first five on both when searching 'Moroccan rugs.' But the site had dropped to 9th on Google when searching 'Marrakesh' and was not in the first 20 Yahoo sites. To remedy a lower listing, 'Marrakesh' should appear more clearly in the first paragraph. The changes in ratings also illustrate that one should stay with the same web host if possible.

To encourage return visits by former clients and would-be clients, I maintain an email list of people who have contacted me about Morocco and its textiles. This is my main promotion tool. Whenever I get new pieces, about three or four times a year, I send out a notice to that list. I always include the option to be removed from the list, though few ask to be. Recently many people use spam filters to decrease the amount of unwanted email, and since my mailings are to a list, some get returned. I can go back and send messages individually, but this is very time-consuming and sometimes it still does not work.

In fact my site appeals to a certain market or 'niche,' inhabited by a certain kind of clients. The buyers and repeat visitors like the handmade, individual style of the textiles and they often find an irregularity appealing rather than undesirable. Some have been to Morocco and want a reminder of their trip. Many like to hear about the women weavers and are consciously buying to benefit them rather than the merchants. Some buy because of the very modest prices. A few quotes from emails give a sense of what people like about the site.

I've been looking at your Moroccan textile website and I love it. I am a weaver, though not a rug weaver, but I have an appreciation for the art and the work that goes into the rugs. I'll check the website periodically for new rugs and pictures and stories.

If you see Jamila, you can tell her from me that she is a real artist; her sense of balance and proportion expressed in the colors and composition of the rug makes the whole room calm and warm. I have two other rugs of similar design, and they're just lumpy by comparison.

I really like your web site and most of all, the prices!!!! I have been surfing the web for a long time looking for Moroccan rugs and you really have the CHEAPEST prices. All the other sites seemed to be charging at least $250 to $400 dollars for a single rug. Ridiculous!!

The rug and pillow (from Zahra Aarab) arrived yesterday.... Perhaps I'm crazy, but when I opened the box, the carpet seemed to smell of wood smoke, adding charm to this very elegant and comfortable piece. From the outset, I was dubious about the sequins, but the first time I walked through my living room late at night to see stars on the floor, I was enchanted!

I've just come back from a trip to Morocco and was appalled by the cost of these same articles; obviously it is the MiddleMAN who makes all the money. I am pleased to see that you are making sure the women who make the articles are those who are getting a well deserved income.

I just wanted to thank you and the women weavers of Morocco for this great service. I have been shopping for a rug and have found it difficult to locate a retailer who sells rugs that do not exploit the weavers or who do not rely on child labor. I was very pleased to come across your site. Not only can I feel good about the purchase of this rug, it is beautiful as well!

A possible source of publicity would be to post a few items for sale on eBay, the Internet auction site. Sellers doing this are allowed to mention their web sites as sources of more items, which is basically an advertisement. I tried this just once and did not generate many inquiries, but feel that once is not a sufficient test. However, to sell on eBay may require a US credit card or bank account so could be difficult for some international groups.

In 2003, I had several opportunities for publicity for the site through print media and television. The site was found by a researcher for CNN International's program *Design 360*, and by Tiziana Alterio, an Italian journalist who specializes in technology in developing countries. In both cases, they found me on the web (a benefit of web presence) and arranged to visit the Moroccan weavers to make films. The Italian video appeared on the Italian station RAI 3 in May 2003, and the CNN program was aired on CNN International and CNN Financial in 164 countries several times during July and August 2003. The Italian program led to many site hits but only a few rug sales, perhaps because the site is in English. The CNN program was broadcast in English and led to inquiries and orders from several parts of the world, including Germany, Japan, Australia, and the United Arab Emirates.

In November 2003, the site was the topic of a 90-second CNN 'non-commercial' for Nokia. There was a series of non-ads that described interesting projects, and my work with rural women weavers was one of them. A CNN crew spent three days filming the 90-second spot and did a beautiful job, but did not manage to include my web address. Consequently, I got *no* orders. The lesson: be sure your web address is included in any publicity. In February 2004, I had the opposite experience. My local newspaper, the *Philadelphia Inquirer*, did a story on my work for their Home section and included the site address, and there were 600 hits on my web site the day it appeared. In addition, it was syndicated and appeared in papers all over the US, and this led to more orders.

The *Inquirer* article had an unexpected but wonderful consequence, one that fulfilled my goal of the site leading to better understanding between cultures by its inclusion of information on the weavers. Not all sites will have this aim, but many of those that focus on women might, and often my women clients seem especially interested in such information. I was contacted by a Philadelphia family, whose daughter was having her *bat mitzvah* soon, and they planned to visit a friend in Morocco to celebrate. The mother emailed and asked if I thought they might also visit the village of N'kob, whose weavers are on my site. I said I would have to contact my assistant and village association president, Si Brahim, and asked if she would like to say the family is Jewish. She said 'if that's OK,' so I did so. Si Brahim said 'Sure! Everyone is welcome. We're not those racist kind of people.' In fact the family did visit, both parents and the young woman plus their Moroccan friend, at a time I was there too. The American and Moroccan families liked each other immediately. In addition, the young woman donated money she had collected as a *bat mitzvah* project to the village association (eight of whom were present) to put toward building their multi-purpose room.

Another opportunity for publicity came, when I was invited to participate in the First International Folk Art Market in July 2004 in Santa Fe, New Mexico. Again, I was found on the web by an organizer and invited to apply for the competitive selection. The goal was to have local artisans and their crafts present, and to get wholesale orders to boost their business. In this case I was assisted by a Peace Corps Volunteer in Morocco who was working with a cooperative that could mass produce textiles for large orders. He photographed rugs for the selection, and helped the artisan get her visa and tickets once she was chosen. I attended at my own expense to translate, and her rugs sold very well, although there were no large orders (true for nearly all the participants). Two lessons emerge from this experience: a web presence opens doors, and Peace Corps Volunteers can be helpful in such enterprises. They could be a good resource in training local people in computer and web skills among other things.

While site visibility seems largely due to technical factors and not related to gender, the media interest and visits were related to the fact that the site works with and benefits Moroccan women, and the fact that illiterate women are linked with this high-level technology. In addition, the majority of my clients are women. This may be because women are more likely to purchase handmade textiles, but also because my site presents information about, and often a photo of the weaver in addition to just a rug, which especially appeals to many women clients.

Benefits of Selling on the Internet

One can examine the benefits of selling online in various domains. Increased sales and profits would be a definite benefit, but one also wants to examine how this affects women's lives. How are the profits used, and who makes that decision? Do increased sales empower women? Do increased sales have an effect on the tradition of weaving? Do Internet sales offer any other benefits?

Increased Sales and Profits

From October 2002 to August 2003, several items were sold online from both sites, 27 from N'kob, and 23 from Ben Smim. By August 2004, sales were 74 and 42 items respectively, so sales have increased. However, in a meeting with the N'kob weavers in November 2002, I heard that they were holding their rugs for Internet sale, thus missing other opportunities and perhaps decreasing sales. I had told the weavers that they could sell their rugs whenever they wanted, realizing they might need cash for an emergency. At the meeting it became clear that they *did* understand this point, and were not holding the rugs at my request, but because the price they had asked of me was higher than they could get locally: they were holding out for the higher price. Both sales and profits have therefore, increased.

Although there is no statistical evidence from N'kob, the above indicates that the profits women earn from Internet sales are higher than what they would earn locally. I also asked what the *difference* in price would be between a piece they sold locally and through the Internet. While they could not give me a specific number or percentage difference, they did say that locally they were paid low-season and high-season prices, and they were quoting the high-season prices on the Internet. In fact, Si Brahim reported that some women were getting more that that. One woman sold an older rug and quoted about US$415, while she would have received US$165 (low season) or US$225 (high season) from a local middleman. Another quoted US$75, while locally she would have received US$35 or less. In both cases, the women almost doubled their prices on the Internet.

Other sample sale prices provide perspective on women's earnings. One of the most expensive rugs sold in N'kob cost US$610 on the Internet, and the weaver got US$500 or 82 percent of that, with the rest used for processing and handling. For comparison, US$500 is about the monthly salary of a local primary school teacher. On the other end of the price scale, a small rug sold for US$125 on the Internet, and the weaver got US$50 or just 40 percent of that, since many handling costs are fixed. However, US$5 is a reasonable daily wage for unskilled labor, so US$50 is not negligible.

In Ben Smim, two students from the nearby Al Akhawayn University studied the effects of Internet sales for the women weavers (El Mahdi and Proberts, 2003). In terms of profit, the research found a clear result in one woman's statement that 'In the *souk* [weekly outdoor market], we make no profit. With the middleman, we make some profit. Online with Susan and Habiba, we make the highest profit possible' (ibid.: 13). However, from the women's reports it appears that the 'highest profit possible' is only about 100 dirhams more than what they could get locally. If this is the case, they should be advised to raise their prices. On the other hand, the project assistant Habiba, had hearsay evidence that one woman got 2,000 dirhams more for her rug on the Internet than she would have received locally. This needs more research. The students also validated what I knew anecdotally, which is, that almost no woman calculates her costs in making a rug. They use their own wool or buy yarn little by little, and give their own time no value. Thus, calculating a real profit is difficult; the best one can do is to compare the prices one would get from different buyers.

Other Benefits of Internet Sales

The research of El Mahdi and Proberts revealed other, unexpected benefits of Internet sales for the women of Ben Smim, who often sell their own rugs at the weekly outdoor market or *souk*.

First, it saves time, effort, and various costs, such as travel expenses. Second, it is more convenient, as the women do not have to stand all day in the hot sun when selling at the *souk*, wasting time, and being vulnerable to men's gaze, which is a common concern. The women do not have to leave home, and can use their time for home duties or other kinds of work. Third, the woven items are saved from being damaged from exposure to dirt/dust, and sunlight, which would fade the colours. Fourth, the online retail price for each item is higher [although not by much, as discussed in further detail below], which raises their profit margin. Fifth, the women receive payment in full, rather than selling the item on credit, as often happens in the *souk*, where customers pay it off little by little (El Mahdi and Proberts, 2003: 13).

While some may wonder if the Internet project is restricting the mobility of these Ben Smim women, keeping them out of the *souk*, in this area women are *not* secluded at home; if they were, they would not be allowed to go to the market and sell their rugs. They still go to shop for food and household supplies, if they wish.

Uses of profits

At both sites I ask the weavers what they will do, or have done, with the profits from their sales. In both places it seems, the main use of income from rug sales is to meet family expenses for food or school clothing, and supplies for children. When I asked one Ben Smim woman to whom her rug profits belonged, she said 'the family.' The money was put in a box in their home, and anyone who needed it could use it for things like school supplies, or transportation, and room rent for a daughter at the university in a nearby town. If they were considering a larger purchase, the woman and her husband would discuss it. In their research, El Mahdi and Proberts found similar uses of the profits. All but one of their six informants used their earnings for basic needs like clothing, food, or medicine (2003: 19).

In N'kob, unlike Ben Smim, women do not go to the weekly market; men buy all household supplies including food, and also clothing for the women and children. Men handle all the money, selling the rugs and spending the income for family needs. Women's weaving income has been crucial to these families, many of whom grow crops which have been very limited by the several recent years of drought. In fact, when I asked one woman what her husband did for a living, she said 'He waits for me to finish my rugs!' She was joking—sort of. Recently one of the women said something like 'You know how men are. When they decide to buy something, they buy a lot of that one thing, and forget other things that we might need. For example, he'll spend the money on a lot of flour and sugar, and not the clothing or the books the children need.'

Thus, men in N'kob have more control, and women less, over the profits from weaving than in Ben Smim. As a feminist, I wanted to see the N'kob women realize at least some direct profit from their work, but as an anthropologist, I knew that one cannot and should not impose such decisions. Instead I used the participatory approach, and asked a meeting of N'kob women how things could be arranged so that women would get at least some of the money from their rugs. One wise older woman said, 'Tell the men that if they would give us a little present when we finished each rug, it would encourage us to work faster to finish the next one.' In October 2004, I asked a group of women how many had tried that—and 11 had!

A few women reported their income being used for non-basic needs. One in Ben Smim was going to buy gold earrings for her marriage-age daughter, and another bought furniture for her home. Another woman re-invested in sheep:

> Only one informant, the one who kept a close account of overheads, the most educated one, was seen to plan ahead, as she buys sheep with the money gained from sales.... This accumulation of sheep provides her with a continual supply of wool for future weaving jobs; in times of financial trouble, it is a source of food; or as a commodity, the animal(s) can be sold off quickly and easily, as there is always a market for sheep. (El Mahdi and Proberts, 2003: 19)

Less money was being used for non-immediate needs in N'kob, although there was no systematic study. Sometimes a man would buy his wife or daughter, clothing as a 'gift,' and some women began to use some of their earnings to travel and visit relatives. In fact, recent information from the field indicates that several N'kob women are *retaining* a portion of profits and using it for clothing or jewelry—or in one case, a new blender. In addition, one of the best weavers said she would like to save money to start her own rug workshop with a sister and have employees ... and to sell the rugs on the Internet.

The Weaving Tradition

N'kob and Ben Smim differ in the local strength of the weaving tradition. The textiles they make are different, and there is a larger tourist and to some degree Moroccan market for the N'kob textiles. With a better market, N'kob textiles are more in demand, and nearly all young women are trained to make them, starting to learn around the age of 10. In the northern town of Ben Smim, there is little market for their mostly flatweave (sometimes called *kilim*) textiles, which are often decorated with sequins. In fact, in another town nearby, women rarely weave for sale any more. One said that the price was not enough to cover the materials and all her hard work; it was just not worth it. While some Ben Smim women still wove rugs to sell,

> ... the survey indicated that generally speaking the tradition of weaving is waning. The majority of informants agreed that young Berber women are being taught to weave by their mothers, especially after leaving school, although some informants stated that young women are not interested in learning to weave, saying that they are more interested in hair, make-up and fashion; the young women do not want to practice the art of weaving because it is too demanding physically, and is not profitable due to the mass production of modern blankets and carpets in factories .... (El Mahdi and Proberts, 2003: 14)

Another factor operating in Ben Smim is probably the generally higher level of education of women (and men) in northern vs. southern Morocco. A higher percentage of girls go on to school in the north, and they concentrate on their studies instead of weaving. Further, it is hoped that their studies will lead to more profitable jobs. In the south, weaving itself is profitable and other jobs unlikely, and this reinforces the general trend to only educate girls to a certain level, often till primary school.

The Internet, by increasing the number of sales, can help to keep the weaving tradition alive. The young women in the Ben Smim area, few of whom now learn to weave, may be encouraged to do so with the prospect of better sales. In fact, my college-educated assistant, Habiba, had only made one rug in her life—but it sold on the Internet, and this led her to weave another.

INTERNET SALES AND WOMEN'S EMPOWERMENT

The concept of women's empowerment is much-discussed but often not well-defined. One of the groups to examine empowerment and its measurement most carefully is the Swedish-based Kvinnoforum, a consultancy organization. They note that one cannot define empowerment simply, and working with several African NGOs came up with a working definition.

The working definition sees empowerment as all those processes that make women take ownership of their own lives, and that these processes can take place on *individual, group and societal level*. These levels are mutually reinforcing and the relationships between them as well as between people are important to study. Empowerment can be approached as a holistic process of gaining control, influence or ownership over one's life and this process can be studied in various aspects of the women's lives. (Kvinnoforum et al., 2001: 43)

For the purposes of this essay, we can see if selling textiles online gives these Moroccan women more control, influence or ownership over some areas of their lives. Although there is no systematic analysis yet on this question, there is some anecdotal evidence. In Ben Smim, the researchers concluded that:

> This project is empowering because: it does not reduce the level of control of their own work/products, as they can sell items elsewhere whenever they want; the women set the prices of items themselves; and they are exposed to a new, larger global market, which means they are more likely to generate income for their own benefit. This constitutes women's increasing of self-reliance, and their right to make choices and influence change through control over economic resources. (El Mahdi and Proberts, 2003: 22)

The above focuses only on the selling aspect, and in fact women also largely control their traditional sales to middlemen or at the *souk*. The one greater element of control with Internet sales is that they can set the final price. The researchers go on to give evidence:

> ... an informant reported that weaving provides her family with a source of income, and as a result, they are able to survive. In that manner, she is a breadwinner, which allows her to have marginal (sic) power in family decision-making. She compared her situation with that of non-weaver women, who passively accept decisions made by their husbands. (ibid.)

In this interview, the woman said that with her money she bought exactly what she wanted, while women without weaving income had to ask their husbands to bring the things they needed or wanted, and often the men did not.

In the early stages of the project in N'kob, it appeared that women had no control over the income from their weaving, and in fact never saw it, since the men handle sales. However, in June 2003, I was surprised to hear that *some* women, especially the two women leaders, did have some control over their earnings. While they were reluctant to state amounts, these women were given 'something' after the sale of a rug to use as they liked. They might buy a scarf or make-up or jewelry, unlike the necessary items their husbands would buy. One woman said she used her earnings to travel, visiting her daughters in Moroccan cities, quite a treat for someone living in a village of 700 people. In the past, she would ask her husband if she could go and he would refuse. Now, she says, when he says no she replies that she'll use her own money, and is then free to go. Other women said that when Si Brahim paid their husbands, they at least saw how much money came in, while they had no idea for rugs sold at the *souk*; this often led them to ask for some of the money. Some mentioned that they felt 'braver' or 'stronger' (*za'm fe rasi*) when their rugs brought in money; one might call that more self-confidence. By October 2004, the younger woman leader said she kept *all* the money from the sales of her rugs. However, I cannot generalize this change in control of income to the whole village: these women get some of their earnings, with the majority still use it for family needs. In addition, not all the men give the women a share. I heard that some men were 'nicer' than others about sharing the money. Further, the two we heard most about were the women leaders, older and with strong personalities, and that probably played a role. When I asked one young weaver what she did with her earnings, she laughed and pointed to her father's belly; I would expect young brides or unmarried daughters to have less access to their earnings.

Another aspect of empowerment relates to women in groups, and that was a factor in N'kob. I held several group meetings there, with women and men separately. While all villagers are officially in the village development association, men are more involved in its functioning and discussions at meetings. Women have meetings with local development field workers about matters of concern to them, like health and nutrition, and they learn more than make decisions. In my meetings, women made decisions about rugs and Internet sales. For example, they were concerned that others could copy their unique local rug designs from Internet photos. I agreed this was possible and asked if they wanted to remove some or all of the photos—and all said no. Making decisions in a group is another way for women to become empowered. They also learned some empowering techniques in group meetings. Finally, the development field worker said villagers recognized that some of women's profits were used, through the village association, to help in village projects like latrines for the school. Thus, villagers could see that women's labor has benefits beyond their immediate families.

CONCLUSION

Considering all the constraints encountered when trying to sell rural women's weaving on the Internet, one might think it unlikely that this project would work. One needs to find assistants to train so the project will be sustainable, and women with enough education are often rare in rural areas. The assistants need training in weighing, measuring, and photographing the rugs, and later in web skills to put products on line. They also need access to equipment like scales, cameras and computers, and to infrastructure like electricity and phone lines that will give them access to the Internet and international communication. Dealing with international currency transfer requires access to bank accounts and inexpensive ways to transfer funds, as well as pricing products to tolerate fluctuations in currency value.

Yet, the project *is* working, and women in two small Moroccan villages *are* selling their rugs on the Internet. The project's goals, of finding a larger, worldwide market for the women's rugs, and allowing them to keep a larger share of the profit, by eliminating middlemen, are being met. Women's profits are mainly used to sustain the family by buying food, clothing, school supplies, and medicines. Women in a few cases use the money for more personal things like jewelry, clothing, or travel. One question was whether this project would help to empower women by giving them more control over their earnings, and through that over other aspects of their lives. At this point this seems to be truer in Ben Smim than in N'kob. One of my current goals is to locate funding for research to better understand the implications of Internet sales in these women's lives, as well as to fine-tune the selling process itself, to make it easier to replicate in other parts of the world.

This use of technology to encourage development relates to gender in various ways. Some readers may expect Morocco, as a Muslim country, to have conditions that consistently limit women's experiences, including access to and use of technology. In a general sense that may be true, since women have a lower literacy rate and would thus find Internet use, especially in French or English, difficult or impossible. In several regions their movement is more limited than that of men. For example, that is true in N'kob compared to Ben Smim, where women can market their own rugs. Yet, the data presented here, illustrates that one cannot be limited by such generalities. As would be predicted, at one site (N'kob) I could not find a woman with enough education to be the project assistant and recruited a man. Yet, at the other site (Ben Smim), I found a woman with more education, camera, and computer experience than the man assistant.

The Women Weavers OnLine project still has some rough edges, and suggestions / solutions are welcome. However, rural Moroccan women are selling their rugs on the Internet since November 2001, and some are using their profits to have a greater control over their own lives. I see this use of Internet sales as a model for overcoming the marketing bottleneck that isolated rural artisans face worldwide, and of securing to them a larger share of the profit from their products. In my more optimistic moments I envision a worldwide women's craft site on the Internet. In addition to benefiting the citizens of developing countries, we would all be enriched by having access to their unique creations.

REFERENCES

El Mahdi, Asmae and Proberts, Darlene. (2003) 'A Case Study of Marrakesh Express: Women Weavers Online', Final project for the class 'Women and Economic Development' at Al Akhawayn University, Ifrane, Morocco.

Kvinnoforum, Organisation for Rural Associations for Progress in Zimbabwe, Women's NGO Coalition in Botswana, Namibia National Association of Women in Business, and the Community Development Foundation in Mozambique. (2001) *Measuring Women's Empowerment: A Report from a Pilot Project on Methods for Measuring Women's Empowerment in Southern Africa*, Chapter 2, http://search.qweb.kvinnoforum.se/sites/qweb/measuring/report.htm.

Pollock, Scarlet and Sutton, Jo. (2003) 'Women and the Internet: Participation, Impact, Empowerment and Strategies', Womenspace Consultation Report, presented at the United Nations Division for the Advancement of Women, Expert Group Meeting in Seoul, South Korea, November 2002, http://www. wmn.ca/uncsw/consult_report_e.htm.

Rice, Marion. (1995) 'Issues Surrounding the Integration of Technology into the K-12 Classroom: Notes from the Field', *Interpersonal Computing and Technology: An Electronic Journal for the 21*st *Century*, 3(1): 67–81 (Also archived as Rice IPCT3N1 on listserv@guvm.georgetown.edu and available at http://www. helsinki.fi/science/optek//1995/n1/rice.txt).

Royaume du Maroc. (1994) *Recensement General de la Population*, Ministere de la Planification, Rabat.

Skuse, Andrew. (2001) 'Information CommunicationTechnologies, Poverty and Empowerment', Social Development Department Dissemination Note No. 3, Social Development Department, Department for International Development, London, http://62.189.42.51/DFIDstage/Pubs/files/sdd_dn3.pdf.

8   VIRTUAL COMMUNITY BUILDING FOR NETWORKING AMONG WOMEN

ISABEL ZORN

> We the representatives of the peoples of the world, ... declare our common desire and commitment to build a new kind of society, the Information Society ... In this society, new technologies, in particular Information and Communication Technologies (ICTs) become an essential tool, accessible to all, for the attainment of a more peaceful, prosperous, and just world based upon our common humanity in all its diversity. (ITU, 2003a: 1)

This quote from the first paragraph of the Draft Declaration of Principles (ITU, 2003a) of the UN World Summit on Information Society (WSIS) needs to be looked at carefully. The first WSIS was held in December 2003 to determine key challenges brought about by the evolution of the digital media. Information and Communication Technologies (ICTs) are meant to play a great role in 'building' the 'Global Information Society'. Building this global information society is currently a key issue in the UN and influences new principles in development policies.

This raises important questions: Is the achievement of the development goals of the UN Millennium Declaration more easily achieved just by implementing more ICTs in nearly every world region? Are all ICTs equal or is the current emphasis on Internet technologies erasing the importance of radio in some countries and regions? Will knowledge, information, and communication, which 'are at the core of human progress, endeavour, and well-being' (ITU, 2003a: 1) really feed people, close the gap between the rich and the poor and solve problems where other development strategies have failed?

The WSIS Draft Action Plan lists the necessary steps to reach the global Information Society, an example being connecting all villages with the Internet by 2010. Only roughly 10 percent of the world population is connected to the Internet, and only 6 million people can use the Internet in Africa, where even the number of telephone lines is about the same as in New York city.[1] The question as to whether building the global information society will truly help the people rather than the western multinational ICTs business expansion, still remains open. Wade (2001) doubts the conclusions of the World Bank Report (2000), which states that the solution to the digital divide is to supply more ICTs.[2] Another important issue is the gap between women and men using and profiting from ICTs.

Women's access to Internet Technology is generally much lower than men's, and this is true not only for the South but also the North: 'women accounted for 38 percent of users in the United States, 25 percent in Brazil, 17 percent in Japan and South Africa, 16 percent in Russia, only 7 percent in China and a mere 4 percent in Arab States' (UNDP, 1999: 62). By June 2001, it was reported that women account for a surprisingly low 37 percent of all users in Germany, 40 percent in Brazil, 44 percent in Taiwan, and 46 percent in Mexico, whereas they have outdated men in the USA, where 52 percent of users are women' (Nielsen Net Ratings, 2001). Despite the impressive growth of Internet usage by women, they do not yet profit from new technologies as much as men do. Considering that ICTs will be pushed from many sides to support development, an important question is: How can Internet technology be designed and applied in order to improve women's lives and women's access to information, education, and independence? This chapter describes the design and implementation of an ICT tool for women in cases where these are accessible, because we believe that visionary settings and applications are needed before equal access is realized. The UN report shows, that 'when there is an enabling environment, ICTs can provide diverse avenues for women's social, political, and economic empowerment' (UN Division for the Advancement of Women, 2002: 3).

This chapter presents a way of empowering women in the North and South (who already have Internet access) by building virtual international communities which can be suitable for women to participate in and benefit from international exchange. It describes ways of building such an enabling environment for women and of transferring the relevant technological competencies. Hence the Virtual International Women's University (*vifu*) project aims at describing virtual women's communities as tools for transferring knowledge and information, international mentoring and support, and the transfer and acquisition of technological competence. This may, thus, be one way of promoting women's participation in actively designing the information society. However, the emergence of ICTs may bring even more barriers to women's access to equal resources, power, and participation. As a group, women are often in weaker positions, have less resources, and less access to technologies. Hence ICTs may even increase the existing gap between advantaged and disadvantaged groups in society. These challenges must be faced if ICTs are going to be more widely implemented and more easily accessed and used. This chapter will argue, that the specific technical, and social design of ICTs is critical for the success or failure of a certain development initiative.

Virtual Communities: A Tool for North-South Communication and Development?

Basically, a Virtual Community (VC) is a community like any other, except that it consists of digital or virtual communication, and 'meetings' between people (Rheingold, 1993) who are part of a group or community where common interests are shared, and information is exchanged. This changes the concept of communities being characterized and constrained by location. Traditionally, people belonged to place-based communities. Because a virtual community is no longer place-based, some diverse concepts emerge.

Often VCs only meet virtually. This implies, for example, that written-only communication and anonymity are some of the key concepts. New possibilities for access, control, knowledge, power, identity, and roles emerge. Usually VCs are organized rather democratically among users with common interests who start building a group identity. These communities usually are a pool of important information, a source of mutual support, and help in various aspects, that is there are learning communities, health communities, communities supporting political activities, etc. As the group meets virtually via the Internet, a specific potential for VCs is their internationality and their possibility for a diversity of its users. Barriers of class, age, location, gender, race may be (but are not always!) lower than in 'real' life.

Access, education, technological know-how, financial and other resources, and social status are not equally available to all people. In general, women have less access than men, even though great differences exist among women. Overcoming these obstacles is not an easy task as access to ICTs and online time is a huge issue. Whereas the immersion of ICTs is seen as a great opportunity for people's empowerment per se, ICTs by themselves are not going to bring about change.

To participate in such communities, women need to have Internet access, knowledge about appropriate communities, the ability to speak and write a common language (often English), time to indulge in this communication, the will to network internationally, and last but not the least, some technological knowhow. The essay acknowledges that participating in VCs is an option only for some privileged groups. However, it argues that the potential for cross-cultural and local communication, for exchange of information and mutual support, and for transfer of knowledge may make VCs interesting tools for some women to find support for both their individual lives and their wider local network. VCs may be tools to access information which otherwise would be out of reach. They have some potential to become tools for democratic and free transfer of knowledge and non-censored political information between North and South (if use and access to ICTs are given—of course the limited use of ICTs in the South implies limited participation in VCs).

Despite their interesting potential, VCs face a variety of constraints. Many international VCs are not truly international but are dominated by one region or nation, often the USA. Additionally, many VCs are male-dominated, and Balka (1993) reports that even in some public feminist groups, men make up the majority of active users. Many Internet applications do not have gender sensitive designs. Even though VCs offer the potential for democratization, they are often promoted for the economic interests of IT companies, and commercial interests of online shops.

Gender and Technology

Technology development can be seen as a social activity which is influenced by existing social structures, values, and practices. Kramarae points out that technological processes have often been studied from the vantage point of men's experiences. She challenges us to 'develop a more inclusive understanding of the social relations and ideologies of technological processes' (Kramarae, 1988: 7), and suggests that putting women at the center of analysis might help to discover new questions as well as fresh approaches to old questions.

Technology can be both a means to overcome gender concepts and to reinforce them. In her 'Cyborg Manifesto', Haraway (1991) discusses the potential of cyborg technology as a tool for both confusing and reconstructing the boundaries of gender. In many cultures, ICTs are seen as a male field, and often the development of ICTs is performed in a rather male-dominated environment. On the other hand, educated women who deal with technology may know more about technology than the average man, and women and men who are not affiliated with technology may experience similar obstacles.

While this essay focuses on 'women and VCs', it does not imply that women can be characterized as a homogenous group. As a group, women are marginalized on the Internet, yet, as individuals they differ greatly in aspects such as class, income, education, culture, location, and age, and may sometimes have more similarities with men than with one another. Therefore, it might be counterproductive to narrow it down to only one perspective from which the experiences of women with computer and communication systems can be viewed, as such a perspective may deepen polarizations and inequities rather than expose and remove them.

With this essay I do not want to specify women-only concepts, but describe a specific experience in a Project both geared towards and performed by women, which may offer insights for other situations as well. Women are often seen as promoters of change and development. Women as a group are marginalized on the Internet and in IT development. Often IT solutions are developed in a homogenous (often male-dominated) culture and hence the risk that other groups' (i.e. women's) perspectives will be forgotten and IT solutions would not be geared to their needs. The case study presented in this essay reflects the experiences of highly educated women with high aspirations who belong to privileged groups in their societies. Discussing this case, which was developed for this particular group of women, might help to discover new questions and insights which could be transferred to other projects and other target groups as well.

THE VIRTUAL INTERNATIONAL WOMEN'S UNIVERSITY (VIFU)

As shown above, Internet use is very different globally, because of which we can only talk in terms of a digital gap, rather than a 'global village'. As women and users from the global South are underrepresented on the Internet, vifu is an interesting example of a community connecting several hundred women users from more than 100 countries.

Since summer 2000, vifu has been networking 700 young students, researchers, journalists, NGO activists, artists, and others via the server www.vifu.de. Vifu is a virtual community, an electronic network, a virtual library, and a source of information and communication for women. But despite the word 'university' in its name, vifu does not offer courses or open distance learning. Vifu resulted from the International Women's University (ifu), which in 2000 offered a three-month face-to-face (f2f) postgraduate course in Germany. The 700 participants worked on global challenges around water, information, migration, city, work, and health. The work was characterized by five methods of doing research and teaching: inclusion of the gender perspective in all issues, interconnection of science and arts, interdisciplinarity, interculturality, and support via ICTs. After three months, the participants returned to their countries all over the globe, and the vifu server is an important tool for continued networking ever since.

Characterization of the vifu Virtual Community

Five years after the end of the f2f program, the vifu networks are still active. The server showed access from more than 105 countries in a one month test period and also opened up to non-ifu participants. The vifu server developed more and more as a global network of women—academically rooted, but aiming at practical changes. Its users see it as an extremely valuable medium for finding and continuing international contacts, for planning collaborative projects and activities, for transferring intercultural perspectives and communication, and for mentoring of inspiring role models.

The Participants[3]

Many of the participants are alumnae of ifu 2000 who have at least one university degree with many having higher degrees. Participants are usually students and researchers, even professors. Others are journalists, politicians, and artists. Of these, 75 percent are engaged in NGOs, while 40 percent are in more than two NGOs. Many are politically active and are organized in local communities and networks, often women's networks. This helps in transferring information from the virtual vifu network into local projects which may not be connected to the Internet, and vice versa, as information from such initiatives finds its way into the vifu network through the mediating participants.

Even though participation is often limited to those from the privileged classes in their societies, we see the flow of information via these users (as key participants) to other groups and local networks. 'Connections' thus spread out in many directions including to women without Internet access. Here the concept of 'bridging ties' is valuable. People who belong to multiple groups act as bridging ties (Wellman and Berkowitz, 1988). Kavanaugh et al. (2003) explain that when people with bridging ties use communication media, such as the Internet, they enhance their capability to educate community members, and organize, as needed, for collective action. In their empirical study they show that people with bridging ties across groups on the Internet have higher levels of community involvement, civic interest, and collective efficacy than those without such bridging ties.

The participants come from more than 100 countries: 26 percent from Asia-Pacific; 21 percent from Germany (the host country); 15 percent from sub-Saharan Africa; 11 percent from Middle and Eastern Europe; 10 percent from Western Europe; 9 percent from Latin America; 5 percent from North America; and 3 percent from North Africa and West Asia. Thus, more than 50 percent are from developing and transitional countries where access to Internet is difficult. This was and is a crucial criterion for the specific development and designing of the server.

The Technical Media on vifu

The platform was set up using mainly open source software (Linux, MySQL, Apache, php, etc.), thus reducing costs and dependence on companies. Open source software also enabled the development team to adapt the software to the specific needs of the vifu Project. The base philosophy was the implementation of efficient low-tech rather than glittery high-tech, as many users may not have access to the newest technical equipment. On the site a variety of specific mailinglists and discussion forums can be found as well as an expert directory and webpages of the many projects dealing with gender specific global issues. The main mailinglist, the students' list, in which all 700 participants were subscribed, sees an average of 3–10 mails and postings per day. Even participants who do not write their own postings, send appreciative mails to the administrators.

The use of discussion forums had its peak in the pre-ifu-phase, when those forums were the only way to get in touch with each other. In order to use such forums, users have to be online constantly for reading and writing. Since every participant received her personal vifu email address during the f2f ifu phase, email, and the mailinglists are the preferred medium for communication. These solutions offer possibilities for a quick download of information so that reading and writing can be done offline for participants with slow, expensive, and occasional Internet access. Offering every participant her individual vifu email address seemed to help overcome barriers to Internet tools as many use their vifu addresses, which can be used via both a webmailer or an (offline) mail program (via POP3 connection). Vifu users call themselves 'vifuties' and state that they would host and welcome any traveling vifutie in their house.

Vifuties wanted to develop an expert directory, as they wished to be able to find each other's contact data for future cooperation in a database. Thus, the team developed a directory according to the users' suggestions and needs. The data can be updated anytime by the users themselves. Online chat was offered in 2002. The chat is used with much pleasure by the participants. However, chat times must be appointed via the mailinglist: A specific day and time (we find 1 P.M. London Greenwich time works well) needs to be set, otherwise users find themselves alone in the chat. On these occasions users happily 'meet' each other and chat informally with a feeling of truly 'seeing' each other again.

In 2002, a content management system (Postnuke) was set online, offering members and newcomers the possibility to publish information on the WWW without any knowledge of webdesign or html. The system is called 'information oasis'. One of the reasons for developing this system was the need to be able to present platform activities to interested parties and possible sponsors, as the mailinglist activities were invisible to the public. However, active acceptance of the information oasis is not yet very high, despite its potential.

In 2002, a virtual library was also developed where diverse files on global gender issues can be found, such as websites, articles, films, radio shows, and artwork, mainly related to the topics 'water' and 'information'. Participants can use the library for online publication of their own papers and products.

POLITICAL AND SOCIAL DYNAMICS OF ONLINE NETWORKING

Analysis of the current active vifu networks (www.vifu.de/network/) shows that they are used for conference and event announcements; searches for experts (to help in certain topics and for conferences, book publications, presentations, translations); international job announcements; political information and information control; founding of NGOs; funding information; international cooperation; collaborative publications; collective action and mentoring. Participants describe the value of the vifu community in emails sent to the development team or to the students mailinglist:

Vifu is the sun of our every day! (Participant from Morocco)

What VIFU has done is the empowerment of women through easy access to information. More importantly, it has engendered global solidarity in strengthening personal relationship among activists, academics, and change agents the world over. I continue staying connected with human rights lawyers in Africa, with educators in Latin America, with activists and social workers in Asia—all these were possible because VIFU was the technological conduit where life-relationships are nurtured and kept alive.

In a few days I will be in Ghana to connect with our sisters S. (human rights lawyer from Sierra Leone), M. (former member of parliament in Ghana) and S. (academic and activist from Bangladesh) [names coded by author]. Our work brings us to a common place at a common time. VIFU has made possible that these encounters lead to countless possibilities where we can make a difference in the lives of other women. (Participant from Philippines/Germany)

These quotes show the community spirit of the participants and illustrate their motivation for participation.[4] The most important element of the virtual community is the non-specific asynchronous student mailinglist. The diversity of the discussed topics inspires the participants to develop new ideas which may lead into collaborative activities. The following three case studies reflect the dynamics of these activities and may illustrate the synergies and the interdependence of technical and social processes, and procedures in the VC.

Case Study I: VEINS—Virtual Encounters in North and South Politics

Many ideas and activities are born in the student mailinglist. The mixture of topics and information is highly appreciated by participants who do not want it organized into separate topic-specific media. They expressed that the mix of personal and professional, of informal and official information, and communication is what makes the mailinglist and network attractive.

When for example—during the West Asian Intifada and after months of reports in newspapers and on TV—a participant from Palestine described her personal situation after Israeli soldiers came into her house and threatened her and her daughter, the shocked community brainstormed about possibilities for action. They sent out articles to be published in national newspapers, started phone calls to embassies, and created an online petition. They decided to organize a virtual conference to have a better understanding of the historical background in West Asia and the principles of peace and conflict in society. The participants designed a call for papers which was sent out internationally, decided on a code of conduct, and determined chairs and moderators. The name of the conference forum was discussed and invented by the users: VEINS—Virtual Encounters in North and South Politics. VEINS characterizes the structure of the vifu netcommunity itself, which is seen as a channel (or vein) for an intercultural flow of academic as well as more 'bloody' issues. The title of the first conference in May 2002 was: 'War, Peace and Conflict in Civil Societies: The Case of Palestine'. Corresponding to the wishes of the community, the conference platform was designed by the vifu development team in Germany. The objectives were:

- Use of Open-Source Software.
- Use of only few and previously introduced services in order to reduce technical barriers to participation.
- Good (= used and accepted) explanations and help functionality.
- Participation of a wider public, thus opening the vifu community.
- Possibility of anonymous participation due to the 'hot' issue and to reduce barriers to participation.
- Possibility of individual deletion of one's own postings.
- Possibility for chair person to delete postings which contradict the code of conduct.
- Possibility of trying out the technology before presenting one's own posting to the public by installing a 'test' forum next to the 'conference' forum.
- Offering a discussion room, a room for position papers, an information board for a collection of relevant articles and webpages, and an informal Café-room.

The conference proceeded for three weeks and concluded with more than 100 postings and a collection of more than 30 articles and webpages on the information board (http://www.vifu.de/network/conference.html). It provided much information on a conflict that has global relevance and provided diverse view-points from different countries which usually are not available in one's own national media.[5] It was interesting, however, that some users who had previously been very active in the closed mailing-list, remained rather silent in the virtual conference, or continued writing comments to the mailinglist but not in the public discussion forums. This could be due to three reasons: (*a*) the greater publicity of such a virtual conference without knowing exactly who the public is; (*b*) the higher technical, financial, and timely effort of posting digital information on a website; and (*c*) the possibility of being found with one's name and (critical) opinion via search engines.

Balka (1993) finds in her studies on women's online behavior in several communities, that many women prefer reading postings to writing their own postings. However, these 'peripheral' members may be an important group of participants in a community, as vifuties describe. For example, a participant from Germany wrote:

> If I do not always participate in the debates, it does not mean that I am not interested in your mails. I am here, I am reading, and I am thinking about the things you say. There are many times when I had wanted to speak up on a certain topic but never found the time. But reading your letters and thinking about them made me an invisible part of the discussion and helped me to reinforce or change my own mind.

Case Study II: One For All, All For One

Another impressive example of virtually-initiated real action started even before the f2f phase. Ifu did not limit its web presence to a static presentation of program information but also technically enabled interaction with and among users and potential ifu participants from the first day. Discussion forums were provided for activity and communication. Virtual communication among the participants started around three months before the f2f phase. When it became clear that a virtual participant from South Africa would not be able to participate in the f2f phase in Germany, the other participants—all strangers—brainstormed ways to realize her physical participation. The community was created. What had started out as some loose communication among women now became—enabled by the adequate technical support—a community of action.

The idea to pledge money virtually was born. When sufficient money was pledged, a German participant opened a bank account where money was transferred, and communication was started with the German embassy in South Africa to speed up visa processing. And the virtual participant, who started such a collaborative action based on trust and commitment, was thus able to participate physically in Germany and speak at the official opening ceremony. This success intensified the community spirit of both the virtual and the entire f2f community members.

Case Study III: WINS—Women's International
Network of Sustainability

During the last days of ifu, the idea to form an international NGO
was born. Communication on this issue was partly supported via
the vifu server, and after some time the Women's International
Network for Sustainability (WINS) was formed and officially
registered. WINS (www.wins.at) aims to support sustainable
development of local communities and their environments from
a gender perspective. As all the WINS members knew each other
from ifu 2000 and could stay in touch with each other via vifu, a
high level of trust and competence could be expected from the
members. Many of them were engaged in developing their local
communities and via the WINS network fundraising, public
relations, knowledge transfer, etc. could be improved.

A participant from India was engaged in a project to improve
drinking water conditions in villages in the north Indian desert.
She set up a five-year project with the aim of improving efficient
water and well use, improving women's education, and empowering women who could then claim access to the village council
sessions. Funding for this project was needed. Information about
the project spread to the online and offline networks. An Austrian
member of the WINS network, who had connections to foundations, and government agencies in Austria, learned that these
institutions were obliged to spend some development aid funds
to so-called 'gender equality' projects. She informed them about
the Indian project and they agreed to finance the project's first
year.

These three examples are all based on trust, community spirit,
collective action, and computer-mediated communication (CMC).
In case study I, the personal description of a political situation
led to an increase in interest for information and to a process of
democratic political activity. By using an adapted platform for this
objective, participants acquired technical skills at the same time.
In the other two case studies, information from one participant
led to an increased support of finances and organization, case II
on an individual basis and case III on a broader basis, using other
non-technical networks.

All the case studies illustrate how the mere ability to inform
one another can lead into action and support, sometimes even

without a huge effort. They show how the existence of a network provides the possibility of directing the flow of information, energy, and finances. Without ICTs, without the virtual community, none of these collective activities could have happened. But a VC does not simply happen, as the ways of designing these technical and social processes are relevant to how it functions effectively.

Principles and Guidelines of Server Development

The server development was started in 1998 by Prof. Heidi Schelhowe and Barbara Schelkle at the Humboldt University, Berlin.[6] The second development phase started in 2002 and was performed under the guidance of Prof. Schelhowe at the University of Bremen.[7] The server was developed socially and technically by an all-women team according to the following principles:

- Participation of users in the process of server development.
- Parallel strengthening of technological curiosity and competence.
- Furthering of the users' community spirit.
- Constant requests for users' feedback, suggestions, and ideas.

The development team considers these principles crucial for designing successful and sustainable VCs especially for people who are not seduced into using technology by the mere fact that it is readily accessible. All new developments were constructed with the perspective of sustainability even after the funding for the server disappears. This led to a process of searching for development solutions that would enable the users themselves to execute the necessary tasks of continuation in server administration and the maintenance of its contents.

A technology deterministic tradition has been dominating research in the field of CMC (Baym, 1995). In current research, if and how user activity can be influenced and raised by the kind of technical design and structure offered is still an open and interesting question. Nancy Baym's (1998) model of 'the emergence of online community' emphasizes the complex interplay between the participants, the context, and the technology. She identifies five pre-existing structures of online communities: external context, temporal structure, system infrastructure, group purpose, and participant characteristics. These had to be considered when developing the vifu server and were of great help in understanding the activities on the server. Much of the server development was inspired by Jenny Preece (2000) who points out the critical inter-dependence of social and technical issues in designing online com-munities, and gives valuable guidelines on designing usability which focuses on human-computer interaction, and planning soci-ability which focuses on social interaction.

Our understanding is that design and structure can influence users' activity, but even more weight is given to the ways of the technological development _procedures_. We believe that a cooper-ative and transparent process of technology development with the continuing possibility of user-developer interaction helps to further not only users' activity but also their loyalty and bond to the platform and virtual community. At the same time, techno-logical understanding and skills can be furthered. The principle for this procedure is to transmit the notion of a technology that is alterable and can be adapted to the people as opposed to the notion of dumb users who do not understand the logic of 'intelligent' technology. 'Make the server your own' characterizes this open and transparent collaborative procedure.

This process can be illustrated by the following example: At some point, the development team saw the need to make the com-munities' activities visible on the server in order to attract funding and sponsors. The team came up with an additional system (Postnuke) that offered communication spaces structured in certain topics, such as 'Jobs', 'ICT', 'Water', 'Postcards', etc. Users did not use them as much as the unspecific general mailinglist and discussed the pros and cons of this structure. From their comments it became obvious, that what they liked about their community was the broad variety of messages. Personal greetings and comments; requests for accommodation while attending a conference; and descriptions of a personal situation in Palestine led to more communication on these issues which, in some cases, inspired the creation of a virtual conference or a sensitive exchange on religious fundamentalism. If the structure of technology forced people to sort their initial posting/comments into certain topics, much of these postings would have never been written. One of the participants expressed the need to keep communication and people in a context and her rejection of communication via structured topics in a clear and poetic way:

> Although I do understand the cons of unwieldy Inboxes and 'wasting time', to me, a major part of the problem has always been that women are supposed to fit in boxes. That women are put into cupboards. Drawers. Kitchens. Pedestals. Small spaces. Small shoes. Short skirts. Inside curtains. The problem with 'everything in its place' is that issues get compartmentalized and distanced from each other to the extent that we learn only about the boxes that apply to us—we lived this out at the physical site of IFU in Germany.... Me, I do like all the news upfront—otherwise I might miss finding out important information. (Taina ... in the box of Canada)

The vifu development process of 'Make the server your own' can be characterized by Baym's (1998) notion of the complex interplay between participants, the context, and the technology and Preece's (2000) notion of the interdependence of the social and technical issues, and by extending these notions with the idea of a constant emphasis on interaction between users and developers. It is possible that this process has influence on the kind of communication happening on the server. Users are constantly asking questions, leading to sharing of technical information. When designing new functionalities, much effort was spent on explaining this well, with the objective of transferring technical competence, and raising curiosity and interest in these new technologies. The beneficial side effects are that users take on responsibility for the server. Users recommend participating in awards and other competitions, express their concern about the end of funding, and take on some administrative tasks.

The way the vifu community functions can be explained partly by Wenger's (1998) description of 'community of practice'. Key issues for Wenger and the vifu community are learning, identity, and meaning. One of the objectives of the server development was to make the use of the server meaningful. Users produce meaning by exchanging their ideas and thoughts virtually with one another. Many users describe how the vifu communication makes them aware of certain issues, how it makes them sit and think. Because of the strong sense of identity, the meaning produced via vifu communication seems to have special weight. Producing an identity was an objective of both the f2f ifu and the virtual environment. The vifu users call themselves 'vifuties' and hereby express their new identity and also their identification with the server itself. We assume that building this identity is one of the main reasons for vifu's success. Learning takes place in many activities, sometimes as intended learning (i.e. the virtual conference), and sometimes unintentionally (i.e. through discussions on the list, by learning technological skills due to the wish to participate in the community).

> I love to receive these mails 'automatically'—and hence lots of food for thought, a sense of being connected even if not always 'visible' on the list myself. (Participant M.F. on the student mailing list, 31 October 2002)

> As a woman from the global south with the so called limited Internet access, I value all the information and discussions that go on this list. I may not be a regular contributor, but I regard the list as my window to the world. (Participant L.E., 31 October 2002)

Designing International Virtual Communities for Women

Due to the lack of resources, the relevance, and practical advantage of Internet use must be clear and obvious before women invest their time and money in using it (Green and Trevor-Deutsch, 2002). The important question is thus: How to design relevant Internet offers and enabling environments in order to let women profit from the options and potentials of international information exchange through the Internet?

VCs help women to use and benefit from Internet applications much more than when they feel isolated in the use of the Internet and technology (even better if they are additionally supported by local f2f communities). For the design of such applications, it is important to keep in mind the diverse technical infrastructure in different regions. In some regions the accessible technical equipment necessary for Internet use may not be of the highest technical standard. This may mean the reduction of technical high-end features and implementation of efficient low-tech rather than glittery high-tech.

Usability and easy-to-find technical support are highly important as many users may not have enormous technical skills. Technical support should be as personal as possible. For example, a support aid does not have to be an impersonal email address like 'support@webmaster.com' but can be a friendly sentence like: 'If you need help with any task or have questions and ideas, please contact Ms. <Name> (including a photo if possible) under the following email address: <name>@vifu.de'.

Help buttons are hardly clicked; it seems that women would rather ask a person than try out help buttons. However, when the vifu support person sends back a friendly informative email suggesting a specific help link, then the help instructions are read and used. A well designed platform offers the possibility of raising users' interest and curiosity in technological issues. And thus the use of the platform may lead to an increase in a woman's technological skills. The beneficial strategies of raising these skills are described as follows.

The availability of a simple community tool, such as a mailinglist, offers the possibility of coming back to the community with questions. The introduction of a new tool or technology once in a while —when a new topic comes up through users—can raise curiosity and technical skills. It seems necessary to introduce new tools only when a new issue or task comes up, and not just because of developers' fascination for a new fancy tool. This tool, with instructions, will first be introduced in the mailinglist. This procedure combines technical and social aspects of learning and acquiring technological skills. Every new tool requires a 'social initiation', determining the relevance and benefit of a tool for a certain context for instance, in the vifu mailinglist, the issue of forming an alumni association came up. For brainstorming ideas on this issue, the development team suggested a certain date to discuss using the chat tool. The chat tool had existed on the server before but was hardly used. When participants agreed, how-to-use-chat instructions were sent to the mailinglist. During the determined appointment, around 30 participants used the chat, with many of them sending how-to questions to the mailinglist when something did not work for them. Many participants said that they had never used a chat tool in their life before and asked for another round!

In the next chat round, some participants were appointed moderators, administrators, and instructors. This again helped to spread technological skills and confidence and unburdened the development team in the process. In vifu, due to technical requirements (and diverse software components), it was necessary to install several different user registration processes for the expert directory/webmail access, the chat, the information oasis. This proved to be a huge barrier for many participants. If registration is needed then only one registration should be needed.

A content management system can provide opportunity and space for women to offer their own content and publish on the WWW without necessarily needing technological knowhow on webdesign or HTML. The vifu Information Oasis offers space to other groups and networks for opening new topics on their own. However, it seems that mailinglists may be a more convenient tool for some women to spread their information.

The procedures of the technological design should be given more attention. It is certainly not always possible to let (all?) users participate in the design and development process. However, transparency and clear communication of new steps and ideas between users and developers can help find out users' needs, problems, and requests. This procedure may also help raise users' loyalty to the platform and their sense of belonging to the community.

The sustainability of a web project and virtual community is an important issue. Many web projects die once their funding ends. To ensure sustainability for the vifu server, community, and network even after funding for server development ends, the development team started handing over more and more administrative rights to users. Some women were responsible for password changes, others for new registrations, someone else administered the information oasis and organized content, someone else keyed in data into the virtual library, etc. As of January 2005, the server and the community are still well, even though funding ended in December 2002. However, after a severe hacking attack in November 2003, some services were destroyed and had to be closed. This led to many questions and requests from the participants who asked for services to be resumed. They expressed their appreciation when the server returned online after a short break for repairs showing their strong identification with the vifu community.

Conclusions:
Potentials of Building Virtual Communities for Women

Despite the growth in the number of Internet users, issues of inclusion and exclusion remain important. Some of the main reasons, especially for women, are lack of resources and Internet access, lack of relevance, lack of an enabling environment, and technological competence.

Because of uneven global development, Internet Technology can exacerbate the gap between North and South, but at the same time, can be applied to help overcome barriers. Virtual international women's communities may be meaningful tools for some women to benefit from the Internet and from international exchange. They may offer a space for providing relevant content and communication as well as offer an environment for raising technological competences. Such communities should be designed in a way that makes them attractive for women to join, otherwise they are not a supporting 'technology' for gaining access to information and participation, but an additional excluding barrier. Such a design includes both technical and social aspects.

The designers of virtual communities should offer possibilities for users to extend their skills and participate in the designing and development processes. These users (usually belonging to the better educated classes) may become multipliers of the information exchanged via the community and transfer such information and technology skills into local networks, especially when they act to bridge ties and are members of several communities. Thus, these communities may become places of uncensored intercultural communication and provide a space for informal support, and knowledge exchange.

Such a network proves to be a valuable resource to women and their networks in other countries, and to an increase in tacit knowledge which cannot be found in books or in the mainstream media. The procedures and social processes of designing such networks and technology should be given attention to make them more user-oriented and gender sensitive. Changing the perception of ICT as a fixed and stiff technical product into a process of user-developer interaction resulting in tools and services that reflect this process, may be a way to raise more women's interest in technology.

NOTES

1. More alarming information (UNDP, 1999: 62):

   Thailand has more cellular phones than the whole of Africa. There are more Internet hosts in Bulgaria than in Sub-Saharan Africa (excluding South Africa). The United States has more computers than the rest of the world combined, and more computers per capita than any other country. Just 55 countries account for 99 percent of global spending on information technology. In several African countries average monthly Internet connection and use costs run as high as US$100—compared with US$10 in the United States. African users had an income seven times the national average, and 90 percent of users in Latin America came from upper-income groups. Buying a computer would cost the average Bangladeshi more than eight years' income, compared with just one month's wage for the average American.

2. A useful overview on current resources on ICT and Development can be found in Cummings 2002.
3. All information about participants taken from the official ifu evaluation: Metz-Göckel (2002).
4. More examples can be found on the vifu information oasis under 'loveletters', http://kitkat.informatik.uni-bremen.de/vifu/Phoenix/html/
5. Diverse international viewpoints were also exchanged after the attacks on the US World Trade Center in 2001. Women from Bangladesh expressed how mainstream media news related demonstrations falsely to Muslim fundamentalism by showing a photo of (some) demonstrators leaving a mosque. A huge international friendly debate started and it became clear how much prejudices on Islam are transported via the Western media and how difficult they are to overcome even among well educated friends. And after US president Bush declared the 'axis of evil', South Korean participants explained how Bush's accusation of North Korea influences politics in South Korea and even in Asia.
6. See Kreutzner et al., 2002 about the guiding principles of user orientation, participation and interactivity.
7. See Büschenfeldt et al., 2003 about the community and library development.

REFERENCES

Balka, Ellen. (1993) 'Women's Access to Online Discussions about Feminism', *The Electronic Journal of Communication*, 3(1), http://www.mith2.umd.edu/WomensStudies/Computing/Articles+Research Papers/online-access-feminism.

Baym, Nancy. (1995) 'The Emergence of Community in Computer Mediated Communication', in Jones, S.G. (ed.), *Cyber Society: Computer-mediated Community and Communication*, Sage Publications, Thousand Oaks, CA, pp. 138–63.

Baym, Nancy. (1998) 'The Emergence of Online Community,' in Jones, S.G. (ed.), *Cyber Society 2.0: Revisiting Computer-Mediated Communication and Community*. Sage Publications, Thousand Oaks, CA, pp. 35–68.

Büschenfeldt, Maika, Plutat, B., Schelhowe, Heidi and Zorn, Isabel. (2003) 'Information Architecture and Networks at vifu: Virtual International Women's University: Continuation of the Project in 2002', in Kreutzner, G. and Schelhowe, H. (eds), *Agents of Change: Virtuality, Knowledge, and the Challenge to Traditional Academia*, Opladen, Leske + Budrich, pp. 161–77.

Cummings, Sarah. (2002) 'Reader: Information and Communication Technologies in Development', Prepared for the conference 'Global e-quality: Rethinking ICTs in Africa, Asia and Latin America' held on 25–27 March 2002 in Heerlen/ Maastricht, The Netherlands, Produced by Royal Tropical Institute KIT, Amsterdam (Available at http://www.infonomics.nl/globalequality/papers/ Reader.pdf).

Green, Lyndsay and Trevor-Deutsch, Lawry. (2002) 'Women and ICTs for Open and Distance Learning: Some Experiences and Strategies from the Commonwealth', The Commonwealth of Learning, http://www.col.org/wdd/Women% 20and%20ICTs.pdf.

Haraway, Donna J. (1991) *Simians, Cyborgs, and Women: The Reinvention of Nature*, Routledge, New York.

International Telecommunication Union. (2003a) 'World Summit on Information Society Declaration of Principles', Draft May 2002, WSIS/PCIP/DT/1(Rev.1)-E, http://www.itu.int/wsis/documents/doc_multi.asp?lang=en&id=624 l 626.

———. (2003b) 'World Summit on Information Society Action Plan', Draft May 2002, WSIS/PC-2/DT/3-E, http://www.itu.int/wsis/documents/doc_ multi.asp?lang=en&id=624 l 626.

Kavanaugh, Andrea, Resse, Debbie Denise, Carrol, John, and Rosson, Mary Beth. (2003) 'Weak Ties in Networked Communities', in Huysman, M. and Wulf, V. (eds), *Communities and Technologies: Proceedings of the First International Conference on Communities and Technologies*, C&T 2003, Kluwer Academic Publishers, Dordrecht, Boston, London, pp. 265–86.

Kramarae, Cheris (ed.). (1988) 'Technology and Women's Voices: Keeping in Touch', in Kramarae, Cheris (ed.), *Technology and Women's Voices*, Routledge, New York, pp. 98–115.

Kreutzner, Gabriele, Schelhowe, Heidi, and Schelkle, Barbara. (2002) Nutzerinnenorientierung, Partizipation und Interaktion als Leitprinzipien: Die virtuelle Internationale Frauenuniversität (vifu) (User Orientation, Participation, and Interaction as Guiding Principles: The Virtual International Women's University), in Neusel, A. and Poppenhusen, M. (eds), *Universität neu denken (Thinking University Anew)*, Leske und Budrich, Opladen, pp. 231–43.

Metz-Göckel, Sigrid (ed.). (2002) *Lehren und Lernen an der Internationalen Frauenuniversität* (Teaching and Learning at the International Women's University), Leske und Budrich, Opladen.

Preece, Jenny. (2000) *Online Communities: Designing Usability, Supporting Sociability*, John Wiley & Sons, Chichester.

Rheingold, Howard. (1993): *The Virtual Community: Homesteading on the Electronic Frontier*, Harper Perennial, New York.

UN Division for the Advancement of Women. (2002) 'Information and Communication Technologies and their Impact On and Use as an Instrument for the Advancement and Empowerment of Women', Report of the Expert Group Meeting, EGM/ICT/2002/Report, http://www.un.org/womenwatch/daw/egm/ict2002/reports/EGMFinalReport.pdf.

UNDP. (1999) *Human Development Report 1999*, UNDP, New York, http://hdr.undp.org/reports/global/1999/en/.

Wade, Robert. (2001) 'How to Harness Information and Communication Technologies (ICT) for Wealth Creation in Developing Countries, and What Donors Can Do to Help. Or, When are Development Fads Beneficial?' (Draft document).

Wellman, Barry and Lerkowitz, S.D. (eds). (1988) *Social Structures: A Network Approach*, Cambridge University Press, New York.

Wenger, Etienne. (1998) *Communities of Practice: Learning, Meaning, and Identity*, Cambridge University Press, Cambridge, UK and New York.

World Bank Global Information and Communication Technologies Department. (2000), 'The Networking Revolution: Opportunities and Challenges for Developing Countries', http://www.infodev.org/library/WorkingPapers/NetworkingRevolution.pdf.

PART III

The Politics and Policies of Gender and ICTs

GENDER-NET: A POLITICAL GOAL OF COMMUNICATION TECHNOLOGIES

DORA INÉS MUNÉVAR M. AND JUAN ABURTO ARRIETA

Gender inequalities prevent women from freely accessing the resources available for the care and the conservation of health; the exercise of reproductive rights; permanence in the education system; obtaining and possession of housing, employment, finances, wealth, and technology; in short, the benefit of material conditions of life that guarantee their active and productive participation in society. This discrimination determines women's exclusion, and women constitute the poorest people in every society and social estate. These circumstances constitute an almost insurmountable impediment to the enjoyment of all kinds of resources, among them technological ones, and in particular, communication technologies.

Science and Technology Studies of European origin are oriented by the intention to extend the reach and the pretensions of traditional sociology. Studies of science, technology, and society of North American origin have a more humanist and pragmatic vision. These two perspectives differ in regard to the facets of the social dimension. The first adopts the assumption of social conditioners as factors that contribute to the genesis and acceptance of scientific-technological products. The second is expressed in the social consequences of science and technology; that is, in the ways in which they affect forms of life, and social organization. As a result, not only is the system of social organization the object of sociological analysis, it is also the subject of scientific investigation.

Based on these considerations, we introduce the configuration that we call here, Gender-Net, as a decisive tool to promote the quality of life of women using human communicative processes that are communitarian in scope, and employing the socio-cultural, and political goais derived from this tool. In principle, this intention forces us to think about the power relations unfolded by the Internet as a technological product and, simultaneously, technological inputs geared to achieving gender empowerment goals. In the same sense, gender and technology articulate as components of social processes, whose foundations interrelate closely until they constitute a confrontation that takes place in cyberspace. It is a situation where the production and consumption of circulating technological products in the network continues till it turns into a network of power. The woven patterns of this network can be examined as symbols; as cyber symbols, both cultural, and political. We maintain that it is possible to make use of the Internet to contribute to necessary social change and interrogate the digital divide, potential and real, through tools of communication technology, like Gender-Net.

Power of Symbols and Cyber Symbols

The symbolic dimension of technological resources has been explored from a gender perspective through the ways that these resources contribute to maintaining women and men in their culturally constructed places. Greater emphasis is usually placed on analyzing the production and consumption of technology, specially with regard to the power it wields in daily life since, 'as a symbol, technology is still setting the joint between masculinity, control, and dominion' (Lie, 1991 cited in Cockburn, 1992: 96). In other words, women, rendered invisible throughout history, have remained and seem destined to remain in anonymity most of their lives, in the different fields of family, school, university, science, and technology. By their historical and cultural position, men keep their essential image of hunters, who, in search of their prey, remain on the lookout for further opportunities. The scheme is no different with the Internet.

Feminist critiques of science and technology have denounced androcentric characteristics in the production of scientific knowledge and its technological applications. Meanwhile, they have emphasized that women in science use different ways to know and discover knowledge. The work of feminists has been important in reformulating the sociological nature of science and technology.

Thus, in the first place, feminism rejects the image of science as an objective and neutral enterprise. There are today, multiple studies identifying sexism and biases generated in scientific processes. Notable among them, are those which, from a socio-cultural perspective, have been centered in the analysis of interests and attitudes necessary to make science and produce technologies. In addition, there are those, that have questioned personality features, ways of thought and perception, self-confidence levels, learning strategies, cognitive styles, and sexual stereotypes in science, all subjects that can be influenced by the confrontation between intellectual stereotypes that benefit men, but degrade the intellectual capacity of women.

A politicized science that validates gender-biased views of the nature/culture dichotomy has justified and perpetuated the social, legal, and political inequality of women. The thread of a repeated deterministic argument has served to render the role of women throughout history suspect; all the more so, given the virtual absence of women in science and technology jobs and as producers and users of the Internet. Gender conditioning seriously affects the development and diffusion of technology and, therefore, improvement in the quality of life; yet another reason to study this situation in some detail so as to find necessary socio-political solutions.

In this sense, the transformation of social relations derived from the use of technological resources like the Internet invites a reframing within the scope of the 'Information Society.' We must approach it like a symbolic universe and consider the diversity of protagonists, the multiplicity of scenes, and the wealth of values, images, and words told and written. This introduces us to the Internet as a tool designed to register, process, and reproduce individual and collective memory. Thus, we define an alternate citizenship on the Internet network as an expression of the human condition.

An interesting feature of the Internet and 'cyberspace' is their evoking of the human, social, and personal condition: both the best and the worst of humanity is or will be on the Internet, as well as the relations it makes possible, all of which is transformed through anonymity. We can now chat with unknown people and develop with ease, an intense and deep relation, independent of social conditions or conventions like sex, sexual preference, origin, age, economic position, educational background, or geographic location. No other mass media has offered this facility of contact between people and groups before. For this reason, it is very easy to fall into the trap of assuming that the Internet is already a worldwide mass media, a universal one, as universal as its citizenship despite its excluding origins. The universality of the notion itself is questionable. According to the numbers, the occasional and permanent *Netizens* (Internet citizens), add up to about 800 million. If we match this number with the world population (in December 2004 humanity reached 6.4 billion), it appears that less than 13 out of 100 people have access to the Internet. This small and extremely privileged group of people has the facility to communicate directly among themselves, without intermediaries or delays. If to this limitation, we add others like language, interests, tastes, preferences, social roles, and access to technological resources, we come to the conclusion that we are as alone as on the Internet as in the real world.

It is in this peculiar falsification—properly hidden by interested sectors—that the danger lies.[1] Only a few people have the power to impose on the Internet, their vision, their conception of the cultural order, and the dimensions of the relations between human beings. This way, they can offer—and hide—the information that best serves their purpose.

COMMUNICATION TECHNOLOGIES AS A GENDER ISSUE

The regulation of different aspects of life by an assembly of institutions—the school, the church, military service, business, political parties, the family, science—and its control over technological resources is maintained through certain political traditions rooted in patriarchy. In this context, the political product of rational actions and a rational political order—a necessary condition for the exercise of individual self-determination under liberal models of democracy—depend on innumerable exclusions, a significant one being gender. The visible result is that those women and men who appear to be subjects are in fact considered objects of power: they are divided into white and non-white, heterosexual and non-heterosexual, adult and non-adult, rich and poor, all fighting for group affirmation. Thus, institutional structures have remained in place to assure the unequal participation of women and men in social, economic, political, and religious spheres. Their ways of regulation have become naturalized and act as sources of power to maintain unequal gender relations. Recognizing and analyzing the central position of gender in social life and technological products is the departure point for problematizing the formulation of science and technology policies. This, therefore, is also the dimension underlying the political goals of the tool that we have termed Gender-Net.

Any system that generalizes the masculine dominion—with special weight attached to technological production—goes beyond the limits of human performance, and does so, based on the relational component that crosses and extends human life: power. Therefore, its analysis demands attention to every action performed by both women and men. In this regard, we can reconsider the words of Bebel, in his book *Women and Socialism* (1879), to illustrate the patriarchal reaction against the political participation of women after the French Revolution: 'competition, hunting, agriculture, politics, efforts of all types, are privileges of man; there is left for woman the care of children, domestic work, the sweet restlessness of maternity. Impudent women, why do you want to become men—gender is not yet enough divided? What else do you need? You should remain as you are in the name of Nature instead of looking for the dangers of so stormy a life. Be happy making us forget you all'. Today, this view of gender roles can be applied to the use of communication technologies.

Transferring this perspective to the Internet represents the extension of the male hunting territory, one which has no imaginable limit: his prey are people, information, contacts, communication, services from and towards everybody. The small Internet elite has served the common interests of few and neglected the majority. It has simplified interrelations, the interchange of information, thoughts, and opinions among them, as well as the quick agreements, the coinciding of objectives and purposes, the efforts to coordinate (synergy), to succeed in common results that benefit members of 'the virtual' elite communities. The Internet not only guarantees communication between interested people, but also the free flow of thought, with the real possibility of reaching more people. The illusion of the efforts of massive, instantaneous communication at the lowest possible cost was never more promising;

and it shapes a new reality which needs to be questioned from a gender perspective.

So far, questioning development in terms of power, gender, technology, political interests, exploitation, decision making, and the sources of financing has been allowed only as a variable in social studies dealing with the production and consumption of technological resources. This tendency is explained by the threads which 'determine [that only] masculine interests have influence in certain technological options' (Cockburn, 1992: 99). These masculine interests have been significant in defining the symbolic uses of communication technologies, as well as the symbolic expansion of the Internet.

Symbolic Uses of Communication Technologies

In a symbolic sense, the authority that regulates the presence of people interested in communicating by cyberspace, anchored in instantaneity and simultaneity, is a way to dominate greater space. A factor limiting communication through the Internet belongs to the cultural realm: local expressions, signs, and symbols may not mean exactly the same thing for people from different cultures. In fact, the risk is that the message conveyed might be the opposite of that which was intended. Another aspect that affects most relations of power comes from its symbolic effects in social life. This aspect—invisible but recognized as legitimate—makes possible cultural interchange founded on the shared belief that the network offers all sorts of products, goods, and services. Its effectiveness depends on certain forms of knowledge circulating between those who access the tool, that is, of the ways in which each person shares the legitimacy of the power that unfolds with the technology and its social, and personal reach. Power also determines the freedom of communication on the Internet. It is a communication system threatened by its bad use and abuse.

We have to be conscious that the principles governing technological production pass through discovery and social construction. Discovery, taken as a process of mobilization of support among rival ideas, shows its relation to the social basis of technology so that 'they are apt for sociological analysis, especially design and technical content' (ibid.: 98). This implies, first of all, that after discovery, we have to 'examine kindly to what extent the logic of this expansive dominion not only affects other groups, but, in the first place, the internal relations of the group of women and men that puts them in practice, the set of private and public relations as well as the contradictions between women and men of the dominant groups and women and men excluded from participation in the benefits' (Moreno, 1996: 99). One has to remember that social interests—essentially lucrative—appear as a motivation for developing scientific knowledge. As a symbolic expression, these interests include not only the guidelines for financing scientific development and technological projects, but also the definition and execution of science and technology policies, as follows:

- Cognitive interests prioritize measurements in which, knowledge is considered to have its structural source in innovations; it is a fundamental aspect of scientific development.
- Ethical and political interests are present to activate the direction and control of science, as well as its reach, and limits.
- Technological interests tied to the effects of science as public property contribute to economic productivity and industrial applications.
- Economic and profit interests decisively determine the course and direction of the use and advantage of communication technologies.

However, all societies have ways of adapting to technological changes, although it is also true that their stratification levels determine this to a large extent. In particular, the production and the consumption of technological resources transform society and its people, encouraging social change that stems from this technological change, as well as the need to respond to new demands that result from this change. In the same way, technological change creates mechanisms of extended reproduction, promotes the division of labor, and increases the number of specialists in support of the improvement of labor productivity. If this increased productivity derives from women—specially from women conscious of its potential, contributions, innovations and lasting social, cultural, political, and economic effects—it can decisively contribute to extending the critical mass of women with the capability, resources, and will to change gender relations. This comes within the scope of a more just society, based on an equitable distribution of power in all its modalities as a source of common benefit.

SYMBOLIC EXPANSION OF THE INTERNET

Several key studies dealing with the advances and diffusion of the Internet highlight the sexist and undemocratic nature of cyber symbols in terms of democracy, citizenship, knowledge, information, and empowerment (Berman and Weitzner, 1997; Buchstein, 1997; Gardinali, 1996; Gousgounis, 1998; Katz, 1997; Rodota, 1995; Spender, 1997; Street, 1997):

The Symbols of Democracy: In Western culture, the ideological construction of democracy lies in the preoccupation to define what are women and men, as well as in demarcating who can participate in the public realm and how. This is a premise that underpins the origin of the modern State. The notion of selective citizenship is built. The contents of words, contemporary institutions, and objective conditions, are a political-conceptual configuration destined to exert a determining weight in European history: citizenship is based on a direct relation between the particularity of the individual and the majority of the universal (humanity) (Bonacchi, 1995: 41). This conception shaped the logic of social law, incorporating asymmetric relations and defining the construction of ideas and values within which certain oppositions—by themselves arbitrary—are reflected, justifying exclusions and inclusions.

The Citizenship Symbols: As a result of the previous symbols, the modern concept of citizenship constructed over the last two centuries, has based itself on an expulsion of the feminine element. This concept not only obviates the feminine element at the constituent moments, but is defined and constructed in direct opposition to it; on the other hand, it serves to affirm the identity of a masculine subject. Once released from the will of the old regime, the subject tries new definitions and relations for himself at the moment in which fresh roles in the social and political field are to be defined (cf. Bonacchi and Groppi, 1995). The role assigned to the feminine reference in this context resulted in the women being deprived of their individuality in contrast to masculine citizens. This situation originated processes of negotiation and renegotiation of women's rights with their bases in the dynamics of interdependences that characterize relations between specific subjects within the familial nucleus and, through them, in the social assembly.

The Knowledge Symbols: Conscious of their real situation (which is rooted in culture), women set out to construct a feminist epistemology which would help bridge the gap between social and natural sciences, in an attempt to create an alternate vision of science. In other words, they tried to place science in the service of knowledge (cognitive foundations, representations), and action (political, social foundations), and to rethink technology. Technology was now understood as a particular spatial organization—of ever increasing complexity—and as a product of the scientific task, and at the same time, as an input (and product!) of power. Consequently, women's access to and reconception of science constitutes a means of empowerment, which must occur in the political context of the quality of life.

The Information Symbols: Shortly before the beginning of the 21st century, the internal and external aspects of communication technology entered the scene. The 'internal' aspect (the discoveries, new developments, innovations, and inventions) has proved difficult—even counter-productive and auto-destructive. On account of the demand volume of the 'outside' (uses, advantages, and applications), women's presence in both sides of the Internet has multiplied substantially. The Internet and the world cannot work efficiently without the decisive and irreplaceable presence of women.

The Symbols that Promote Empowerment: The availability of mobile personal communication, data storage, and data transmission has doubled as empowerment tools. This occurs in a manner that gradually reveals different levels of empowerment. However, the opinions of women must be taken into account and given a political-legal character if women's demands are to be viable. Therefore, it is necessary that civic or communitarian organisms be present to gather those opinions, synthesize them, and give them an ample, discursive, and real presentation, one that permeates the life of women and men, girls and boys.

Gender-Net: A Means to Obtain Our Desired Goals

The preoccupation to transform the asymmetric conditions between genders involves, in principle, a way of thinking based on the existence of otherness, of heterogeneity, and plurality. It creates a space where it makes sense to recognize multiple political subjects for the building of strategies and the use of tools that can lead to real change and social transformation to benefit humanity. An indispensable requirement of this possibility is respect for the material right of difference—tolerance, and acceptance; a notion as political as equality. If it were not this way, in the words of Celia Amorós (1996: 57), 'my difference would not be recognized, this is to say, valued by the other one as worthy of the same respect as the one that appears in front of my own point of view like "his difference" in front of me.' Perhaps for this reason, the conscious action of and by women, when demonstrating their heterogeneity and diverse developments, has established different guidelines and policies between which countries of the North and South are today differentiated. Women's actions have enabled them to advance their understanding of the subordinations which they share, although these vary for reasons of class, race, ethnicity, in addition to other cultural variables like age, or sexual orientation.

The efforts of countless feminist groups during the last 40 years serve as a frame to affirm that our mentality had changed to a certain extent by the time we entered the 21st century. But this is no where near to a total acceptance on the part of power in general and men as individuals, of the active presence, with rights, contributions, and expectations, of women in the social and cultural context; all the more necessary in the globalized world. This causes us to consider more deeply the dominion of scientific progress, the control of techno-science over science, and technology as well as the challenge to ensure that its use is inclusive of and beneficial to women. In short, it helps us debate and question our own perspective, the means to produce science and the use of technology, as well as the control of the processes of its production and consumption. Therefore, in effect, national, regional, continental, and world-wide research and development policies, along with those of science and technology, must imbue scientific formation and technological production with the autonomy to promote development by means of overcoming social contradictions. They must recognize and respect cultural, racial, ethnic, and gender differences, whose holders have the right to profit. Any science and technology to service the needs of the people begins with the right to communicate, advances access and enjoyment of the available technological resources and finishes with the right to enjoy its profitability effects.

Although it is certain that there is a more or less valid legal and accepted frame to resist gender discrimination, we consider that there still remains a lack of force to obtain changes in attitudes, mentalities and behavior of society in general, and men in particular. A possible means within the reach of women comes from viewing communication technologies as sources of empowerment for the exercise of citizenship. This, however, calls for democratic societies with a new coinage.

CAPACITY OF COMMUNICATION TECHNOLOGIES

'To know it is to be capable' is a statement that has become commonplace without having lost its wisdom. In the valuations of the poorest of women, lack of education, and political and cultural impossibility, historically maintained, disallows access to, use, and the taking advantage of technological resources. And this is not through inaction or lack of praxis. All the efforts that poor women have made, all the products of their work have almost always been for the exclusive benefit of somebody else.

It is necessary, therefore, with the initiative of women's movements, to place in the agenda of the governments, the national, and international organizations, the urgent and undelayable improvement of the quality of life of women in general and the poorest women in particular. It is necessary that facilities be planned and organized so they can access—and indeed do access—the technological resources that allow them to take the best decisions, so that they can simultaneously take the best political actions for their own social benefit. The intention is that they free themselves from the exploitation that they have suffered from the history of humanity, so that surpassing the historical conditions they have been placed under, they can help other women be valued as individuals. Empowerment through knowledge, and the use of communication technologies is the desired goal.

An Internet for the Dissolution of Obstacles

Until now, the programs directed to work towards these goals and the attendant strategies have operated by means of information directed through/by/for women. These seem effective to understand and assimilate the real contribution of their potentialities, results and products, and to demonstrate that it is possible to undertake initiatives to unveil power relations. Power always, until now, has been considered an asymmetric relation of oppression. Existing conditions—subjective and objective, theoretical and practical—that frame power relations from a gender perspective lead us to the resources of communication technologies in the way in which the communication processes are the key to sensitizing and constructing new citizenships, even virtual ones.

The fact that the freedom of expression, ostensibly present in every form of communication, is invariably mediated through relations of power, proves that no participatory process is entirely independent of the same notion of power that characterizes society. This is because communicative processes are intertwined with an assembly of social relations that denote power, status, and the corresponding availability of resources. The Internet network now hopes to surmount these obstacles present in virtual relations, which are nothing more than a mere reflection of the human condition.

The benefits of the network are tempered by the knowledge that the services the Internet can provide are not within the reach of poor people and are limited to the well-off. Isolation, as far as communication is concerned, is one of the main features of poverty and has as much to do with the non-availability of material-mass media, as with the restrictions in access to knowledge. Telecenters and community centers aimed at imparting information and communication technology for the low-income group, has been devised to remedy this situation.[2] Telecenters are an alternative to personal and corporate uses of the Internet, and are intended to benefit the entire community in general and women in particular.

Christina Courtright (2000) states that 'the phenomenon of the telecenters, also called Internet cabins or centers of communitarian access, is growing everywhere in the developing world as a mechanism to provide to the local population an access way to the

Internet to improve their economic and social conditions.' To what degree can we consider the use of the Internet through telecenters as an example of achieving development through communication technology? The author asks herself this question before concluding that 'the telecenters tend to be created to harness development in their respective places.' She continues, 'The provision of information over interactive communication has been prioritized, the potential impact of the telecenters is less than accounted for because the suppliers do not have enough understanding of the information demand.' While insisting upon the need to promote an increased participation of the community in this kind of an initiative, she seems to suggest that those towards whom these resources are directed, are, however, never consulted about their own information and communication needs. She adds that it is imperative that such initiatives be related to 'the local needs, the literacy levels, the language, and the culture.'

Although telecenters are intended for communitarian use, the truth is that their use is mostly at an individual level. It is necessary to move beyond the personal use of Internet resources—chat and email—and on to attaining the common objectives for cultural transformation. The ones who best adapt themselves to these uses define subjects of common access that can be employed by those who will participate in consultations, investigations, and surveys.

Rather than take decisions on our own, we need to listen to and identify people's needs while deciding where telecenters will be set up, and to adapt them to those requirements. Specific processes must be considered for each community, always from the viewpoint of participative communication for empowerment, in agreement with the formative and educative needs of women as its prompters. If we have now clarified that telecenters must develop in a context within which communication paves the way for empowerment, we must go into the details of our proposal: Gender-Net, and the ways in which it would operate, who will communicate what, with which particular objectives, means, and strategies. It is while answering these questions that the persons and motivations that give content and reason to these means will be exposed, thereby hastening communication processes for communitarian proficiency from a gender perspective.

Gender-Net as a Technological Communication Tool

The recognition and acceptance of the right to enjoy the benefits of available technological resources will be the means to strengthen diverse positions between women and men. Only with the inclusion and participation of each person in the production and consumption of technological resources—with their political, social, and economic loads lightened through joint rights directed to take care of group differences—will it be possible to weaken the oppression and repression in cyberspace. These are elements that constitute the basis of the redefinition of some foundations that, from a gender perspective, not only recognize diversity, but also raise crucial debates regarding the circulation of ideas on the genuinely democratic uses of the Internet and their effects on a virtual citizenship. This is framed in its capacity as a medium that goes beyond information, and deals with understanding and knowledge.

For this reason, it is imperative that communities agree among themselves on their list of priorities, organized according to immediate and intermediate needs. On this, they must coordinate the formation of their internal structure. On this same basis, they will ascend to a second communication level when coordinating with the other geographic communities, therefore yielding larger organizations. This is what will imbue them with the appropriate strength. Communication objectives and actions can be taken only after the mechanisms and participants in the interlocution have been defined.

This communication level will be arrived at, once properly organized communities call attention to and invite to a responsible, serious, and formal debate the local, governmental, and international organizations that are to receive the former's list of demands. This movement will have to be transformed into communitarian development—empowerment—projects, raised from a macro vision: health, potable water, sewage systems, education, public services, production, employment, consumption, commerce, and transport. It is clear that the communities will have to actively participate in obtaining resources for the attainment of their objectives; in the measurement, attainment, evaluation, and spreading of results. Community participation is crucial for a genuinely democratic state, legitimately guarded by the common welfare, in which the interests, opinions, and rights of women are properly taken into account. Viewed in this context, Gender-Net becomes a specialization of a macro communitarian project instead of being merely a space for women who debate subjects of women.

Gender-Net fits within the category of gendered communitarian needs and has as much to do with men as women in that, men are the other half of humanity with material and subjective needs communicable towards the transformation of unequal gender relations. In the beginning, as a first stage, Gender-Net will attempt to educate women with a view to strengthening their collective empowerment. One aspect of this will involve sensitizing the community towards the purposes and objectives of Gender-Net, and placing selective teams in charge to maximize participation. The next step would involve collecting information from the women of the community, learning about their education levels, their interests, opinions pertaining to individual, gender, and community problems, and possible solutions that would be implemented by the Gender-Net project in each community. This exercise will help identify objectives, people, as well as their particularities, extent, resources, times, and costs of the program.

Gender-Net will essentially be a mass media, something like a 'supertelephone' or a 'superfreeway' that will allow the registration of participative proposals and consensus on objectives, means and projects, as well as provide the community with feedback and storage facilities. It is important that most of the communitarian work be done within the community, free from all trappings of technology. This community is also to be kept properly informed of the political and cultural advances made possible through Gender-Net. All the compiled information is to be at the disposal of those who produce it. This is an attempt to shrink the digital divide by extending global communicational networks to change existing socio-cultural relations between women and men.

Gender-Net and the Digital Divide: The digital divide stems from asymmetric power relations in which few hold and profit from the political and economic power that comes from exploiting both the work force and natural resources. It results from and through the formation of the so-called 'Information Society/Civilization,' wherein every real relation in society is mirrored in cyberspace. The main feature of this new civilization is the vast amount of educative and material resources it possesses, whose use greatly increases its wealth, much to the detriment of other less fortunate societies outside its purview.

It is naïve to believe that the problems faced by these enormous majorities will be solved magically once they have a new material means which could improve the quality of their lives. Our first priority should be to see to it, that the material resources under consideration benefit those most in need of them. Here, we count on knowledge and the appropriate experience to maximize cultural utilities, rather than economic ones. It is clear that this initiative must go towards removing gendered obstacles for communitarian development.

In the context of computerized communitarian communication, we define development as the substantial and durable improvement in the quality of community life through synergistic, coordinated action over a specified period of time, which is monitored, evaluated, and financed by specific and definite agents. This development must have clearly defined objectives and measurable goals, which take subjective changes into account along with collective needs.

Gender-Net Phase I: Global Communicational Gender Context: A good departure point will be the analysis of the quality of community life through these telecenters. Specific gender data compiled will serve to describe the particular communitarian configuration of each Gender-Net node. In its beginnings, the organization, as an educative center, can be thought of as storing communitarian information, and as a space for debate. As a specific project for Gender-Net, we can consider the experiences of groups of women in telecenters and other similar initiatives whether or not in technological environments.[3] This pilot project needs a site, technical material supplies for its operation and maintenance, interdisciplinary specialized personnel, and the raising of definite communitarian objectives in the context of a gendered global communication.

Gender-Net Phase II: Sensitization and Awareness for Sociocultural Change: Gender-Net is not, and cannot be, a short term project. If its purpose is to help redress an unfair historical situation, it must face formidable forces, active ones like vested interests, as well as passive ones—attitudes, behaviors, uses, and customs. If women without distinction will be the first to be sensitized in the project, men have also to be taken into account. At this stage, it is possible to consider a sensitization of social, cultural, political, economic, and legal organizations. Further political goals are complex, and need to be promoted by groups of women before they make a significant difference in everyday life.

Gender-Net Phase III: Towards Changes in Gender Relations: When society has recognized the necessity to take all women into account, it will be able to consider changed relations between women and men, and girls and boys, to the benefit of both sexes. The beginning of the third millennium has brought about an awareness that it is no longer possible to sustain the cultural domination of one half of humankind—a domination originally premised on biological fact. As a result, more and more people, both women and men, have engaged in an interrogation of the causes, effects, and conditions of asymmetrical power and gender relations, offering opportunities to the hitherto marginalized from the possession and exercise of power. This constitutes a conscious bid for freedom, a goal that is gradually being constructed outside the existing systems of education. Viewed in this context, Gender-Net appears as a challenge for change.

A Provisional Conclusion

If women have suffered the most under historical relations of power, it is necessary that they be allowed free access to the opportunities aimed at improving the quality of life, specifically in terms of social relations. In order to initiate this change, we propose using telecenters, an expression of the Internet, and their communitarian influence on the macro-social level. Telecenters are used for the configuration of Gender-Net with the purpose of allowing women access to the knowledge, communication, education, debate, co-ordination of theories and practices that they are constantly faced with in local, regional, continental, and world-wide contexts.

Recognition of the right to communicate on the part of both women and men will give Gender-Net credibility. But it is also necessary: (*a*) To circulate these ideas among women's movements across cultures; so that they can be raised to governments, national, and international organizations and be included in their respective agendas; (*b*) To promote consciousness at each operative level to help women reach their goals; (*c*) To equip Gender-Net with human, material, and technical/technological resources; (*d*) To extend its presence to the historical context drawn up by the first quarter of the century in order to assure its continuity; (*e*) To periodically evaluate its accomplishments, take advantage of the experience gathered, and correct possible deviations; and (*f*) To strengthen Gender-Net as a tool of communication technologies with an essentially political character that can bring about a change in gender, and other social relations.

There is no doubt that everything has to begin by sensitizing organizations—local, regional, continental and world-wide—to the need to harness the Internet at the educative, communicative, social, and cultural levels, and include it in the political agenda to aid the allocation of human, material, and financial resources. Telecenters would then have to be multiplied so that Gender-Net could become the means of expression, communication, debate, and coordination among the women of the world. Preference will be given to women involved in helping women activate their communicative processes from a gender perspective to advance their life chances in the third millennium.

Sitting before a computer to debate the digital divide will not help unless we are aware of the gender problems facing the community. Efforts will not amount to much if we are not clear on how to raise corresponding solutions, less still if new knowledge does not circulate on the matter, and if the technical operation is not guaranteed either. This statement points to the fact that Gender-Net must be a multi- and inter-disciplinary project managed by people with technical knowledge, in social sciences, health, rights, education, psychology, administration, and management. Active participation of women is as essential in this process as is the consciousness of the necessity to change gender relations.

Notes

1. The deep crisis into which e-commerce has fallen is no more than a reflection of the effects and illusions of the supposed magnitude of the Internet, as well as the effects and conclusions of the real motivations of the *Netizen*.
2. A site, which 'serves as a meeting place for people interested in telecenter practice and research'. Information on the International Development Research

Centre's (IDRC) PAN Networking and Acacia telecenter initiatives is included, along with links to resources produced by others working in the field. The site is intended to foster learning and understanding of international telecenter experiences, issues and lessons (IDRC Telecenter Research, in http://www.idrc.ca/pan/telecenters.html).
3. Gender Equity Issues and New Information Technologies, http://www.educ.sfu.ca; Gender Center for Sustainable Development, WIRC Women's Information and Research Centre, http://www.wirc.mn.

REFERENCES

Amorós, Celia. (1996) 'Feminismo filosófico español: modulaciones hispánicas de la polémica feminista igualdad-diferencia (Spanish Philosophical Feminism: Hispanic Configuration of the Feminist Controversy Equality-Difference)', *Revista Deval*, No. 3, pp. 47–78.

Berman, Jerry and Weitzner, Daniel J. (1997) 'Technology and Democracy', *Social-Research*, 64(3): 1313–19.

Bonacchi, Gabriella. (1995) 'O contexto e os delineamentos' (The Context and the Delineations), in Bonacchi, Gabriella and Groppi, Angela (Organizadoras) (Organizers), *O dilema da cidadania: Dereitos e deveres das mulheres (The Citizenship Dilemma: Rights and Obligations of the Women)*, Editora Universidad estadual Paulista, Sao Paulo, pp. 26–47.

Bonacchi, Gabriella and Groppi, Angela. (1995) [Organizadoras) (Organizers)] *O dilema da cidadania: Dereitos e deveres das mulheres (The Citizenship Dilemma: Rights and Obligations of the Women)*, Editora Universidad estadual Paulista, Sao Paulo.

Buchstein, Hubertus. (1997) 'Bytes That Bite: The Internet and Deliberative Democracy', *Constellations*, 4(2): 248–63.

Cockburn, Cynthia. (1992) 'Abriendo la caja negra: la tecnología en los análisis de la sociología feminista' (Opening the Black Box: The Feminist Sociology and its Analyses of the Technology) in *Sociología del Trabajo: Revista cuatrimestral de empleo, trabajo y sociedad (Sociology of the Work: Journal of Employment, Work and Society)*, ST 15(Fall): 91–107.

Courtright, Christina. (2000) 'La comunicación para el desarrollo y el Internet: Un análisis del contenido de las páginas Web de algunos Telecentros de América Latina y el Caribe' (The Communication for the Development and the Internet: An Analysis of the Content of the Web Pages of Some Telecentres of Latin America and the Caribbean), Indiana University, December 2000, http://php.indiana.edu/~ccourtri/paginas-telecentros.html.

Gardinali, Paolo A. (1996) *Cybervillains and Vigilantes: The Construction of Social Order on Usenet*, American Sociological Association (ASA), USA.

Gousgounis, Nicolaus. (1998) *The Challenge of the Discussion Lists on the Internet and the Production of Social Knowledge*, International Sociological Association (ISA), Pedagogical Institute, Athens, Greece.

Katz, James E. (1997) 'The Social Side of Information Networking', *Society*, 34, 3(227): 9–12.

Lie, M. (1991) 'Technology and Gender: Identity and Symbolism', Paper presented at the 4th IFIP Conference on Women, Work and Computerization, Helsinki, Finland, July 1991.

Moreno, Amparo. (1996) 'Crisis de la racionalidad androcéntrica en la sociedad de la información' (Crisis of the Androcentric Rationality in the Society of the Information), in Radl, Rita (Editora) (ed.), *Mujeres e institución universitaria en occidente. Conocimiento, investigación y roles de género (Women and University in the West: Knowledge, Investigation and Gender Roles*, Memorias Congreso Internacional Universidad Santiago de Compostela. Santiago de Compostela, pp. 95–100.

Rodota, Stefano. (1995) 'Essere "Cittadini" nella dimensione delle nuove technologie della comunicazione' (Being "Citizens" in the Context of New Communications Technologies), *Inchiesta (Inquiry)*, 25(109): 91–95.

Spender, Dale. (1997) 'The Position of Women in Information Technology, or Who Got There First and with What Consequences?', *Current-Sociology/Sociologie-Contemporaine*, 45(2): 135–47.

Street, John. (1997) 'Remote Control Politics: Technology and "Electronic Democracy"', *European Journal of Communication*, 12(1): 27–42.

10 Thinking BIG to Accelerate Gender Equality and Transformation in the ICT Arena

GILLIAN M. MARCELLE[1]

The international community has made progress in recognizing that the Information and Communication Technologies (ICTs) revolution should not proceed as a technologically deterministic law onto itself, but must be shaped by human values. The need to align development in the ICTs arena with human development objectives is now widely accepted. However, to date, these re-shaping efforts have been relatively silent on the need to include gender equality and the promotion of women's empowerment as central tenets of the transformation effort. In this regard, the ICTs arena trails behind peace and security, education, health, human rights, and trade, for example, where there is acceptance that there can be no meaningful progress without a consideration of gender equality and women's empowerment.

There is thus an urgent need to fill the gap between the concept and practice of gender equality in the ICTs arena and to develop effective strategies for concerted action. These actions are needed to ensure that women secure access to the potential benefits of the ICTs and to minimize potential unequal distribution of benefits associated with the ICTs revolution. ICTs cannot fulfill their potential for use as a tool for gender equality, women's empowerment, and human development unless decision-making and participation in the ICTs sector undergo a fundamental change.

This chapter outlines a conceptual framework which can be used to open space for gender equality and women's perspectives to contribute to reshaping the ICTs revolution. The approach sets out a three-phased process consisting of: Buy-in; Implementation; and Growth and reinforcement (BIG). This action oriented conceptual framework is used to analyze four critical areas of intervention— ICTs policy making; ICTs applications for promotion of women's economic empowerment; ICT-enabled health and education services and ICT-mediated public life participation.

The BIG approach argues that the first step in the transformation process of the ICTs sector is the redefinition of the raison d'être for the expansion and application of its services. The approach further suggests that growth in the ICTs arena should become embedded in a set of efforts to promote human development rather than remaining an end in itself. Without this link to human development, ICTs will remain a technological side-show, the applications and services will continue to be the playthings of the global elite, and the digital divide statistics will continue to be alarming.

Insertion of positive human values and aspirations such as equity, equality, and justice into the ICTs arena introduces an ethical dimension, without which the ICTs revolution remains shallow, and unconnected to the central development problems of poverty, insecurity, disease, and growing inequality. This dimension cannot be introduced without concerted action and negotiation among the interested stakeholders. However, without it, ICTs infrastructure and applications may continue to enjoy unprecedented diffusion rates, but will only provide benefits to the rich, and privileged, excluding the poor.

The BIG approach also implies changes in the means used to promote ICTs sector development. Rather than pursuing only limited reliance on market-mediated tools of liberalization, privatization, and deregulation, it argues that other non-market mediated mechanisms should be deployed. The BIG approach defines options that enable ICTs services and applications to be made available to all citizens rather than only those consumers who can pay market determined prices. Implementing these options will require creativity and inventiveness on the part of all actors. It is also clear that non-market mechanisms are a necessary component of this pro-development ICTs strategy to compensate for market failure and to optimize social benefits. In the people-rather than profit-centered ICTs revolution envisaged here, democracy, transparency, and participation become the bases for governance of the sector rather than just empty rhetoric.

Why We Need to Think BIG:
Antecedents of the Conceptual Framework

As noted in Marcelle (2000a), the intellectual foundation for a transformative intervention in the ICTs arena can be developed by drawing on feminist theory on social relations and feminist analysis of organizational change (Goetz, 1997; Kabeer, 1994), feminist perspectives on globalization and macroeconomic change (Jackson and Pearson, 1998), as well as other strands of engagement on transformation of the ICTs sector (Hammelink, 1997; Mansell and Wehn, 1998). This essay argues, that precisely because feminist perspectives on change tackle many of the issues that remain most intractable, such as the organizing values and premises of the ICTs sector, and its intersection with market-based globalization, it is essential to draw on their work. Policy literature and other influential texts, particularly those not written by feminist scholars, do not tend to treat gender equality as a central theme (Mansell and Wehn, 1998; World Bank, 2002). This is an example of conceptual silence and emphasizes the need for scholarship and action to close this gap.

Application of a gender lens to ICTs took off in 1995. The United Nations Commission on Science and Technology for Development (UNCSTD) undertook a comprehensive study of the relationship between gender, science and technology (S&T), and development (UNCSTD-GWG, 1995) for the Fourth World Conference on Women in Beijing in 1995. The Report established that there are gender-specific aspects of the ways in which S&T systems interact with societies and their developmental processes, and conclusively showed that in a wide range of technological developments there are significant aspects of differentiation in levels of access to, control over, and benefits resulting to women and men. The barriers facing women in S&T fields from environment to energy and agriculture included unequal access to education and training, unfair distribution of financial and technical resources, limited participation in decision-making and control, socialization pressures, and the devaluation of women's knowledge.

Furthermore, the UNCSTD Gender Working Group (GWG) studies concluded that women, particularly those in developing countries, face gender-specific barriers (socialization, labor market segmentation, unequal access to education and training, etc.) in harnessing ICTs for their benefit. But these studies also found that there were potentials for ICTs to provide women with opportunities for expansion of their economic enterprises, as well as for positive social, political, and cultural change. However, the UNCSTD Study addressed neither gender relations within firms in the ICTs sector, nor how the organization of the ICTs sector reinforced existing gender inequality.

Marcelle (2000b) focused on how ICTs sector policy reform could be altered to include human development as a core rather than a secondary objective. Using empirical case material from the African region, this Study provided a basis for the claim that unless the purposes of the ICTs sector are redirected away from purely private sector interests, it will continue to under perform in its contribution to development aims. A singular focus on maximization of profit and reliance on market mechanisms leads to classic market failure with under-investment in social and institutional capital, restrictions on growth of supply, and lack of creativity in stimulation of demand.

There have also been important contributions from Asian scholars on the effects of rapid diffusion of ICTs on gender relations within firms and markets (Mitter, 1999). The results from those studies, while not particularly encouraging, provide evidence that rapid diffusion of ICTs has produced some beneficial impacts for women as a result of actions by trade unions, women's cooperatives, enlightened private sector firms, and the state.

In addition to work by scholars and researchers, there have been many practitioner-led interventions that have attempted to galvanize action on gender and ICTs at national, regional, and international levels. There has also been a focus on providing basic ICT literacy training for women, and training women activists to use ICT tools for social and political advocacy. There is a growing trend for NGO-led programs to assist with strengthening the capacity of civil society to engage in the ICTs development policy space. One of the most significant of these efforts is the work of the ITU Task Force on Gender Issues, which has the potential to become an influential body in terms of changing practices within firms in the telecommunications and information technology sector, and within the global regulatory framework for telecommunications policy. The Task Force (known by its French acronym

BTD) was set up in 1998 as a quasi-advisory body established within the Division of the ITU responsible for development activities. Since its inception it has worked to fulfill its ambitious mandate of 'ensuring that all programs and projects of the ITU Bureau for Telecommunications Development take into account a gender perspective' (www.itu.int/itu-d/gender).

In July 2002, the Task Force on Gender Issues was reestablished as the ITU Working Group on Gender Issues. In the same year, the ITU-BDT also finally appointed a Senior Gender Adviser, but has still failed to set up a fully staffed gender unit to implement a strategic program. However, the Working Group still struggles with a host of problems, including lack of legitimacy and authority, inadequate financial resources and budgetary insecurity, potential for co-option of its mandate, fragmentation of effort, lack of integration with ITU staff functions, voluntarism, and lack of formal decision-making and governance arrangements. All of these problems can be considered as barriers erected as traditional institutions resist transformation.

The international women's movement has taken steps to accelerate the participation of women and gender advocates in the policy making aspects of the ICTs sector at both national and international levels (see, for example, www.genderwsis.org, www.apcwomen.org). However, these efforts to strengthen the policy and advocacy capability of gender equality advocates are severely hampered by under-representation of women at the decision-making level. In moving forward on a more collective and less fragmented basis, gender advocates may require new ways of working to challenge leadership and negotiation styles. This author's assessment is that efforts to 'mainstream' gender equality in ICTs take place in silos. The groups of women's organizations involved in lobbying and advocacy through the Beijing processes have few lines of communication with staff members of telecommunications and IT firms and organizations. There is also little agreement on what the priority advocacy issues are, and on definite strategies and tactics.

The development of the BIG framework reflects on this 'conceptual silence and ambiguity' regarding gender equality in mainstream global efforts to align ICTs and human development; feminist research and analysis of transformation in spheres such as trade and human rights; recent studies of the integration (or lack thereof) of gender analysis in ICTs projects, and conceptual work on gender analysis of ICTs policy (Marcelle, 2002). Recent reports prepared for the UN-DAW Expert Group meeting on gender and ICTs, including an online conference on the impact and use of ICTs as an instrument of women's empowerment and advancement, provide an updated assessment of the extent to which women are able to participate fully in the ICTs arena (Hafkin, 2002; UN-DAW, 2002).

The framework is also informed by praxis. The author has been involved as an external change agent for including gender perspectives in the work of the ITU and the UN-ICT Task Force, has worked with NGOs that are lobbying for inclusion of gender equality issues in ICTs policy and practice, and has advised international organizations on gender and ICTs program development. The impetus to develop a conceptually based guide for action is based on the assessment that although there has been relatively good progress on women's organizations making use of ICTs as tools, there is insufficient effort to develop strategies to rethink the value and purposes of the ICTs sector and to shape practices of policy and regulatory bodies. It is for this reason more than any other, that this work, in progress of developing a conceptual framework that guides action, will hopefully stimulate more effective action on the part of gender policy advocates. The article is organized in four sections; the conceptual framework is presented in Section two; applications of this framework to four areas of intervention are discussed in Section three and the final section offers concluding remarks.

THINKING BIG: A CONCEPTUAL FRAMEWORK TO GUIDE TRANSFORMATION OF THE ICTs ARENA

The BIG (Buy-in; Implementation; and Growth and reinforcement) approach is a conceptual framework that can be used to guide actions that lead to transformation of the ICTs arena. The changes that are advocated aim to ensure that the ICTs sector facilitates meaningful participation of women, promotes gender equality, furthers the empowerment of women, and advances human development. The main issue is: How can efforts to integrate gender equality and accelerate transformation of the ICTs arena be achieved?

Taking up from the problem assessment summarized earlier, the BIG approach argues that a combination of (1) conceptual/strategy development and (2) focused collaborative action is required to accelerate progress. First, the definition of the term 'ICTs arena' is used here in an all encompassing sense to include ICTs production units (companies that make equipment or produce services), ICTs services and applications (telecommunications, information technology services such as software, multimedia, e-commerce, etc), ICTs equipment, ICTs policy, and regulatory bodies operating at national, regional, and international levels, as well as the technical bodies involved in setting technical and industry standards for the ICTs infrastructure and services. Further, the ICTs arena is defined to include both intermediate and final goods and services. This comprehensive definition recognizes that ICTs infrastructure, services, and applications in addition to being final goods and services, are often integrated into the value-chains of production and consumption of other sectors. For example, ICTs are used as intermediates or inputs in the production of other goods by the manufacturing sector and as means for delivering services such as news, entertainment, education, training, finance, tourism, etc. As a result of this sprawling and pervasive nature, it is often difficult to measure the boundaries of the sector and to identify decision-makers. These characteristics also mean that a full analysis of women's roles and contributions must take account of these multiple facets.

Many of the earlier academic studies have focused on women's employment participation in specific segments of the ICTs production process (Mitter, 1999) and NGO activism has typically centered around women using ICTs for social and economic empowerment. However, when the full range of the ICTs arena is specified, it becomes clear that providing equal opportunity for basic ICTs literacy and enhanced competence also impacts on employability and has indirect effects on women's economic activity in sectors that have the potential to use ICTs to increase efficiency, improve quality, and widen market access. Another implication of this definition is that it includes decision-making structures within the ambit of the ICTs arena (Marcelle, 2000b).

Second, the framework emphasizes that while the majority of ICTs infrastructure, services, and applications are designed and produced by private sector companies, universities and research institutions, the conditions for their production are influenced by a much larger set of actors. For example, public sector decision-makers set the rules and monitor operations of companies, and private citizens are employed by ICTs companies, and also consume and use ICTs equipment, services, and applications in their daily lives. This interaction between profit motivated companies, citizens using ICTs services, consumers buying ICTs equipment, services, and applications and public sector institutions carrying out oversight, makes for a complex terrain. This complexity means that when designing a strategic approach, variation in context is centrally important. It is not possible to develop a *one-size fits all* strategy for the inclusion of human development objectives in the ICTs arena.

Third, the ICTs arena is technologically intensive where decision-making requires a minimum level of familiarity with and competence in computers, telecommunications, and information technologies. Meaningful participation as a producer or competent user is assumed to require additional competence, increased knowledge, and deeper understanding of the underlying technologies. The implication for gender advocates and other change agents is that they must acquire and continuously develop a familiarity with and confidence in technological issues if they are to engage effectively.

Fourth, ICTs are considered to be socially constructed. Therefore, the impact and outcomes resulting from their production and application are influenced by social and economic factors, such as income level, gender, race, class, etc. Finally, since ICTs are not considered to be gender-neutral, there is an explicit focus on identifying and explaining the ways in which the ICTs arena is gendered and on devising strategies to change unequal gender relations. The process of unearthing the gendered nature of the ICTs arena, influencing gender relations, and reducing inequality is explicitly deemed to be a political process involving conflict, bargaining, and negotiation over change and transformation of power relations as well as access to resources. It is expected that change agents (internal and external) will meet with resistance and will have to devise strategies to overcome resistance.

The framework argues that simultaneous and proportional efforts in the two spheres of concept/strategy development and focused collaborative action are more likely to yield results. The BIG approach argues that advocates and change agents who are guided by grounded concepts are likely to better explain the imperative for change, to identify the nature of challenges, and to anticipate resistance. It further suggests that collaborations are more likely to have a wider and more sustained impact, since these draw on a broader range of talents, skills, and experiences. The path of transformation proposed is one that takes full advantage of multiplier effects. As shown in Figure 10.1, the BIG approach suggests that limited collaborative action and inadequate concept development (quadrant 1); scholarly activity which defines aspects of the gender digital divide but is divorced from concrete grounded activity (quadrant 2); or a series of actions which may be well coordinated but are not aligned to the strategic objective (quadrant 3), will not produce maximum acceleration towards transformation (quadrant 4).

Figure 10.1
Three Phases of the BIG Approach to Transformation of the ICTs arena

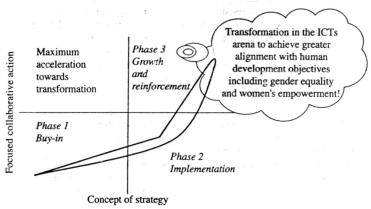

The three phases (see Figure 10.2) are described as follows:
The **Buy-In** phase focuses on reducing conceptual silence and ambiguity, and generating the impetus for collaborative action. The main tasks associated with this phase are problem identification, clarifying the underlying philosophy, as well as forging

Figure 10.2
Strategies for Applying the BIG Approach
to Transformation in the ICTs Arena

Phase	Main Features	Recommended Strategies
Buy-In (Intellectual and Social Capital Intensive)	• Confusion • Fragmentation • Little or no coordination • Lack of legitimacy • Active and passive resistance • Small pilot projects • Limited impact	• Research and analysis • Develop and articulate a compelling case • Develop tools for analysis and advocacy • Develop models of organizational collaboration • Communicate with decision makers to raise awareness and counteract inertia and resistance • Build support base
Implementation (Financial Capital Intensive)	• Improved clarity in defining strategic objectives and good practices • Increased collaboration • More deployment of projects of appropriate scale • Less resistance • More integration of gender equality objectives • Moderate impact • Risks of co-option and dissipation of strategic intent	• Build community of practice • Undertake focused interventions to assist producers • Develop specific campaigns around allocation of adequate resources • Build critical mass of women decision makers • Improve evaluation and monitoring mechanisms • Share results • Continuous leadership and capacity development
Growth and Reinforcement (Social, Political, Intellectual and Financial Capital Intensive)	• Conceptual clarity • Widespread implementation • Innovative approaches emerge • High impact	• Reinvigorate and sustain conceptual and strategy development • Undertake R&D to identify technology-based solutions • Share insights with development community • Identify champions and converts among the ICTs decision makers • Expand and update awareness raising campaigns. • Begin again using insights and experience!

agreement on shared objectives. In this phase, change agents are likely to have various interpretations of the cause of gender-based discrimination and also to have multiple objectives for promoting gender equality in the ICTs arena. At the beginning of the intervention cycle, there is often little common shared understanding of how to counter gender-based oppression and accelerate transformation. It is likely that the inputs for this stage will be varied, and there is much to be gained from reviewing the experiences gained through multiple sites of experimentation. This phase is likely to produce a catalogue of problems, and will encounter different types of resistance. However, this phase also provides the ferment which over time, can result in appropriate strategies to counter resistance and challenges. It is often the frustration and disappointment with small-scale experimentation, lack of in-depth analysis, insufficient evaluation, and limited information sharing that prompts change agents to improve their organizational collaboration. The need to reach decision-makers can also lead to the forging of alliances among scholars, institutionally located gender advocates, and NGOs.

The **Implementation** phase is one in which projects of appropriate scale are deployed and efforts to integrate gender equality in the ICTs arena proceed to yield moderate impact. During this phase, gender equality and human development objectives are considered to be legitimate aspects of the ICTs arena. There is increased collaboration and communication among scholars and practitioners at national, regional, and global levels. More gender advocates move into decision-making positions and influence the agenda and raison d'être of the ICTs arena. Collaboration with ICTs producers also improves as gender advocates develop strategies to work with and influence the practices of these important actors. Progress is also made in the designing and implementation of evaluation and monitoring mechanisms to assess the impact of projects and programs. During this phase, it is likely that the ICTs for development constituency will begin more effectively to share results with the broader human development constituencies. This is not to say that there are no risks associated with this phase. On the contrary, the risks of co-option and dissipation of fundamental objectives are greatest when mainstream institutions become involved. Coping with these threats requires continuous attention to developing leadership and building capacities of the change agents and their organizations.

In the **Growth and reinforcement** phase, there is a dual focus on refining concepts and tools. These tools are designed based on a careful assessment of prior experimentation and taking account of the implications of the need to accelerate implementation. This phase provides an opportunity to make further progress in increasing participation in areas that have been particularly difficult to penetrate and to improve the effectiveness of interventions. It is in this phase, that the advocates of gender equality and ICTs can draw on networks of support, shared expertise, and political clout to move towards the achievement of overall strategic goals. Progress towards transformation is likely to accelerate significantly when the motor of innovation and technological investment in the ICTs arena, allocates significant resources to serving human development needs. This will only be achieved when there is conceptual clarity and political will is directed at galvanizing this effort. The gender advocacy community cannot achieve this acting on its own, but will make more progress as part of broad based pro-development coalitions.

Several critical success factors are necessary for the BIG approach to achieve its objectives. The approach requires greater collaboration among a range of actors and improved sharing of information, knowledge and expertise, and responsibilities, based on mutual respect and an appropriate division of labor. It requires coordination of a range of focused and strategic actions directed at many levels. The framework also requires diversity and adaptability to the specific context as it will vary according to country, environment, and type of actors involved. The framework does not envisage a linear, well-delineated cut-off between phases, but rather anticipates a messy, non-linear, and chaotic implementation pattern. However, the framework suggests that there are likely to be some sequencing requirements since it is expected that the learning and facilitation effects in the earlier phases will provide a foundation for intermediate and later phases.

This approach requires commitment to the strategic objective, as well as the ability to invest resources (intellectual, financial, and social capital) at every stage of the process. A first step in applying this approach would be to undertake an enquiry to determine the initial conditions and identify the barriers. It would also be helpful to define the intermediate goals, so that progress can be regularly monitored. The second step would involve designing specific strategies that are developed and clarified through the articulation of statements of objectives, indicators, and outcomes. The approach is flexible and can be tailored to suit venues of varying scales and complexities. However, the framework strongly argues that every action, regardless of scale, should be continuously assessed. This ensures that at every stage, alignment, and understanding of the overall strategic objective is maintained rather than dissipated. Reinforcing actions that have the potential to make a positive contribution, and avoiding those that do not, is non-negotiable.

The BIG approach also suggests that there is a need to develop indicators and assessment tools that move beyond instrumental indicators such as simple counts of the number of women in ICTs projects, or women in decision-making positions in the ICTs. The focus suggested is on developing outcome and impact indicators on how the goals of empowerment and gender equality are advanced. The international agencies that are currently engaged in developing indicators for the Information Society should be made aware of the need to do more to integrate gender statistics in their input indicators. These agencies have yet to make any significant moves towards the development of outcome or impact assessment indicators, which are more complex and difficult to design and operationalize.

APPLYING THE BIG APPROACH

This section provides an illustration of how the BIG approach can be applied to four possible sites of intervention where ICTs can contribute to women's empowerment: ICTs policy making; ICTs applications for promotion of women's economic empowerment; ICT-enabled health and education services; and ICT-mediated public life participation (Marcelle, 2002). It is also worth noting that by considering these four distinct issues, many different aspects of the value-chain of the ICTs arena can be discussed. In the policy area, the focus is on transforming decision-making and governance, while in the issues of health and education and public life participation, the focus is on how women's production and consumption of ICTs goods and services can promote gender equality and women's empowerment. In the economic empowerment issue, the impact of ICTs is extended to their role as intermediate product or services.

As noted earlier, the pre-requirement for using this framework is an understanding that all social, economic, and political processes, including the production and/or application of technologies, are gendered. Hence, the first step in applying this framework would be to identify the characteristics of the initial conditions and the types of barriers faced. Second, the framework recommends that specific action orientated strategies be developed to tackle the barriers identified. These strategies will include the definition of intermediate goals, and designing of evaluation and progress monitoring systems. Finally, the framework implies that progress towards achievement of the overall strategic objective is attained by continuous learning, assessment, evaluation, and careful interpretation of experiences.

In the first stage, opportunities should be created to explore the consequences of existing gender relations. Change agents using this approach should construct arguments and marshal evidence that vary according to the context and political environment in which the intervention is being made. However, they ought also to take account of the guidance from Peggy Antrobus, a member of the DAWN Collective, who has insightfully argued that while it is possible to adapt to the context—shifting from justice-based to expediency-based arguments—true transformation will result only from wisdom-based strategies (Antrobus, personal communication). Once there is agreement on the objective of an intervention, change agents can proceed with an enquiry into the initial conditions in the ICTs arena:

1. Are gender equality perspectives understood by decision-makers at all levels?
2. Are gender equality perspectives used by decision-makers at all levels?
3. What types of organizations advocate for gender equality?
4. Who are the champions of gender equality?
5. Is there agreement on why gender equality should be included?

6. Is there agreement on how gender equality perspectives should be included?
7. How much of the financial budget is allocated to gender equality or women's advancement?
8. How are decisions about budget allocations, innovation, and project development made?
9. At what level are women active in the decision-making systems?
10. What are the most common reasons given for not adopting pro-active strategies to enhance the participation of women?

The next stage involves identifying specific actions that respond to the initial conditions and barriers identified. Care is needed to ensure that these actions are appropriate to the spaces where strategic interventions are to be made. Taking these steps to persuade decision-makers is a minimum starting point, since without 'Buy-in', there is little likelihood of further progress to implementation, growth, reinforcement, and transformation. The common features that the BIG approach recommends are, careful research and articulation of the benefits of taking a gendered approach, as well as increasing the number of gender advocates in the center of power and decision-making as a pro-active strategy to counter resistance. For example, in the area of ICTs policy making, the BIG approach suggests that it is the task of gender advocates to push their analyses of ICTs policy making to the technical aspects of this field and to provide hands-on recommendations as to how telecommunication network deployment and licensing can take account of gender equality perspectives. If gender advocates assume the role of technical advisors on these issues more assertively and effectively, their efforts are also more likely to reduce resistance to gender and ICTs as a conceptual issue. Figure 10.3 illustrates suggested actions to secure Buy-in for gender equality across the four areas of concern.

The characteristics of the 'Buy-in' phase suggest that converts and believers in the cause of gender equality will self select and take on leadership. These individuals are likely to come from backgrounds of feminist scholarship, gender analysis, and activists campaigning for gender justice. However, there are some challenges

Figure 10.3
Increasing Buy-in for Gender Equality in the ICTs Arena

	ICTs and Economic Empowerment	ICTs and Education ICTs and Health	ICTs Mediated Public Life Participation
ICTs Policy	*Buy-In:* Focus on undertaking research and conceptual development, influencing decision-makers who currently occupy positions of power and influence and simultaneously build leadership that can occupy positions of power and decision-making.		
	Explain to decision-makers why		
	• Gender neutrality of ICTs is a myth • Democratization of ICTs policy making is beneficial • Gender advocates can add value in the decision-making sphere	• Specific ICTs mediated projects catering to women's health needs are feasible and necessary • Specific action to support girls' training and education in ICTs are necessary	• Women's participation in public life may require specific effort that is feasible and beneficial
	• Subsidized access to ICTs for women is beneficial and feasible • Labor markets discriminate against women's participation and advancement in the ICTs arena		
	Show decision makers how		
	• Women entrepreneurs in the ICTs sector face specific barriers to success and this retards overall growth and economic performance • Emerging firms in the ICTs sector can be encouraged and supported to implement practices which support women's employment	• To provide expert advice on design of gender equitable ICTs-mediated health and education programs	• To design ICTs-mediated governance programs and facilitate women's public participation and integrate with roles and responsibilities
	• To design tools and frameworks to incorporate gender equality perspectives in ICTs policy • Dialogue with gender equality advocates produces useful perspectives on ICTs for development		

Occupy decision-making positions in the ICTs arena to operationalize these recommendations.

associated with institutional positioning and this style of leadership. Gender equality advocates who do not have a background or experience in the ICTs sector, are unlikely to have regular lines of contact and communication with relevant decision-makers. Conversely, most women and men in leadership positions in the ICTs sector do not have familiarity with gender equality advocacy issues. Facilitating interaction between these groups therefore, requires capacity building, and active development of a cadre of *dual skilled* individuals who can make the case for gender equality in the ICTs sector with both passion and competence. The communication process also requires brokers to facilitate regular contact and constructive engagement between ICTs decision-makers and gender equality advocates. In this regard, gender equality advocacy units in global institutions, within the United Nations system and its specialized agencies, can play a crucial role.

The 'Buy-in' phase faces a particular challenge since it is within this phase that institutionally based gender equality advocates and other gender advocates in civil society organizations have to work together. For these alliances to be successful, civil society based advocates must remain convinced that institutionally based advocates will not 'water down' strategic objectives in order to win tactical or careerist advances. Conversely, the institutionally based advocates will have to be reassured that the civil society actors have a sound and realistic understanding of the pressures, tensions, and constraints under which they operate. Building organizational competence for the 'Buy-In' phase is a careful balancing act; these considerations should receive explicit attention rather than being swept under the carpet. The requirements of the 'Buy-in' phase imply that gender equality advocates need to design processes for sharing responsibilities and leadership with other organizations which may have different perspectives, preoccupations, and political histories.

Once Buy-in has been won, change agents should focus on ensuring an increase in the financial resources allocated to implement gender and ICTs projects and programs. These actions define phase two, the Implementation phase. Even the largest gender and ICTs projects currently in place, such as Grameen Telephone, do not involve a proportionate or equitable allocation of ICTs for development budgets and do not register on the scale of large infrastructural projects. The Implementation stage should also be accompanied by intensive evaluation and assessment to ensure that technological folly does not overshadow the original intention of securing transformation. In the Implementation phase, the venue of activity shifts from sites associated with concept and organizational development to those that are operationally focused. Since private sector companies, public sector ministries, regional bodies, and other donor agencies are the main actors in large-scale ICTs service and equipment delivery, change agents should ensure that they focus on shifting the practices of these actors. The main focus of this phase is on ensuring that ICTs and development programs and projects that promote gender equality are not trapped in the perpetual pilot project stage, but move to scale without dissipation of strategic intent.

Since by definition, implementation activity is decentralized, there is an important role for continuous assessment and monitoring. Civil society organizations, scholars, and gender equality advocacy units should be involved, working in partnership with ICTs decision-makers in all stages of Implementation, particularly in rigorous and sophisticated assessment of projects and programs. There will be variation in the rate at which regions, countries, and sectors implement gender equality perspectives in the ICTs arena. Progress will be uneven and non-linear. There is no blueprint, but there are opportunities to experiment and learn. Unlike the way small-scale gender and ICTs projects are implemented currently; the BIG approach suggests that moving to scale should proceed on the basis of close alignment with the conceptual foundation and strategic intent established in the Buy-In phase (Figure 10.4).

The Growth and reinforcement phase combines a focus on expanded implementation, learning, and reinvention. In this phase, the activities are spearheaded by a community of practice that is united by its genuine interest in promoting gender equality in the ICTs arena, and undertakes outreach to a much wider and politically more diverse set of actors in the development community. With these synergies, the champions of gender and ICTs transformation are more likely to increase their impact. This phase builds on the achievements in the earlier phases, as illustrated in Figure 10.5.

Figure 10.4
Specific Actions to Secure Implementation of Gender Equality in the ICTs Arena

Implementation: Focus on translating the results of research, and conceptual development into concrete programs and projects, at appropriate scale and continue to evaluate and assess the outcomes of programs and projects in the light of strategic objectives

Moving to Scale

ICTs Policy	ICTs and Economic Empowerment	ICTs and Education ICTs and Health	ICTs Mediated Public Life Participation
Measure the expenditure of gender equality related ICTs programs and interventions	Support large-scale deployment of ICTs in women dominated areas of production (e.g. agriculture, textiles, craft)	Secure budgets to rollout ICTs based education and health services targeted at girls and women	Increase allocation within e-government budgets to projects which address the specific public participation needs of women
Assess and evaluate the contribution of gender equality perspectives in achieving ICTs for development objectives	Targeted strategies to increase women's employment in the ICTs core sector	Increase women's participation in advanced ICTs training and education programs	Analyze the impact of ICT-mediated public life participation on gender relations
Build and strengthen leadership of change agents	Targeted strategies to facilitate actions to remove the barriers to women's entrepreneurial activity		Develop strategies to cope with 'backlash' effects

Figure 10.5
Specific Actions to Secure Growth and Reinforcement
of Gender Equality in the ICTs Arena

	ICTs and Economic Empowerment	*ICTs and Education, ICTs and Health*	*ICTs Mediated Public Life Participation*
ICTs Policy	*Growth and reinforcement*: Focus on ensuring that ICTs for development include gender equality perspectives and are increasingly aligned with a broader transformation project. This is achieved by building coalitions among groups seeking social, economic, and political justice.		
Increasing Impact	Link the ICTs initiatives to the campaigns and programs aimed at transformation of global economic policy and end to feminized poverty	Form alliances with women's health and education coalitions and campaigns that advocate for the right to education for all	Develop alliances with pro-democracy movements to strengthen response to any negative reactions to increased women's public life participation
	Set a broad agenda that aligns with goals of pro-people social movements and human development coalitions		
	Contribute to debates on the intersection between ICTs and the achievement of the Millennium Development Goals		

CONCLUSION

This article has outlined a conceptual framework that can be used to transform the ICTs arena for the promotion of gender equality, women's empowerment, and human development. The framework is informed by feminist analysis of organizational and institutional transformation, and efforts to integrate gender issues into ICTs and development both at the theoretical, and practical levels. However, it anticipates that efforts to transform the ICTs arena will be fraught with problems and contestation, and acknowledges the difficulties that may arise from attempting any change in this particular political, and economic context. The BIG approach offers a perspective in which resistance is anticipated and responded to, pro-actively. Within this approach, it is argued that a simultaneous focus on conceptual/strategy development and focused collaborative action is needed to produce acceleration in the transformation agenda. The framework implies that shifts are required in how gender equality advocates approach interventions in the ICTs arena and suggests that gender advocates be prepared to assertively negotiate with powerful forces in the ICTs arena, strengthened by their development of conceptually sound and contextually flexible strategies.

The BIG approach identifies several openings for engaging influential actors to secure change. Many influential organizations including the United Nations ICT Task Force have resolved to work to ensure that there is better alignment between expansion and growth in the ICTs arena, and human development goals and aspirations. There is also a commitment to ensuring that broad goals, as encapsulated by the Millennium Development Goals become the *heart* of the World Summit on the Information Society. In parallel, the international community has recognized the importance of gender equality and the empowerment of women, as enshrined in the Beijing Platform for Action. However, these two spheres of activity have not yet had a meeting of minds and as a result, collaboration among actors is scarce. Applying the BIG approach provides a basis for reducing this parallelism and demonstrates the contribution of gender advocates to shaping the Information Society.

The framework has argued for a three-phase process for transformation of the ICTs arena. Where there are opportunities for collaborative action among various bodies, leadership in each phase is likely to be shared among different actors. In the Buy-In phase, strategic actions are likely to be led by academics and civil society actors working with institutionally-based counterparts to persuade private and public sector decision-makers in the ICTs sector to take gender equality concerns seriously in their planning and program development. The Implementation phase sees the leadership shift to actors such as national governments, ICTs producers, and operating companies that can ensure that ICTs and development projects that promote gender equality move to scale. The growth and reinforcement phase sees the issue being taken up by a broad coalition of development change agents, and the greatest impact is realized in this phase.

The BIG approach outlined here is a work-in-progress. The conceptual framework is ambitious in scope and hopefully provides a thought-provoking response to the question of how we can accelerate progress in the integration of gender equality, and transformation of the ICTs arena. Despite its ambitious reach, the intention is, however, very simple—to inspire others and the author to continue the process of bridging the conceptual and operational gap that exists in our efforts to transform the ICTs arena so that it more effectively benefits humanity.

NOTE

1. This article is a revised version on paper prepared for UN-DAW Expert Group Meeting on 'Information and Communication Technologies and their Impact on and Use as an Instrument for the Advancement and Empowerment of Women', Seoul, Republic of Korea, 11 to 14 November 2002.

REFERENCES

Goetz, Anne-Marie (ed.). (1997) *Getting Institutions Right for Women in Development*, Zed Books, London.
Hafkin, Nancy. (2002) 'Gender Issues in ICT Policy in Developing Countries: An Overview', Report EGM/ICT/2002/EP.1, prepared 25 October 2002, UN-DAW, New York, (Available at http://www.un.org/womenwatch/daw/egm/ict2002/reports/Paper-NHafkin.PDF (last accessed 20 January 2005).

Hammelink, Cees J. (1997) 'New Information and Communications Technologies, Social Development and Cultural Change', Discussion Paper 86, UNRISD, Geneva.

Jackson, Cecile and Pearson, Ruth (eds). (1998) *Feminist Visions of Development: Gender Analysis and Policy*, Routledge, New York and London.

Kabeer, Naila. (1994) *Reversed Realities: Gender Hierarchies in Development Thought*, Verso, London.

Mansell, Robin and Wehn, Uta (eds). (1998) *Knowledge Societies: Information Technology for Sustainable Development*, Oxford University Press, Oxford.

Marcelle, Gillian M. (2000a) 'Transforming Information and Communication Technologies for Gender Equality', *Gender in Development Monograph Series*, No. 9, UNDP, New York.

———. (2000b) 'Getting Gender into African ICT Policy: A Strategic View' in Rathgeber, Eva and Ofwona, Edith (eds), *Gender and the Information Revolution in Africa*, IDRC, Ottawa.

———. (2002) Report of Online Consultation organized by UN-DAW on Information and Communication Technologies (ICT) and their Impact on and Use as an Instrument for the Advancement and Empowerment of Women, UN-DAW, New York, (http://www.un.org/womenwatch/daw/egm/ict2002/reports/Report-online.PDF (last accessed 20 January 2005).

Mitter, Swasti. (1999) 'Globalization, Technological Changes and the Search for a New Paradigm for Women's Work', *Gender, Technology and Development*, 3(1): 1–17.

UNCSTD-GWG (United Nations Commission on Science and Technology for Development—Gender Working Group). (1995) *Missing Links: Gender Equity in Science and Technology for Development*, IDRC, Ottawa, and Intermediate Technology, London.

UNDP. (1999) *Human Development Report 1999*, UNDP, New York.

UNDAW (United Nations Division for the Advancement of Women). (2002). Final Report of the Expert Group Meeting on Information and Communication Technologies (ICT) and their Impact on and Use as an Instrument for the Advancement and Empowerment of Women, EGM held in Seoul Korea, November 2002, UN-DAW, New York, (Available at http://www.un.org/womenwatch/daw/egm/ict2002/reports/EGMFinalReport.pdf (last accessed 20 January 2005).

World Bank Group. (2002) Information and Communication Technologies: A World Bank Group Strategy, World Bank Group, Washington, DC.

About the Editors and Contributors

Editors

CECILIA NG is Visiting Associate Professor at the Asian Institute of Technology, Bangkok (Thailand). Earlier, she was Associate Professor at Universiti Putra, Selangor (Malaysia) and Research Fellow at the United Nations University Institute for New Technologies, Maastricht (The Netherlands). Cecilia has conducted research and published widely on gender, development and work, with a focus on globalization, technological change and women's employment. She is an editor of the journal *Gender, Technology and Development*.

SWASTI MITTER is an international consultant on information and communication technologies (ICT) and gender. She was Chair of Gender and Technology at the University of Brighton, Brighton (UK) and Deputy Director of the United Nations University Institute for New Technologies, Maastricht (The Netherlands). She has been a Visiting Fellow at the Science Policy Research Institute of the University of Sussex, Brighton (UK), and at the Center for Women's Studies at University of California, Los Angeles (USA). She has published widely on women and technology, and has advised major UN agencies and the World Bank.

Contributors

JUAN ABURTO ARRIETA, a systems engineer, was working as an informatics journalist in Managua, Nicaragua. He passed away three years ago.

SUSAN SCHAEFER DAVIS is an independent scholar and consultant with a focus on gender in North Africa (Morocco, Algeria, Tunisia, Egypt) and Palestine. She has worked with the World Bank, FAO, USAID and the Peace Corps, and has served as Clerk of the Middle

East Panel for the American Friends Service Committee. She has held teaching or research positions in the US (Haverford College, the University of Pennsylvania, Trenton State College, and Rutgers University) and Morocco (Al Akhawayn University), with work focusing on Moroccan women and adolescence. Her recent publications include *Patience and Power: Women's Lives in a Moroccan Village,* and *Adolescence in a Moroccan Town. Marrakesh Express* (marrakeshexpress.org) shares her knowledge of Moroccan textiles, and supports women weavers in Morocco.

GOVIND KELKAR is Asia Programme Coordinator, IFAD-UNIFEM Gender Mainstreaming Programme in Asia, New Delhi, and the founding editor of the journal *Gender, Technology and Development.* She has taught at the University of Delhi (New Delhi), the Indian Institute of Technology (Mumbai), and the Asian Institute of Technology (Bangkok), where she founded the graduate program in Gender and Development Studies. In addition to co-authoring *Gender and Tribe* (1991), she has co-edited *Feminist Challenges in the Information Age* (2002) and *Gender Relations in Forest Societies in Asia: Patriarchy at Odds* (2003). With a focus on gender relations in Asia, she has contributed numerous articles to scholarly journals.

GILLIAN M. MARCELLE, an ICT policy specialist based in South Africa, runs Technology for Development (TfDev), a strategic consulting practice. She holds a Visiting Fellowship at the Science Policy Research Institute of the University of Sussex, Brighton (UK). Earlier, she held a variety of positions, including with BT, Oftel, Analysys, and JP Morgan Chase. Her most recent book is *Technological Learning: A Strategic Imperative for Firms in Developing Countries* (Edward Elgar, 2004). Gillian serves on the Board of the UN ICT Task Force, and has been active in gender equality issues on a number of civil society bodies including the WSIS Gender Caucus and the ITU Working Group on Gender Issues. She is a member of the editorial board of the *Southern African Journal of Information and Communication.*

DORA INÉS MUNÉVAR M. is lecturer in Social Theory and Gender Studies at the Department of Human Communication, National University of Colombia, Bogota. She holds degrees in Speech Therapy, Law, Criminal Law and Sociology of Education. Based on these fields, she combines an interdisciplinary approach to her research, teaching, and consultancy on educational law, and gender issues. Her recent contributions are "Power, gender and academic work" (*Poder y género en el trabajo académico*) and "Academic productivity at National University" (*Productividad académica en la Universidad Nacional*). She conducts research into human communication and cultural processes; relations between power, gender and knowledge in relation to academic work and productivity; and science, technology and medicine.

VEENA N. is at present living in the jungles of southern India, where she is documenting the culture, knowledge, and traditions of the Soliga adivasis. She works with the Vivekananda Girijana Kalyana Kendra in B.R. Hills. She has been the Assistant/Managing Editor of the refereed journal *Gender, Technology and Development* published from the Asian Institute of Technology, Bangkok (Thailand). She has also worked as a sub-editor/journalist with leading newspapers in India and Thailand. She has conducted research on gender and ICTs in India and Southeast Asia.

MARTHA ROLDÁN is Senior Researcher in the Sociology of Work, Development and Gender of Conicet (National Council of Scientific and Technical Research of Argentina). She is also Professor at FLACSO (Latin American Faculty of Social Sciences) in Buenos Aires, Argentina, where she directs a project on informational-communicational development and the engendered construction of a NIIDL (New International-Informational Division of Labor). She co-authored (with Lourdes Benería) *The Crossroads of Class and Gender* (1987). Her latest book is *Globalization or Mondialisation? Theory and Practice of Productive Processes and Gender Asymmetries* (*¿Globalization o Mundiali-zación? Teoría y Práctica de procesos productivos y asimetrías de género*) (2000). She has published widely in Spanish on issues relating to the New International Division of Labor.

CZARINA SALOMA-AKPEDONU is Assistant Professor of Sociology at the Ateneo de Manila University (Philippines). She is Board Member of the International Sociological Association Research Committee on the Sociology of Science and Technology. She has recently completed a study of the technological elite in the

Malaysian automotive and information technology industries. Her book *Doing IT in the Philippines: Globality, Gender, Knowledge, and Information Technology* is soon to be published by the Ateneo de Manila University Press.

GIRIJA SHRESTHA is the Regional Secretariat Management Officer of the UN-HABITAT/Urban Management Programme–Asian Institute of Technology (UMP-AIT) Partnership. Prior to this, she was a researcher in Gender and Development Studies at AIT, and an architect/urban planner in the Housing and Physical Planning Department, Government of Nepal. Her areas of interests are Gender and Housing Technology, Urban Planning and Governance. She recently co-authored (with Dev Nathan) "Leasehold Forestry for Livelihoods of the Poor in Nepal" in the book *Globalization and Indigenous Peoples in Asia: Changing the Local-Global Interface* (Sage, 2004).

ISABEL ZORN is a researcher at the Centre for Digital Media and Education, Department of Computing Sciences, University of Bremen (Germany), where she works on the interlinkage of technology design and education. She was responsible for the scientific management of the International Symposium on Gender and Information Society GIST 2004, *www.e-gist.net*. In 2003, she evaluated 100 e-learning modules for Gender Mainstreaming criteria and co-developed a guideline for gender-sensitive e-learning design. She was closely involved with the development of the vifu server and virtual community building among international scholars. Recently, she co-authored "Good Practice Strategies for Gender-Sensitive Design of E-Learning Modules" (*Good Practice für die gendergerechte Gestaltung digitaler Lernmodule*) in *Campus 2004— Have Digital Media for Universities Grown up? (Campus 2004— Kommen die digitalen Medien an den Hochschulen in die Jahre?).*

INDEX

If my heart could speak it
would ~~in motioning~~ call for you
If my eyes could roam
they would navigate towards you

If my soul could be free of my body
I would be left lifeless for it would
~~my soul will embrace~~ ~~engulf you~~ seek you
~~almost beautifying~~
leaving me in a state ~~as I am~~
~~however~~ of destitute
~~From~~ You are my true desire
~~of all senses and~~
    sensually, spiritually, eternally.

Beds of snow, white and soft.
~~Yet~~ Comforting yet fragile
~~As the sun rises it melts~~
In its temporality though, lies its beauty
Layers of flakes piling,
~~tirelessly~~ against ~~profuse bodily~~ melting tops
As it settles into cushions + pillows
~~Amongst its~~ ~~before it set~~

case studies - brilliant but lacde men!

very - good reference

politics - skeptical .... - need to be, but good
aware . [?] works
ii moving
forward

.'. è 3 parts must be read
contingentially . iv order
fo i read ~ to be aware .

well compiled

very good women's voices
tep lacde in other bookes .

very good balana of troy

& deadmen,
& praetorius / odeon
& pdriay master as .

untouched - onpin
- ural

2 0 0 2 6 5